Navigating Legal Research
&
Technology:

*Quick Reference Guide to the 1,500 Most Common Questions
about Traditional and Online Legal Research*

Compiled by:

JOEL FISHMAN, PH.D.

DITTAKAVI RAO, M.A., M.L.S.

Bridge Publishing Group LLC
Getzville, NY
2010

Navigating Legal Research & Technology : Quick Reference Guide to the 1,500
Most Common Questions about Traditional and Online Legal Research

Copyright © 2010
Joel Fishman and Dittakavi Rao

Published by:
Bridge Publishing Group LLC
39 Concetta Court
Getzville, New York 14068
United States of America
Phone: 800.758.3010
Email: mail@bridgepublishinggroup.com
Website: http://www.bridgepublishinggroup.com

Typesetting by: Wordstop Technologies (P) Ltd, Chennai, India
Website: http://www.wordstop.com

Library of Congress Control Number: 2009936266
ISBN: 978-1-935220-32-9

Please note: Special discounts are available for bulk orders. Please contact Bridge
Publishing Group LLC for more information.

Questions or comments about this book may be directed to
Joel Fishman at fishman@duq.edu

Biographies of Authors

Joel Fishman is the Assistant Director for Lawyer Services of the Duquesne University Center for Legal Information/Allegheny County Law Library. He earned his B.A. degree in 1967 from Hunter College, M.L.S. from Queens College in 1973, and M.A. and Ph.D. degrees from the University of Wisconsin-Madison in 1969 and 1977 respectively. Dr. Fishman is the author of more than 200 publications including books, articles, and book reviews. He is the author of *Bibliography of Pennsylvania Law: Secondary Sources* (1993), *Judges of Allegheny County, Fifth Judicial District, Pennsylvania (1788–2008)*, co-author of *Pennsylvania Legal Research Handbook* (2d ed. 2008), Associate Editor, *The Pennsylvania Constitution: A Treatise on Rights and Liberties* (2004), co-author, *Searching the Law* (2d, 1999; 3rd ed. 2005), and more than 20 volumes of Pennsylvania court reports. He won the American Association of Law Libraries "Call for Papers" competition in 1995 for his "Reports of the Supreme Court of Pennsylvania" and the 2005 Connie E. Bolden Scholarship Award for his twenty-five years of writings on Pennsylvania law and bibliography from the State Court & County Special Interest Section of the American Association of Law Libraries. Dr. Fishman is co-director of the Pennsylvania Constitution Web Site at Duquesne University School of Law.

Dr. Fishman has taught legal research courses at the University of Pittsburgh for twenty-five years, Robert Morris University for eighteen years, and Duquesne University Paralegal Institute for five years. He participates in the teaching of first-year law students at Duquesne University Law School and teaches courses in the Continuing Legal Education program offered by the Center for Legal Information.

Dittakavi N. Rao is the Associate Director of the Duquesne University Center for Legal Information / Allegheny County Law Library. Mr. Rao earned his B.S. and M.A. degrees at Andhra University, Waltair, India. He earned his M.L.S. in 1978 at the University of Pittsburgh. Mr. Rao is the author of the *Pennsylvania Paralegal Computer Research Handbook*, published by American Lawyer Media, and *Pennsylvania Legal Research Web Sites* (an Internet website that can be accessed at www.pennsylvanialegalresearch.com).

He is also the co-author of the *Pennsylvania Legal Research Handbook*, (2d ed. 2008) published by American Lawyer Media, and *Computer Assisted Legal Research*

Made Easy in Pennsylvania, published by the National Business Institute. Additionally, he has published several legal bibliographies, pathfinders, as well as several legal research and library science articles.

Mr. Rao has taught Manual Legal Research, Computer-Assisted Legal Research, and Advanced Legal Research for several years at the Duquesne University School of Law and the Duquesne University Paralegal Institute. He also has taught library science at the University of Maiduguri, Nigeria and North Eastern Hill University (visiting fellow), Shillong, India.

Mr. Rao was voted the Outstanding Law Librarian of 1998, and was awarded Duquesne University's President's Award for Staff Excellence in 1994. Mr. Rao has also served as President of the Western Pennsylvania Law Library Association (WPLLA) from 1993 to 1994. He is the co-columnist, with Professor Frank Y. Liu, of the bi-monthly column, "In the Stacks," for *Pennsylvania Law Weekly*.

Introduction

Why we developed this book

There are several good books on legal research that are used both by law school and/or paralegal students. These books provide general information on both manual and online legal research. However, they overlap in content, provide the same types of illustrations, and provide only a minimal standard introduction to electronic research in using the Internet, Lexis, and Westlaw.

Having taught legal research for almost fifty years between the two authors, we understand that students learn legal research. In beginning legal studies students generally have little or no knowledge of law books. Whether teachers use lectures, powerpoint, or some other method of instruction, students are usually at a loss to quickly follow and pick up different terms. Frequently, students have a wide range of questions in trying to understand the details of a research problem. This has led us to believe that instruction will be helped through a different reading approach in legal research, the question-answer approach.

Our work reverses the traditional legal research book by addressing students' questions that they ask in class. All legal research instructors will recognize many of the questions that we post here in our work. Even the most elementary legal terms we have tried to include in the work, general definitions, practice and procedure terms, and legal research definitions of most of the works familiarly treated in first-year law school or in paralegal courses.

Legal research has changed considerably over the past two decades. With the introduction first of electronic legal research using Lexis and Westlaw, and then the introduction of the Internet, legal research has radically changed from manual research to both manual and electronic research. The capability of researching a large amount of primary sources—case-law, constitutions, statutes, and administrative law regulations and cases—online means that electronic legal research for many researchers today means a limited use of manual research. Even secondary sources are coming online through Lexis, Westlaw, and Loislaw, thereby giving even more opportunity for researchers to reject manual legal research. Given the fact that almost a generation of law students have been using electronic legal research means that there has been a significant decline in using manual legal research. Almost any law librarian today can provide stories of how lawyers/law students/paralegals are not familiar with book research.

For the past quarter century, the growth of interdisciplinary studies —critical legal studies movement, for instance has meant that an increasing number of scholars and students are using legal sources without formal training in them. While it is recognized that a standard work may be a worthwhile resource to read, a question-answer book may also answer the researcher's immediate questions without reading extensively through textbooks.

Since the 1980s, there has been a significant growth in legal assistant or paralegal training. The advent of paralegal training institutions, the increase in the number of administration of justice/criminal justice/legal studies programs in undergraduate and graduate institutions has lead to increasing interest in legal research. As the law becomes more interdisciplinary, students from outside of the legal forum, these students need to learn legal terms and legal research techniques. The authors have had airline pilots, nurses, pharmacists, doctors, and other professionals who wish to improve their knowledge of law and legal research techniques as students.

In addition, the increasing fees demanded by lawyers has led the general public to visit law libraries to do their own legal research. While some questions are quite easy to answer, many problems really do require a lawyer's attention. However, questions posed by them have also been incorporated here.

In conclusion, based on our instruction, performing reference services for faculty, students, and the general public, we have drawn upon our experiences to create this work.

Acknowledgments: We wish to thank our colleagues for reading over the manuscript and making suggestions for improvement: Amy Lovell, Manager of Database Systems at Duquesne University Center for Legal Information; and Ann Orsag, Director of Library Services, Buchanan, Ingersoll and Rooney; and Penny Fishman for her useful suggestions. Mr. Milan Komljenovic, Manager of Information Technology, at Duquesne University Center for Legal Information, for his technical assistance in the preparation of the work; Ms. Lisa Marie Mason, Court of Common Pleas of Allegheny County, for her word processing expertise; and Mr. Jerry Schaas, student intern from the University of Pittsburgh, GSPIA, for proofreading the document. Any errors are, of course, are own responsibility.

We wish to thank Brian Jablonski at Bridge Publishing Group LLC for his support in publishing our book.

Joel Fishman, Ph.D.
Dittakavi Rao, M.A., M.L.S.

Master Table of Contents

Detailed Table of Contents

CHAPTER 10: COURT RULES 207

CHAPTER 1

INTRODUCTION TO LEGAL RESEARCH

Introduction: Law as a field of study has its own terminology, sources, and method of citing that is necessary to learn for someone who wishes to become competent in the field. This first chapter provides an overview of the legal field including general questions dealing with research and the profession of the law.

A. GENERAL QUESTIONS

What is legal research?

Legal research involves finding and using relevant information to solve one's legal problems. Legal research requires the use of both primary sources (constitutions, statutes, regulations and case law) and secondary sources such as encyclopedias, annotations, periodicals, and treatises to help find and explain primary sources. In addition there are finding aid tools like digests, citators, and indexes to locate both primary and secondary materials.

What is legal analysis?

Legal analysis involves reading both primary and secondary sources in order find the facts and issues needed to answer one's legal problems.

What are the steps involved in legal analysis?

Generally, legal analysis includes gathering the facts, analyzing the facts, identifying the legal issues, and organizing the legal issues.

What are the main components of legal research?

Finding the appropriate source to answer your questions; using that source efficiently by using indices, etc.; and finally updating the information you found in the source.

What are the types of legal research?

There are two types: manual legal research and computer-assisted legal research.

Why is manual legal research important?

Paper research provides the foundation of the American legal research system. Paper research sources have been developed throughout the history of the United States. The paper resources serve as the foundation of the organization and structure of the American legal information system.

Paper research tools were developed through a comprehensive analysis of the hierarchical structure of knowledge of the law. The table of contents and indexes and digests of these tools were developed through the painstaking analysis of individual concepts of law and facts of legal controversies.

Increasingly, these indexes, tables of contents, and digests have migrated from paper products to online versions.

Paper resources are available in greater number than in computer databases. Primary sources as well as secondary sources are not all available online. Nor are historical documents that date back to ancient times (depending on the country one is researching in). Although primary and secondary sources are current in Westlaw and Lexis, there are many websites that are not kept current.

It is not always possible to authenticate documents that are available in the online environment.

The online databases like Lexis and Westlaw are very expensive to use for a wide range of documents. Mastering paper research can reduce the need for electronic research and thus reduce costs.

Why is computer-assisted legal research (CALR) important?

CALR provides full-text of federal and state primary sources including constitutions, statutory law, caselaw, and administrative regulations. A wide variety of currently published secondary sources are also available (e.g. encyclopedias, ALR annotations, treatises, periodicals, and legal newspapers.)

What are the advantages of computer assisted legal research?

As opposed to paper or book-based research the computer assisted legal research (LexisNexis, Westlaw and Internet) has the following advantages:

Fast: Online research gives the researcher the ability to quickly find documents in full text. It also saves time in searching cases for specific fact patterns.

Cost effective: Online research saves time which means more projects can be completed in the same amount of time it previously would have taken to research one project. It saves time from having to physically go to a library to find the materials. It saves costs in photocopying and storage needs by saving electronic documents.

Variety of options for saving the research: Print; save to disk; email and fax. The variety of saving options give the researcher the ability to save materials that will be needed later or even send the materials directly to other people.

Combining your research terms: Online research allows for detailed searching for fact-specific cases on a topic using Boolean and proximity connectors. Searching can also be done through the natural language method.

Current information: Book sources are always "out-of-date" even though they attempt to maintain currency with pocket parts or new releases. Online databases may be updated more frequently, sometimes daily or weekly, as new developments occur.

Searching several types of documents: Online research permits researching of multiple primary or secondary sources at one time.

Documents are linked to each other for easy accessibility: Databases incorporate links between items, e.g., a court case cites a case, statute, code, or rule, and a link ties you directly to that reference for one to read.

Biographies of attorneys and judges: Online databases provide biographical information on judges and lawyers, e.g., Martindale-Hubbell Law Directory, Westlaw Profiler, and Federal Judges at <www.fjc.gov>. In addition, it may be possible to view pictures of various judges and lawyers.

Cases argued by attorneys: Databases have cases divided into segments which include attorneys or counsel to identify the various cases that they have argued.

Opinions written by judges: Databases provide a segment search to locate cases written by judges as majority opinion, dissenting, and concurring opinions.

Flexible: One can retrieve legal documents by their various segments, e.g., cases can be retrieved by docket number, judge, counsel, date, etc.

Efficient: Researchers can find all types of factual information online from calendar dates, stock market prices, quotations, etc.

Cases: Published and unpublished cases available from all jurisdictions from the colonial period to today. Access provides new cases (slip opinions) added on a daily basis.

Secondary sources: Full text databases link primary sources to secondary sources for further research, e.g., encyclopedias, ALR annotations, CLE materials, periodicals, restatements and treatises. The secondary sources also link back to the primary sources online.

Archived databases for primary sources: Researchers can find archives for the past fifteen years of major primary sources by year, e.g., *United States Code Annotated* (USCA) and *Code of Federal Regulations* (CFR). This is helpful to locate text of the law as it existed as of a specific date.

Validation of cases: Databases provide citator services (Shepards on Lexis and KeyCite on Westlaw) to determine the history and treatment of a case as to whether it is good law or not. The system is also available for constitutions, statutes, and rules.

Access to online tutorials: Databases provide online tutorials to assist the researcher in how to use the database if not familiar with it.

Help feature: There is usually a help feature on the commercial databases providing either online assistance, live session contacts, or a phone number to call to speak to an attorney immediately and at all hours of the day.

Site map: Web sites and databases provide site maps for those who need to see all parts of the site easily.

What are Computer Assisted Legal Instruction (CALI) lessons?
Computer Assisted Legal Instruction (CALI) lessons are the products of the Center for Computer-Assisted Legal Instruction (CCALI) which was established in 1982 by the University of Minnesota Law School and Harvard Law School. CALI lessons (tutorials) are written by law faculty and law librarians. Currently, there are over 625 lessons in 32 different areas of law. New lessons are added every year. These lessons serve as a supplement to classroom instruction.

Most of the American law schools maintain a subscription and make the lessons available to the students.

What are fee-based services?
These are online databases purchased from private vendors for a fixed period of time for access to a wide range of primary and secondary sources.

What is effective legal research?
Effective legal research begins with examination and review of footnote rich secondary authority materials such as treatises, encyclopedia articles, law review

articles, etc. and then a careful review of all relevant and controlling statutes and regulations and applicable case law. Hybrid research of both manual and electronic resources such as LexisNexis, Westlaw and open Internet is more effective than only one type of research method.

What is cost effective research?

Cost effective legal research concerns using law books and accessing free Internet sites to obtain primary and secondary materials rather than using fee-based services like LexisNexis and/or Westlaw.

When can I stop my research?

When one begins to find the same documents over again in their research, it is time to stop your research.

What are free Internet services?

Institutions like governments, educational institutions, organizations, and individuals provide information on the Internet that is posted for free to anyone who has Internet access.

Who are the major players in computer assisted legal research?

Westlaw is a full-text database produced by West Group, a division of the Thomson Corporation. Lexis is a full-text database produced by Lexis, a division of the Reed-Elsevier Corporation.

What are the primary authorities of law?

From the legal research point of view, the primary authorities of law consist of constitutions (federal, states, local governments); statutes (federal, state legislatures, and municipal governments); administrative rules and regulations (departments and administrative agencies of the government) and case law (judiciary).

What is the importance of primary authority in carrying out legal research?

The information found in the primary sources are the actual law that people need to follow. It is necessary to cite to primary authorities when conducting legal research. Generally, court decisions are based on the interpretation of the primary materials.

What is blackletter law?

One or more legal principles that are fundamental, settled law. It may also be known as "hornbook law."

What takes precedence among primary sources?

Constitutions are the most important source and are superior to statutes and regulations. Statutes are superior to regulations.

What are secondary authorities of law?
The secondary authorities are not the actual law. These materials include digests, citators, dictionaries encyclopedias, periodical literature, legal newspapers and newsletters, ALR Annotations, and treatises.

What is the importance of secondary authorities in carrying out legal research?
There are two main functions of secondary authorities. Secondary sources help find, explain, and criticize legal issues. Secondary authorities also help in locating primary source materials through the text and footnotes of those works.

What is the difference between federal and state law?
Federal law covers all fifty states while state law covers only the law of one state, e.g., a law passed in Maine has no effect in Iowa.

What is substantive law?
Substantive law includes all topics of law including: contracts, criminal, civil, torts, property, etc.

What is procedural law?
Procedural law is related to the functioning of a court and includes: rules of civil procedure, rules of criminal procedure, rules of evidence, etc.

What is Adjective law?
Adjective law is another name for procedural law, that is, it deals with rules governing practice and procedure within a jurisdiction.

What are court rules?
Each court will have its own rules. These rules explain the jurisdiction over the courts, how to conduct business within the court, e.g., brief writing.

What is the rule of law?
Technically the "rule of law" can be regarded as a principle of sovereignty of the laws over men.
The rule of law is supposed to shape the American legal system according to the political ideals of social stability and predictability (*Dana Neacsu: Introduction to U.S. Law and Legal Research, 2005*)

What are the main legal systems?
There are four dominant legal systems: 1) Common law system (England, USA); 2) Civil law system (Roman, German, Europe etc.); 3) Socialist system (China, Russia, Cuba etc.); 4) Religious systems (Islamic, Jewish, Hindu etc.)

What is common law?
Common law is the Anglo-American legal system based on judicial opinions. In America, it is the acceptance of certain laws and judgments derived from England and updated by the customs, laws, and court decisions of our country created both before and following the American Revolution.

What is civil law?
Civil law is one of the two major legal systems in the Western World originally deriving from the law of Rome and still followed today with in Europe, Latin American, Scotland, and Louisiana in the United States.

What is an adversarial system?
The Anglo-American legal system provides for an adversarial system in criminal law in which a lawyer/advocate pleads a case before an impartial judge or jury.

What is an inquisitorial system?
The European legal system is considered an inquisitorial system of law based on Roman law or Napoleonic Code wherein judge(s) investigate the matter.

What is soft law?
Soft law refers to nonbinding documents or instruments (guidelines, declarations, or principles) that may have use politically, but are not enforceable. For example a UN General Assembly resolutions on terrorism constitutes "soft law." (Marcy Hoffman & Mary Rumsey: *International and Foreign Legal Research: A Coursebook*, 2008)

What is supranational law?
A supranational organization (1) has powers that its member states do not have because they surrendered those powers to it; (2) may enact rules that preempt the laws and regulations of its member states; and (3) may grant rights and privileges to the nationals of its member states, which those nationals may directly invoke. (Marcy Hoffman & Mary Rumsey: *International and Foreign Legal Research: A Coursebook*, 2008) Example is European Union.

What is national law?
National law is essentially the domestic or internal law of a country. It defines the role of government to the people and controls relationships between people. It may regulate foreign persons and entities, but it does not have effect outside the boundaries of a nation. (Marcy Hoffman & Mary Rumsey: *International and Foreign Legal Research: A Coursebook*, 2008)

What is customary law?

Customary law tends to govern areas of personal conduct, inheritance, and marriage. Most often, customary law is unwritten and is dispensed by persons with elected or hereditary roles within a small community. (Marcy Hoffman & Mary Rumsey: *International and Foreign Legal Research: A Coursebook*, 2008)

What is private international law?

Private international law governs the choice of which national law to apply when there are conflicts in the domestic law of different countries related to private transactions between private parties. These conflicts arise most often in areas such as contracts, marriage and divorce, jurisdiction, recognition of judgments, and child adoption and abduction. (Marcy Hoffman & Mary Rumsey: *International and Foreign Legal Research: A Coursebook*, 2008) It is also known as 'conflict of laws.'

What is public international law?

Public international law governs the relationships between national governments, the relationships between intergovernmental organizations (IGOs), and the relationships between national governments and IGOs. It also regulates governments and IGOs across, national boundaries. (Marcy Hoffman & Mary Rumsey: *International and Foreign Legal Research: A Coursebook*, 2008)

What is transnational law?

Transnational law is a broad category that is generally taken "to include all law which regulates actions or events that transcend national frontiers. Both public and private international law are included, as are other rules which do not wholly fit into such standard categories." (Marcy Hoffman & Mary Rumsey: International and Foreign Legal Research: A Coursebook, 2008)

What is comparative law?

Comparative law is "the study of the similarities and differences between the laws of two or more countries, or between two or more legal systems. ((Marcy Hoffman & Mary Rumsey: *International and Foreign Legal Research: A Coursebook*, 2008)

Who are the major legal publishers?

The three major international companies are Thomson, Reed Elsevier, and Wolters Kluwer. Thomson includes West Group, Lawyers Cooperative, Foundation, Research Institute of America, and Warren Gorham & Lamont. Reed Elsevier includes Lexis, Matthew Bender, and Shepard's, Wolters Kluwer includes Aspen, Commerce Clearing House, and Wiley.

How are law books generally updated?

Bound volumes are updated by pocket parts and paperback pamphlets, while looseleaf publications are updated by releases that may be placed in the front or back of the volume or replacement pages.

What is a pocket part?

A pocket part is a pamphlet that fits in the back cover of the book and updates the book's information since the publication of the volume (check copyright date). In a multivolume set, like annotated codes, digests, and encyclopedias, the individual volumes may have different copyright dates as they are not always published simultaneously.

What happens when a pocket part gets too big for the back of the book?

The publisher will convert the pocket part to a supplementary pamphlet that sits besides the bound volume. In some sets, like digests, supplementary pamphlets may also be published to update the annual pocket parts throughout the year. A bound volume and supplement will eventually be recompiled into a new bound volume(s).

What are releases for looseleaf services?

A release is an update for a looseleaf service that provides replacement pages for older pages. Individual pages or small pamphlets can also be placed in the front or back of the volume as a supplement to the main volume.

What are finding tools?

Finding tools, sometimes called search books, include digests, citators, tables and indexes that help identify primary sources. Finding tools are sometimes considered secondary sources, but some classify them as tertiary sources.

Are videos available for legal research?

Videos are available from various legal publishers on a wide range of legal topics. They are available in various formats including DVD format. There are some videos available online at Findlaw.com or Lawinfo.com.

B. LEGAL PROFESSION

How does one become a lawyer?

In the United States, one has to attend law school to receive training in the law to become a lawyer. Law schools today primarily provide three-year programs of instruction.

How many law schools are there in the United States?
There are more than 200 law schools in the United States which are accredited and non-accredited.

How are law schools accredited?
The American Bar Association accredits law schools. Law schools are required to comply with a detailed list of standards to be accredited.

Can unaccredited law schools become accredited?
Yes, once they believe they have achieved the ABA Standards for Accreditation, a law school can apply for provisional and then full accreditation.

Are there any law schools offering online law degrees?
There are some universities offering online law degrees which are not accredited by the American Bar Association; however, they have individual state education department and state bar approval. Currently, Concord Law School, part of Kaplan University, founded in 1998, offers an online law degree program. The school offers a four-year part-time program that will allow the student to take the bar admissions test in California. Students who pass the California bar exam are also eligible to appear for the Wisconsin bar. The school also offers an Executive Juris Doctor (EJD) degree, a three-year part-time program. There are other schools including Northwestern California University School of Law that offer programs as well.

Outside of the United States, the University of London offers a three-year online law school degree program.

What is the role of the American Association of Law Schools (AALS) for law schools?
The American Association of Law Schools serves as a "learned society for the legal profession." The organization provides criteria for admission of law schools and its faculty to the organization. The organization provides additional criteria to the operation of the law school, its faculty, students, curriculum, physical facilities, etc. The web site for the organization is www.aals.org.

Can you become a lawyer if you go to an unaccredited law school?
You may practice in the state that the law school is located in if you pass the bar exam. If you pass the bar exam you may practice in other state's federal courts but not the state courts.

What are the qualifications to become a lawyer?
In order to go to court, one has to pass the state bar exam which is usually a two-day exam, one day for multiple choice questions and the second day for essay

questions. The bar exam is generally given in February and July. The students who graduate in the spring (May-June) generally take the exam in July and are notified in October of passage. February tests are reported in summer.

Students are also required to take the Multistate Professional Responsibility Examination during their law school career or shortly after passing the bar exam. There are specific rules to follow if a lawyer fails to comply with these requirements.

Do you have to take an exam to become a lawyer?
Yes. In all states there is a two-day bar exam consisting of a short answer exam and a second day of essays.

Who gives the bar exam?
There is a state board of bar admissions created either by statute or by court rule to oversee the bar admission rules.

What if you fail the bar exam?
You can practice as a lawyer under the direction of other lawyers, but cannot go into court. You can take the bar exam multiple times until you pass the bar.

What is the case law method (Socratic) of teaching in law schools?
Christopher Columbus Langdell, Dean of the Harvard Law School, introduced the case-law method in the 1870s. He believed that studying and reviewing cases through a question-answer approach between teacher and student was better than the lecture presentation. Case law method is also known as the Socratic method.

What is the curriculum for law school students?
The law school curriculum is a three-year program of study. The first-year consists generally of required courses in legal research and writing, procedure, criminal law, torts, property, and constitutional law. Second and third year students select their own course of study.

Some schools have certificate programs for students who take a certain number of courses/credits (12-18 credits) in a specialty area like taxation, environmental law, international law, etc.

Are there any case briefs available online?
Law School briefs on some topics such as Civil Procedure, Property, Torts etc. are available from Invispress at www.invispress.com/law website. Casebriefs www. ecasebriefs.com is another company which provides case briefs for fee. Some law firms offer their own briefs online for free. For example, Mayer Brown, at

www.appellate.net, offers their briefs for cases argued before the United States Supreme Court.

Are course outlines available online?
Most of the comprehensive legal web sites have links to outlines to courses offered in the law schools under 'law students' heading. In addition to comprehensive sites, web sites such as 4 law school (www.4lawschool.com), Law Student (www.lawstudent.com) also provide links to course outlines.

What are the types of degrees offered by law schools?
There are three levels of legal education. The first degree is the Juris Doctor (J.D.) which is usually a three-year course of study. The LL.M. degree is a Master's degree in which lawyers usually specialize in a specialty area, e.g., labor, taxation, environmental law. The S.J.D. is the Doctor of Jurisprudence which is the doctorate degree in law. It may or may not include coursework and the writing of a dissertation. In addition, many law schools have implemented joint-degree programs with other schools or departments within the university, e.g., J.D. and M.B.A. in Law and Business, J.D. and Ph.D. studies in Law and History.

Do all lawyers appear in court?
No, actually a majority of lawyers do not appear in court. Only those lawyers involved in litigation appear as counsel in court.

Who are trial lawyers?
Trial lawyers appear in court to advocate for their clients. The majority of lawyers do not appear in trials on a regular basis.

Who governs how attorneys practice in a state?
There are boards of discipline within each state which may be under the highest court of that state.

What if you cannot afford an attorney?
There are various non-profit organizations that may be able to provide legal assistance, e.g., Neighborhood Legal Services, organizations such as Y.M.C.A./Y.W.C.A., or specialty organizations, community services, domestic violence, etc.

What is a contingency fee?
Lawyers charge a percentage fee (30%-40%) of the award granted a client either in reaching an out-of-court settlement or an award made in a trial.

What is a retainer?
A client pays a sum of money to an attorney to retain his/her services.

What is the role of legal services?

Legal services, may be named differently in various states, offers low-cost attorney services for civil suits usually, e.g., housing, landlord-tenant, etc. There is a maximum income on the individual to qualify.

What does it mean to do pro bono work?

Attorneys provide free legal service to those who cannot afford their regular prices.

What is *in forma pauperis*?

Individuals who cannot afford lawyers and wish to pursue a court case can file papers with the courts requesting pauper status to obtain services for free, e.g., cost of filing or photocopying costs.

What is a paralegal or legal assistant?

A paralegal is a person trained to assist a lawyer in his practice. A paralegal may take courses in a paralegal program to learn legal topics to assist lawyers.

The American Bar Association defines a paralegal, or legal assistant, as a person qualified by education or training "who is employed or retained by a lawyer, law office, corporation, governmental agency or other entity who performs specifically delegated substantive legal work for which a lawyer is responsible."

While not authorized to give legal advice, a paralegal is responsible for a wide range of functions. Among other things, a paralegal will be the primary contact for clients, do legal research, draft legal documents, and will seek out and interview potential witnesses. While specific duties vary depending upon where they are employed, very often, the work of the paralegal determines how an attorney will handle a particular case. (www.paralegaltraining.net)

Do you need a certain type of degree to become a paralegal?

Programs consist of usually eight to ten courses. Some schools admit those with college degrees; others will take high school graduates.

Can paralegals practice law?

No. Paralegals have to work under the direction of a lawyer.

What is a legal secretary?

A legal secretary is a secretary that specializes in working in a law firm.

C. LEGAL WRITING

What is a legal or office memorandum?

An associate lawyer writes a memorandum upon a particular topic to present to a senior attorney who will use it to provide legal advice to a client?

What are the parts of a memorandum?

A memorandum consists of the following elements:

1. Heading
2. Questions Presented
3. Brief Answers
4. Statement of Facts
5. Discussion
6. Conclusion

What is CREAC Rule in writing a memorandum?

The CREAC Rule is used to write the discussion part of the memorandum.

1. Conclusion (overall)
2. Rule (common law and statutory rules)
3. Explanation (rule proof)
4. Application (of laws to the facts)
5. Conclusion (Mini)

What is a closed memo?

In legal writing and research courses, the closed memo is one of the first writing assignments given to first-year students. The memo deals with a specific problem in which the students are given the controlling statute and one or two cases to prepare a memo without looking at any other sources.

What is an open memo?

The open memo follows the closed memo. Students are given a fact situation in which they have to research primary and secondary sources in order to prepare the memo.

What are the sections included in a sample memo?

A sample memo includes: statement of facts; issue statement; brief answer; discussion; and the conclusion.

Where can I find a sample memo?

In most legal writing books, a sample memo is usually included. It can also be found in an appendix in the *ALWD Citation Manual*.

What is an opinion letter?

A lawyer writes an opinion letter to provide information to the client in order to make a decision.

What is a brief?

An attorney writes a brief as a legal document to convince the court that the client's position is correct and should be adopted.

Briefs differ from memoranda because briefs present an argument and must convince the court and opposing counsel that the position is correct.

What are the types of briefs?
Plaintiff brief, defendant brief, appellant's brief, appelle's brief, and reply brief.

What are the parts of a trial court brief?
A trial court brief contains the following parts:
1. Caption
2. Introduction
3. Questions Presented
4. Statement of Facts
5. Argument
6. Conclusion

What are the parts of an appellate court brief?
An appellate court brief contains the following parts:
1. Title Page
2. Table of Contents
3. Table of Authorities Cited
4. Opinion(s) Below
5. Jurisdiction
6. Constitutional Provisions, Statues, Regulations and Rules Involved
7. Standard of Review (required by some courts)
8. Questions Presented
9. Statement of Facts
10. Summary of Argument
11. Argument
12. Conclusion
13. Appendix(es)

Source: John C. Dernbach et al: *A Practical Approach to Legal Writing & Legal Method* 237 (3d ed. 2007)

What is the record?
The record is the verbatim transcript of the trial court proceedings. It may be sent along with the appellate briefs to the intermediate court for review. It may also include the lower court opinion and orders.

What is an objective memoranda?
An objective memoranda is also known as an office memo.

What is a motion brief?

A motion is the presentation of the request made before the court with an accompanying brief providing arguments in favor of your position.

What is a motion in limine?

Prior to trial attorneys file motions in limine to prevent unwanted testimony or exhibits from being introduced into evidence.

What is a trial brief?

The brief submitted to the trial court presenting the arguments of the plaintiff in the case.

What is an appellate brief?

The brief filed on behalf of the person appealing a lower court opinion to a higher court.

What are merit briefs?

Merit briefs are those briefs written for cases that the U.S. Supreme Court has agreed to hear. They are available at the United States Supreme Court website, Lexis (File name: BRIEFS) and Westlaw (File Name: SCT-BRIEF). They are also available under Preview of the U.S. Supreme Court at the American Bar Association website, www.abanet.org.

What is meant by invitations?

When the Court is considering whether or not to grant review in a case in which the government is not a party, it sometimes issues an order inviting the Solicitor General to file a brief expressing the views of the United States. The brief filed in response to such an order is an *amicus curiae* brief at the petition state, but it is often referred to informally as an "invitation." (www.usdoj.gov)

What does oral advocacy mean?

Oral advocacy deals with trial practice in which the trial attorneys on both sides present their cases before the court.

D. COURT-RELATED INFORMATION

What are the three branches of the government?

The three branches of government consist of the Executive (President), Legislative (Congress), and Judiciary (U.S. Supreme Court).

What are courts of limited jurisdiction?
Some courts, especially federal courts, are limited to hearing cases based on subject matter jurisdiction provided by the Constitution or Congressional statutory law.

What are courts of general jurisdiction?
State trial courts have general jurisdiction over a wide range of topics

What are courts of record?
County courts may function as courts of appeal for lower courts. Courts of record means the proceedings are recorded the first time, in effect a new trial from the beginning (trial de novo).

What are courts of no record?
These are usually the small claims courts below the state trial courts served by justices of the peace, district judges, or magisterial district judges.

What are courts of last resort?
Every state has a court of last resort known as the state supreme court sometimes called a supreme court or circuit court of appeals (MD, NY). Except for Oklahoma and Texas, every other state has one court of last resort. In Oklahoma and Texas, there are two courts of last resort, one for civil and one for criminal.

What is the relationship of the federal and state law?
Under the federal system, the United States Constitution describes certain powers given to the three branches of the government. Under Article I, Section 10 of the Constitution those powers not enumerated are left to the state. Each state has its own constitution that gives the government certain powers that vary from state to state.

What is the difference between a justice and a judge?
It is a matter of designation. Usually, the judges of the highest court of a jurisdiction are called justices, intermediate appellate and lower courts judges are called judges.

What is a justice of the peace, magistrate, district magistrate, magisterial district judge?
A justice of the peace sits on the municipal or local courts below the trial court level generally on "courts not of record." The position has different names in the various states: a justice of the peace, magistrate, district magistrate, magisterial district judge.

What is the role of the Attorney General of the United States?
The Attorney General is the chief legal officer of the United States. The President can request an opinion from him concerning questions of law.

What is the role of the State Attorney General?
The State Attorney General is the chief legal officer of the state. Governmental officials can request an opinion from him concerning legal matters.

What is the role of the Solicitor General of the United States?
The Solicitor General represents the federal government in cases heard before the United States Supreme Court. He also files *amicus curaie* in cases determined to be important to the government. He is sometimes called the "tenth justice" because of his close relationship to the Supreme Court.

What is the role of the city solicitor?
The city solicitor is the chief legal adviser to the local government administration, e.g., Mayor/Council/Manager.

What is the role of the district attorney?
The district attorney is a municipal officer who prosecutes criminal cases within the municipality.

What is the role of the public defender?
The public defender serves as the defense lawyer for those accused of a crime who are unable to obtain private lawyers because of lack of financial resources. Public defenders are present in both the federal and state systems.

What is the role of a sheriff?
The sheriff is responsible to provide service of process upon defendants.

What is service of process?
Service of process is the delivery to the defendant of a summons accompanied by a complaint.

What are the types of service of process?
There are three types: actual (hand delivery), substitute (registered mail), and constructive (by publication in the local newspapers).

What is a law clerk?
A law clerk is a law student who works for a law firm usually on a part-time basis.

What is a runner?
A runner is a person who files papers for the firm in the various court offices.

What is a motions judge?
Judges are assigned to hear various motions and petitions on a daily basis by lawyers or pro se clients. Judges may be assigned on a daily, weekly, or monthly basis.

What is a motions clerk?
The motions clerk takes the papers and keeps the docket of activity on a daily basis.

What is the docket clerk?
The docket clerk maintains the daily court records of papers filed in court.

What is the function of the court reporter?
The official court reporter is a court officer who provides a summary of each court case and works with the commercial vendors to publish the cases.

In trial proceedings, the court reporter is a paid employee who takes a verbatim record of the court's testimony during trial, depositions, or other proceedings where that a record needs to be maintained.

What is the purpose of Law Day and when did it begin?
The American Bar Association first put forward the idea of a national holiday to recognize the rule of law in our society. In 1958, President Dwight D. Eisenhower proclaimed Law Day to strengthen our great heritage of liberty, justice, and equality under the law. The statutory law providing for an annual proclamation can be found in 36 U.S.C. §113.

E. LITIGATION

What is federal jurisdiction?
Federal courts hear two types of cases: those involving a "federal question" and those involving disputes between citizens of different states.

What is venue?
Venue determines where the case will be held based on some connection between the events and persons.

What is jurisdiction?
Jurisdiction is based on the selection of the appropriate federal or state court to adjudicate a case. It is determined by the court, not the parties.

What is original jurisdiction?
Original jurisdiction is the jurisdiction exercised by the court that first hears a case.

What is appellate jurisdiction?
Appellate jurisdiction is the jurisdiction exercised by an appeals court that handles appeals from the trial court on both the federal or state level. On the federal level, the Circuit courts and Supreme Court hold appellate jurisdiction.

What is judicial review?
It is the power of the court to review whether a statute or rule is constitutional under the federal or state constitutions.

What are the things involved in the anatomy of a case?
Pleadings – Motions – Complaint – Discovery – Remedy – Summary Judgment – Appeal

What is a writ?
A court's written order to perform or not perform a certain act. In English history the writ system was part of the development of common law forms that existed until the nineteenth century. A specific writ had to be written for a specific type of case to be presented in the English courts, otherwise the case could be dismissed. The writ system developed in the United States as well and is still used as in appealing a case to the United States Supreme Court in filing a writ of certiorari.

What are pleadings?
A party's filing of formal documents with the court that state the arguments concerning the relevant issues.

What is verification?
Verification is a written statement under oath confirming the correctness, truth, or authenticity of a pleading. In some states a complaint must be accompanied by a verification signed by the plaintiff.

What are motions?
Motions are written or oral applications requesting a court to make a ruling or order.

What is a complaint?
The initial pleading that starts a civil action.

What is a demurrer?
An answer to a civil complaint that contends that even if the facts are correct, there has been no wrongdoing.

What is a remedy?
It is what the court can do to assist a litigant either by providing judgments to the winner of a case or by to refrain the litigant from repeating the wrongful conduct.

What is a summary judgment?
A judgment granted to the defense based on the information provided that there is no issue of fact and the case is dismissed before a trial occurs.

What is declaratory judgment?
A binding judgment issued by the court that defines the legal relationship between the parties and their rights with respect to the matter before the court. A declaratory judgment does not provide for enforcement of the judgment, however. In other words, it states the opinion of the court regarding the matter before it without requiring that either of the parties do anything. See, e.g., *Roe v. Wade*, 410 US 113 (1973). (http://www.law.cornell.edu/wex)

What is an appeal?
A losing litigant takes the lower court's decision to a higher appellate court for review, such as taking a federal district court case to circuit court or taking a circuit case to the U.S. Supreme Court.

What is an interlocutory appeal?
In civil procedure, it is an appeal of a trial court ruling before the trial has been completed. For interlocutory appeals to the United States Supreme Court, it is called collateral order doctrine.

What is the difference between and a court order and court rule?
An Order is particular to a set of facts and circumstances before the court and is applicable to the litigants in that case. A Rule is more generally applicable to parties before the court (Toni M Fine: *American Legal Systems: A Resource and Reference Guide*, 2008)

What is moot court?
Law students in the 2d and 3d year participate in moot court competition. Students write appellate briefs and compete in oral competition before a hypothetical court.

What are oral arguments?
Attorneys present their case before the judges orally.

What is certiorari?
A writ of certiorari is presented to an appellate court to review a case from a lower appellate or trial court. If the court approves the taking of the writ, it is generally called cert. granted. The writ is what is used to bring a case before the United States Supreme Court.

In state proceedings, the writ may also be used, but may also be called different terms, such as allocatur granted or denied in Pennsylvania.

What is cert. denied?
The appellate court refuses to hear the writ of appeal from the lower court. The decision of the lower court becomes final.

What is discovery?
In pretrial procedure, information concerning each side's case is presented to each other. It eliminates the surprise factor at trial. Discovery includes: interrogatories, depositions, requests for admissions, and requests for production of documents.

What are interrogatories?
Interrogatories are the questions lawyers ask to obtain evidence from either party in a suit.

What is a request for admissions?
One side presents the other side with questions that have to be either admitted or denied.

What is request for production of documents?
One side requests the opposing party to produce documents in its possession or control, so the requesting party may examine them.

What is a deposition?
A person gives oral testimony in response to questions that is recorded word for word by a court reporter.

What is an expert witness report?
A report produced by an expert witness that supports a witness's factual basis for his/her opinion on the specific topic.

What are the different types of relief a plaintiff may obtain?
Damages; Injunction; Specific Performance; Restitution; Attorney's fees.

What is non prossing a case?
A judge has the ability to cancel a hearing when a plaintiff has not followed or complied with a court's directions. Non pro gives the trial judge the ability to manage his/her docket.

What is an adjudication?
An adjudication is a formal decree or judgment by a court.

What are the steps involved in a trial?
The American Bar Association provides an outline of the steps in a trial from pre-trial to post-trial procedures in both civil and criminal trials. See http://www.abanet.org/publiced/courts/cases.html

Settling Cases
Pre-trial Procedures in Civil Cases
Jurisdiction and Venue
Pleadings
Motions
Discovery
Pre-Trial Conferences
Pre-trial Procedures in Criminal Cases
Bringing the Charge
Arrest Procedures
Pre-Trial Court Appearances in Criminal Cases
Bail
Plea Bargaining
Civil and Criminal Trials
Officers of the Court
The Jury Pool
Selecting the Jury
Opening Statements
Evidence
Direct Examination
Cross-examination
Motion for Directed Verdict/Dismissal
Presentation of Evidence by the Defense
Rebuttal
Final Motions
Closing Arguments
Instructions to the Jury
Mistrials
Jury Deliberations

Verdict
Motions after Verdict
Judgment
Sentencing
Appeals

What are the types of jurisdiction?

Jurisdiction is divided into three components: subject matter jurisdiction; personal jurisdiction; and notice and opportunity to be heard.

What is subject matter jurisdiction?

Subject matter jurisdiction is a question of authority of the court over the nature of the litigation. i.e. the subject matter presented. Subject matter jurisdiction is conferred by constitution and statute.

What is personal jurisdiction?

Personal jurisdiction refers to the court's power over the person of the defendant, the court has *in personam* jurisdiction. Personal jurisdiction means court's power over the person or the property of the defendant.

What is general jurisdiction?

At the trial level, a federal or state court can hear all types of cases, commonly known as general jurisdiction.

What is limited jurisdiction?

If a court hears a case dealing with a specific subject matter issue, such as family court, traffic court, or probate court, it is of limited jurisdiction.

What is diversity jurisdiction?

Diversity cases involve citizens of different states that are tried in the federal courts.

What is *In rem* jurisdiction?

Courts may exercise jurisdiction over defendants who own property located within the state. When the action is to determine rights to property, the action is *in rem*. An action to quiet title or an action to probate an estate are examples of *in rem* jurisdiction.

What is venue?

While jurisdiction deals with the authority of a court to exercise judicial power, venue deals with the place where that power should be exercised.

What are arbitration proceedings?
In various courts, claimants can take a case to arbitration between one to three lawyers who hear and determine a case rather than going to trial. There is a statutory limit of how much money the case is worth in order to go before arbitration.

What are court rules and orders?
The court issues rules and administrative orders to assist in the business of the court.

What is a criminal complaint?
A criminal complaint is a formal charge against a person.

What is an affidavit?
An affidavit is the written statement by a person that is usually notarized to be considered an official document.

What is a notarized statement?
A notary affixes his/her seal to a document after taking the swearing of a person that the document is truthful.

What is a bench trial?
A bench trial is when the judge sits alone to hear a case without a jury.

What is a grand jury?
A grand jury is called by the district attorney to investigate criminal actions and bring charges against individuals.

What is a petit jury?
This is another way to describe a regular trial jury. The jury hears and makes a determination in a trial.

How many people are on a jury?
Usually 12 people sit on a jury. In some states a civil jury can have as few as six members. A criminal jury usually has twelve, but may have as few as ten members.

What are the requirements to be on a jury?
U.S. citizen, state citizen, and a registered voter within the jurisdiction the person is living in.

What is voir dire?
It stands for "speak the truth." It is the preliminary examination by plaintiff's and defendant's attorneys of prospective candidates to select the members of a jury.

What are preemptory challenges?
Each side in a trial has the right to dismiss a certain number of prospective jurors for no reason. Beyond that number, there has to be a significant reason for dismissal.

What are the types of penalties for criminal actions?
The three types are felony, misdemeanor, and summary offense

What is a felony?
It is a serious crime usually punished by imprisonment or death, e.g., murder, robbery, arson, rape.

There may be degrees of felonies within a jurisdiction, first, second, third degree felonies which will also lead to various lengths of years of imprisonment in the state prison.

What is a misdemeanor?
It is a crime less serious than a felony punishable by fine, penalty, forfeiture, or lesser confinement than in a felony (county jail rather than state prison).

What is a summary offense?
In some jurisdictions, it is similar to misdemeanor or maybe for a lesser type of penalty than misdemeanor. In Pennsylvania, it may include imprisonment only up to ninety days.

What are interrogatories?
Interrogatories are questions asked on both sides to gain information in discovery during the pretrial procedure.

What is injunctive and mandatory relief?
A court, usually following a hearing, grants an order called an injunction telling a party to refrain from doing something. Failure to do so will result in irreparable harm or injury if not approved. A mandatory injunction orders an affirmative act or mandates a specific action.

What is an injunction?
It is a writ issued from a court to stop a certain action.

What are the different types of motions?
There are more than a dozen different motions as listed in *Black's Law Dictionary*, e.g., ex parte motion, petition to the court without letting the other side answer, motion to modify, in post-trial proceedings, a request to change a previous order.

What is a pretrial conference or hearing?

The conference is a meeting of opposing counsel with the judge to review the proceedings of the case, to review evidence, and the issues that will be tried.

What is a long-arm statute?

A law that allows a local state court to exercise jurisdiction over a company or person of another state.

What is forum non conveniens?

The ability to change the location of where a trial will be held based on the needs of all of the litigants.

What is an interpleader?

This is when two people are involved in a lawsuit to collect money from a third party who does not know which one to pay. The court collects the money from the debtor who then is removed from the suit.

What is res judicata?

"The thing has been judged." A previous court has decided a suit and cannot be brought before another court for another hearing.

What are causes of action?

Causes of action deal with the implementation of a civil action complaint. There is a multi-volume set of books called *Causes of Action* (West Group) (KF1250).

Where can one find sample complaints?

Causes of Action is a multivolme set of books (1st series, 30 vols.; 2d series, 29 vols. so far) that review a particular cause of action. Each volume has between five and ten articles. Each article is structured in the following manner (checklists do not appear in every article):

  I.   Introduction
  II. Substantive Law Overview
  III. Practice and Procedure
  IV. Practice Checklists
  V.   Appendix (including sample case and sample complaints)

Each volume has a detailed index and a jurisdiction table of cases.

Where can one find background material on trial preparation of specific topics?

Am Jur Trials (KF8915 A74) is a multi-volume set (113 vols. so far) that contains articles on preparing for trial. Each volume contains at least two or more articles

(articles can be up to 400-500 pages long) on a specific type of trial action, e.g., cardiolology medical malpractice.

What are interrogatories?
Interrogatories are the questions lawyers ask in order to obtain evidence from either party in a suit.

Are there books that cover interrogatories,?
There are several different titles that cover interrogatories including the following well-known titles:
> *Bender's Forms of Discovery* (KF8900 A3B4)
> *Expert Witness Checklists* (KF8961 D36)
> *Medical Malpractice: Checklists and Discovery* (KF8925 M3D36)
> *Pattern Deposition Checklists* (KF8900 D3)
> *Pattern Discovery: Antitrust* (KF8900 D316)
> *Pattern Discovery: Employment Discrimination* (KF8900 D32)
> *Pattern Discovery: Motor Vehicles* (KF8900 D34)
> *Pattern Discovery: Premises Liability* (KF8900 D327)
> *Pattern Discovery: Products Liability* (KF8900 D35)
> *Pattern Discovery: Tort Actions* (KF8900 D333)

What other books cover materials for interrogatories?
Am Jur Proof of Facts (KF8933 A426) is a multi-volume set (1st series, 30 vols., 2nd series, 50 vols., 3d series, 108 vols. so far). Each volume has five to ten articles.

What is the opening statement in a trial?
The opening statement by plaintiff's and defendant's attorneys lay out the arguments and conclusions to be made during the trial.

What is the closing statement in a trial?
The closing statement by the plaintiff's and defendant's attorneys summarize up the arguments presented in the trial for the jury to consider in their deliberations.

What is hearsay?
Testimony provided by a person who does not actually know the facts of a situation but is providing it second-hand.

What is direct examination?
In trial, the questioning of a witness by the person calling the witness to the stand.

What is cross-examination?
In trial, the questioning of a witness by the person opposed to the party who called the witness.

What are jury instructions?
At the end of a trial proceeding, the judge gives instructions to the jury concerning the points of law that they have to determine in order to find the plaintiff guilty or innocent.

What are points of charge?
Points of charge are jury instructions for specific charges by a judge.

What are the types of jury instructions?
There are civil and criminal jury instructions. There may also be general or specific topics that have jury instructions. The instructions may be published on the federal or state level. Also most states will publish their own civil and criminal jury instructions.

In some states they are considered official publications of the court.

What books cover jury instructions?
There are two major sets covering federal civil and criminal jury instructions:
> *Federal Jury Practice and Instructions* (West) (KF8984 D4)
> *Modern Federal Jury Instructions* (Bender) (KF8984 A65M64)

Titles covering individual topics:
> Construction Litigation (KF8984 A65C66)
> *Jury Instructions in Automobile Actions* (KF8994 D674)
> *Jury Instructions in Commercial Litigation*
> *Jury Instructions in Real Estate Litigation* (KF8994 D6752)
> *Jury Instructions on Damages in Tort Actions* (KF8984 E156)
> *Jury Instructions on Medical Issues* (KF8984 A65E22)
> *Jury Instructions on Products Liability* (KF8984 E164)
> *Manual on Employment Discrimination Law and Civil Rights Actions in the Federal Courts* (KF3464 R53)
> *Model Jury Instructions for Business Tort Litigation* (KF8984 A65A5)
> *Model Jury Instructions for Employment Litigation* (KF8984 E39)
> *Model Jury Instructions for Fidelity Cases* (KF1223 M63)
> *Model Jury Instructions for Surety Cases* (KF1045 A65M63)
> *Model Jury Instructions in Civil Antitrust Cases* (KF9066 A5M63)
> *Model Jury Instructions: Patent Litigation* (KF3155 M63)

Sample Civil RICO Jury Instructions (KF8984 S26)
Section 1983 Litigation: Jury Instructions (KF1325 C58S363)

How does one research jury instructions?

In some states jury instructions are part of the state's *Shepard's Citations* or may be available in online Shepard's and/or Keycite. Otherwise one can research the full-text databases in Lexis and Westlaw.

What is the purpose of jury verdicts?

Jury verdict information provides the practitioner with amounts of money awarded in plaintiff tort cases.

Where can one find resources on jury verdicts?

The Jury Verdict Research Series provides summaries in a multi-volume set.

Also Jury Verdict Research and Analysis has national and individual state publications on jury verdicts which are published monthly.

What is the sentencing phase of the trial?

Following the time that a person is found guilty of a crime, there is a period of time between the trial and the actual sentence imposed by the judge. It may also include the time after the imposition to include time for appeals. A judge may or may not impose imprisonment while an appeal is being made.

Are there sentencing guidelines in criminal cases?

Yes, the Sentencing Reform Act of 1984 altered federal sentencing law. It created the Federal Sentencing Commission to draw up guidelines for federal judges to impose on prisoners. These guidelines became effective November 1, 1987.

There is an annual official volume of the *Federal Sentencing Commission Guidelines* (KF9685 A329U55). It is also a volume published along with Title 18 U.S.C.A. and U.S.C.S. and other annotated editions by commercial vendors.

Do states follow the same Federal guidelines?

States may have their own sentencing guidelines that may be part of the statutes, administrative regulations, or court rules.

What is meant by alternative sentencing?

Alternative sentencing is a form of punishment that does not include incarceration in jail or prison. It provides for rehabilitation, deterrence, retribution, and justice.

What is probation?

Probation provides for the reduction of a sentence usually based on good behavior in jail/prison.

What is parole?

Parole is the process by which a prisoner requests a reduction in sentence from an administrative body that reviews parole requests. The agency may grant them or recommendation goes to the governor for his review.

What makes a case appealable?

The litigant who lost the case can appeal to the intermediate appellate court if he can convince the court that the trial court erred and that the error wrongly affected the outcome of the case.

What is meant by standard of review?

Standard of review gives the intermediate court the ability to review lower court cases. Generally, there are three types of standards: "de novo," "clearly erroneous," and "abuse of discretion."

What is meant by scope of review?

Scope of review refers to the appellate court's review of the issues heard by a trial court and level of deference provided by the decision of a trial court.

What is a plea bargain?

A plea bargain occurs between the prosecuting attorney and the defendant to agree to a specific sentence rather than go to trial. It may result in a reduced sentence of years in jail, house arrest, fine, or other reparation.

What is a plea agreement?

A plea agreement is the defendant agreeing to a plea bargain in court before a judge. A judge may decide to keep or reject the agreement based on federal or state guidelines.

II. INTERNET

What types of legal research materials are available on the Internet?

Primary legal research materials such as constitutions, statutes, administrative rules and regulations and cases are available.

Are there any secondary legal materials available on the Internet?

Legal dictionaries, a sort of legal encyclopedia (not like *C.J.S.* and *Am. Jur. 2d*), periodical articles, legal forms, legal directories, public records are available.

What types of secondary legal materials are not available on the Internet?
A.L.R. annotations and legal treatises are not yet available from the Internet except from the LexisNexis and Westlaw.

Is information available from the web sites reliable?
Information available from the government and court official web sites is completely reliable. Links provided by the reputed educational institutions and many commercial sites are also reliable.

How far back is the (archival) information available from these web sites?
Generally, Internet sites are good for the current information. Most of the web sites have archival information for the last ten years.

What are some of the government sites for legal research?
Official sites for the courts such as the U.S. Supreme Court web site www.supremecourtus.gov; Library of Congress web site http://thomas.loc.gov; and Government Printing Office web site www.gpoaccess.gov are few good examples of many government sites.

What are some of the educational institute sites for legal research?
Most of the law school libraries offer a plethora of legal links from their home pages. However, Cornell Law School web site, www.law.cornell.edu; Washburn University Law School web site, www.washlaw.edu; University of Pittsburgh Law School web site, www.jurist.law.pitt.edu are a few good examples of many educational sites.

What are some of the comprehensive legal web sites?
There are several good comprehensive legal research web sites. Findlaw, www.findlaw.com; HeiroGamos, www.hg.org; Megalaw, www.megalaw.com; Law Guru, www.lawguru.com; Virtual Chase, www.virtualchase.com are a few good examples of many comprehensive sites.

What are some of the private individual web sites for legal research?
Law firms from law firms and librarians from the law schools have good web sites for legal research either on a specific topic or comprehensive in nature. Sheela Murthy web site, www.murthy.com; Bit Law web site, www.bitlaw; Dittakavi Rao web site, www.pennsylvanialegalresearch.com are a few good examples of many private sites.

What are the alternative commercial legal research databases to Westlaw and LexisNexis?

Though the LexisNexis and Westlaw are the two most comprehensive full text online legal information sources, Loislaw, www.loislaw.com; Versuslaw, www.versuslaw.com; Casemaker, www.lawwriter.net; Fastcase, www.fastcase.com are a few good alternate sources to LexisNexis and Westlaw.

Are there any legal help sites on the Internet?

There are several legal help sites available on the Internet. Some are free and some are fee-based. LegalZoom, www.legalzoom.com, The Law.Net, www.thelaw.net are few of many fee-based websites and FreeAdvice, www.freeadvice.com, TheLaw, www.thelaw.com, LawHelp.Org, www.lawhelp.org, are a few of many free legal help Internet sites. Sites such as ProSe Law Center, www.pro-selaw.org provides very useful information for pro-se litigants.

III. LexisNexis

Are there any training modules or online instruction to research Lexis?

Once you are ready to conduct a search, Lexis provides a View Search Tutorial link at the bottom of Search Help box. The tutorials cover Search Advisor, Navigating Documents, Research History, etc.

When was Lexis started?

Lexis, "the first commercial, full-text legal information service," has been providing information to the legal community since 1973.

When was Nexis started?

Nexis was created in 1979 to provide access to news and business information. The Lexis-Nexis Group was acquired by Reed Elsevier PLC in 1994.

Do I need to have an ID to access Lexis?

Yes. Lexis-Nexis service is subscription only. Students in the law schools get training and personal IDs in the first year. Any one can obtain an ID for a fee.

What are the different methods of accessing Lexis?

There are three different access sites, www.lexis.com, www.lexisnexis.com/lawschool and www.lexisnexis.com. Each provides a different home page to access the databases.

How do I sign-on?

Enter your ID number in the LexisNexis ID dialog box. And then enter your last name in lower case in the Password dialog box and click on "Sign On."

For privacy and security reasons, last names are no longer used as passwords. All users must create both a Custom ID and a Password.

What is a library and a file?

Information in Lexis is divided into libraries and subdivided into files. Files can be multiple or single titles. Libraries, for example, are Cases —U.S., Federal Legal —U.S., and State Legal —U.S., etc. Within Cases —U.S., files can be Mega, All Federal, All States, etc.

What is the purpose of the Tabs?

It is useful to create a Tab on a specific topic if you use it continuously, since it brings together all primary and secondary sources under the tab topic.

There is an ADD/EDIT TABS link to select or remove tabs.

What are the tabs along the top of the main page?

Search, Research Tasks, Research Advisor, Get a Document, Shepard's, Alerts.

What is Search?

Under the Search Tab are Sources, Guided Search Forms, and Command Searching.

Sources tab provides two options: Recently Used Sources and Look for a Source which provides the major libraries and their files, e.g., Cases —U.S., Federal Legal —U.S., States Legal —U.S., etc.

Guided Search Forms allow the researcher to specify which resources will be searched. Guided search forms are available in Lexis for federal and state law, cases, codes, by area of law, law reviews, and many other categories.

Command Searching provides the ability to enter multiple sources and search commands in one search.

What is the difference between search and advanced search?

Segments and date are available only when you choose advanced search.

What is Research Tasks?

This tab has a selection of major topics that incorporates primary and secondary sources on that topic, e.g., bankruptcy has in addition to primary sources, News and Legal Developments, Collier Bankruptcy Library, Public Records, etc.

What is Search Advisor?

Search Advisor helps you find legal materials based on areas of the law and legal topics. If you are unsure about how to begin your research, Search Advisor is a good place to start. One can run a search on a topic by jurisdiction without inputting any other information in the query box.

Each topic is broken down into subtopics for review, e.g., Legal Ethics contains General Overview, Client Relations, Judicial Conduct, Law Firms, etc.

Like the Search feature, Search Advisor lets you access legal materials in two ways: Choose From My Last 20 Legal Topics, or Look for a Legal Topic.

What is Get a Document?

Get a Document lets one retrieve a document by citation, by party name, and by docket number.

Get a Document by citation obtains cases, statutes, rules, law reviews, etc. by exact citation.

It is essential that you enter the correct citation for the document you are requesting. If you are not certain of the citation, click on Citation Formats link.

Get a Document by Party Name lets one put in at least one of the two parties to a case along with the selection of a jurisdiction. A date may or may not be entered.

Get a Document by Docket Number lets one put in a docket number along with the selection of a jurisdiction. A date may or may not be entered.

If you wish to select multiple documents at one time, use the Get and Print link below the query window.

What is Shepard's?

Under the Shepard's tab are Shepard's, Table of Authorities, Auto-Cite, and Lexcite.

Shepard's allows you to determine the validity of a case or statute and to find other documents by providing parallel citations, case history, treatment of a case, and citations to a case.

What is Table of Authorities?

Table of Authorities provides a list of cases cited in a case along with Shepard's signals, e.g., Roe v. Wade, 410 U.S. 113 cites 143 cases.

What is Auto-Cite?

Auto-Cite allows you to verify the accuracy of a case citation; check a cite to confirm case name, jurisdiction, and year of decision; verify the precedential value of a case; and research a case citation to review prior history and find related annotations.

What is Lexcite?
Lexcite allows you to find both reported and unreported cases that refer to a case law citation.

What is Alerts?
Alerts provides email notification of new documents on a specific topic that you have requested.

Shepard's Alert lets one enter a citation and provide an email notification daily, weekly, or monthly when a case containing your search term is found in new cases on that topic as a cite or full-text format.

What is the History link?
History provides Recent Results and Archive Activity. Recent Results lists your searches for the previous 24 hours. Archive Activity lists the previous 30 days of research activity.

What are the research methods to retrieve information from the databases?
There are three methods to retrieve information: Terms and Connectors, Natural Language, and Easy Search.

What is "Terms and Connectors" search method?
The researcher uses Boolean connectors —and, or, not —along with connectors that let's one connect words together within a sentence, a paragraph, within a certain number of words of each other, etc. The symbols are:

And searches words anywhere in the document

Or searches listed words but usually think of synonyms, e.g., landlord and tenant or lessor and lessee

And Not Excludes any words that follow and not in search request, e.g., Puerto Rico and not Puerto for just Rico cases.

! Exclamation point replaces any ending to a root word, e.g., dissent!

* Asterisk substitutes a single letter within a word, e.g., wom*n searches for woman or women.

Connectors
/n finds two words within n words of each other; n can be up to 255 words

Pre/n finds two words in the same document with first word preceding second word by n words, e.g., cable /1 television

/s finds words in same sentence

/p finds words in same paragraph

What are Search Commands?

At Least require a term or terms to appear a certain number of times within a document

All Caps require a term to be in all caps to bring up selected words, e.g., AIDS

Caps restrict search to find terms in which capital letters appear anywhere in the term, e.g., SuperVga, SUPERVGA, Supervga.

No Caps search to find terms with no capital letters in the word

Plural search is restricted to only plural forms of a word

Singular search is restricted to only singular forms of a word

What is Natural Language search method?
Researcher enters regular sentence or key words and the computer will return answer based on relevancy. This may result in more or less results than Terms and Connectors search.

Please note that the default number of results for Natural Language is 100 results. The default number or results for Terms and Connectors is 3000 results.

What is Easy Search method?
This search form is a simple, uncluttered user interface, without details of more advanced search options (no segment selection or date restriction drop-down menus; no mandatory terms field; etc.). When a user runs a query in Easy Search, the system evaluates the search behind the scenes and automatically determines whether to use Boolean logic or plain English/Freestyle type search algorithms. The user does not need to know LexisNexis search commands or connectors, or follow any particular syntax, to run a query.

What is Suggest Terms for My Search?
Once you key in a word or term, clicking on this link will provide synonyms and core terms associated with the word you entered.

What is Check Spelling?
The link will check the spelling of your search request and point out any misspellings to correct.

What are the segments?
Segments will vary from file to file. For example, each case is broken down into its various segments or parts. The researcher can select segment and add the variable (judge's name, attorney's name, etc.) to the segment and then place it in the search box provided above. It is possible to just type the segment(s) name in the query box.

Cite
Cites
Concur
Concurby
Core-Terms
Counsel
Court
Court-Text
Decision
Disposition
Dissent
Dissentby
Headnotes
History
Judges
LED-Headnotes
LN-Headnotes
LN-Summary
Name
Notice
Number
Opinion
Opinionby
Opinions
Outcome
Overview
Posture
References
Summary
Syllabus
Writtenby

What are date restrictions?
Restrict by Date provides standard restrictions as well as the ability to limit dates to a specific time period.

Standard restrictions are
No Date Restrictions
Previous Week
Previous Month
Previous 6 Months
Previous Year
Previous 2 Years
Previous 5 Years
Previous 10 Years
From date to date inputting mm/dd/yyyy to mm/dd/yyyy

What are Date Formats?
Valid date formats include using just numbers or months abbreviated as Jan., jan., Jan, Jan, January, January. Years can be in full number —1999 —or abbreviated at 99.

What does Focus function do?
Once a search is completed, the Focus function lets one reduce the number of hits and find more relevant documents by adding additional terms.

How can I edit my search?
If a search returns too many cases and/or irrelevant cases, click on the Edit Search link to take you back to the original search. You can then revise or add new terms to the original search. Lexis also helps by providing a link to Suggest Terms for My Search for more related terms to your research question.

What is More Like This?
More Like This limits the search to Core Cites or Core Terms. Core Cites refers to cases with similar citation formats. Core Terms are key words found in the document that you can select from to locate other cases on the topic.

What is More Like Selected Text?
More Like Selected Text lets one highlight a phrase or sentence and then search libraries for other cases containing the exact phrase or sentence.

How does one view the documents results?
Lexis will display your search results in four choices: Cite, KWIC, Full, and Custom. One can select a default display by any of those four formats.

Cite provides a list of the documents by citation only.

KWIC provides a list of the documents with a block of text on either side of the search terms printed in bold type. The default is usually 25 words on either side of the search terms, but can be changed (up to 999 words) if you click on the KWIC link.

Full provides full-text of the documents.

Custom provides a list of available segments which can be selected for view (all or some may be chosen).

What features are available in Delivering Documents?

Lexis provides different methods to obtain the completed search documents: Fast Print, Print, Download, Fax, Email, and Text Only.

Fast Print allows you to print from an already formatted setting, such as name of the printer, font type, font size, etc.

Print lets you select each time how the document is to be printed. The format may be in citation, KWIC, or full text; word processing format (Word, Word Perfect, Adobe PDF, TXT file, or Generic (RTF) format); and font type and font size.

Download lets you download your documents in Format (various word processing formats), Document View (cite, KWIC, full, custom), and Formatting Option (font type) and font size. One can print all documents, a selected number of documents, or a specific document.

Fax lets you fax a document to yourself or someone else with an added brief note attached.

Email lets you send documents to a person as an attachment.

Text Only function removes all graphical elements from the documents.

IV. Westlaw

When was Westlaw started?

Westlaw is the product of West Group. West Group has been providing information to the legal community for over 120 years. West Group, a division of the Thomson Corporation, was formed in 1996 when West Publishing and Thomson Legal Publishing merged. Westlaw was created in 1974.

How do I sign on?

Once you are on Westlaw's home page (www.westlaw.com), type your Westlaw password in the "Password" box and then type your last name in "Client ID" box.

If I am a law student can I sign on to www.westlaw.com or www.lawschool. westlaw.com?

If you are a law student you will be better off signing on to www.lawschool.west-law.com which will link to a wide variety of resources of particular interest to law students, such as information about events and Westlaw training opportunities at your school; The West Education Network (TWEN); study aids; state bar information; career planning materials; and job listings in the Law Student Jobs Online and Attorney jobs Online databases.

What is West OnePass?
When you register your Westlaw password, you will be prompted to West OnePass to create your own easy-to-remember username and password.

What are the advantages of West OnePass?
With West OnePass, you can use a single username and password to access information and services from many West Web sites, including lawschool.westlaw.com, westlaw.com, west.thomson.com and westlegaledcenter.com.

What are Tabbed Pages?
Tabbed pages in westlaw.com are organizational tools that help you focus your research and save time.

How do I select my Tabbed Pages?
Click My Westlaw link at the top of any page. A list of available tabbed pages is displayed. Select the check box next to the name of each page that you want to have available when you sign on to Westlaw.

How many Tabbed pages can I select?
You can select a varied number of tabbed pages. You can add and remove tabbed pages whenever you want. You can also personalize your tabbed pages. In addition to the 6 tabs that you set, you can click on the blue link and add up to two more tabbed pages for this research session only. You can share your personalized tabbed pages via email.

What is Research Trail?
The Research Trail makes it easy to keep track of your Westlaw research and return to research tasks you completed previously.

How do I save my searches to my research trail?
A new research trail is automatically created each time you access Westlaw and automatically saved when you end your research session.

How long are my searches saved?
Each research trail is available for 14 days after it is saved. You can download or email research trails.

What is Trail Notes?

The Trail Notes feature enables you to create notes about a particular task or research session. You can use these notes as a personal record or share your notes with others.

How can I add Notes to my research trail?

While viewing a research trail, click Add Note for the research event to which you want to add notes. Type the note in the Text box and click Add Note.

What is a database?

The information in Westlaw is organized into more than 30,000 databases. To run a query you have to first select an appropriate database.

What are the types of databases?

Generally there are two types: General or large databases and specific purpose databases. For example you can retrieve a United States Supreme Court case from the Supreme Court database (SCT) or all federal cases database (ALLFEDS) or all cases from all state and federal jurisdictions database (ALLCASES).

Which database should I select?

The charges are more for a larger database. It is a good practice to choose a specific purpose database to retrieve information.

How can I choose a database?

Westlaw provides several methods to choose your database: Database Wizard (bottom left on directory page); Westlaw Directory (tab on the homepage); Recent Database Feature (under search these databases on left side of the page); Favorite Database Feature(under recent database); and IDEN database (enter IDEN in search these databases box that will provide you with a list of databases for the word you have entered).

What is scope of a database?

Scope is a Westlaw feature that provides detailed information including search tips. The scope icon (a small letter I in a circle) is available next to database identifier.

What are the fields and restrictions?

Field restrictions are the different sections of a court case that can be separated into fields and searched independently.

How can I enter my research query?

In the Query Box, one can search using Terms and Connectors or Natural Language. KeySearch is an additional search engine that is accessible from the top blue bar and walks you through various topics. KeySearch is discussed below.

What is 'terms and connectors' search?

Terms and connectors are divided into several parts: Boolean connectors include using the words "and," "or," and "not." "And" connects two words or terms located anywhere in the case. "Or" is the use of synonyms in searching cases. "Not" eliminates words close together that one does not wish to have together, e.g., RICO cases, but not Puerto Rico. (Note that NOT must be entered at the very end of the query.)

Cases can be broken down into the various fields:

Annotations	Judge
Attorney	Lead
Author	Notes
Caption	Opinions
Citation	Prelim
Concurring	Prelim and Caption
Court	References
Credit	Source
Digest	Substantive Doc
Dissenting	Summary
Document Type	Synopsis
Document Number	Synopsis & Digest
End	Text
Historical Notes	Title
Index	

What are date restrictions?

Westlaw provides date restrictions for use in searches:

Unrestricted	Last 30 days
After	Last 60 days
Before	Last 90 days
Between	Year to date
Specific	This Year and Last Year
Last	Last 3 Years
Today	Last 10 Years

What is 'natural language' search?
This is the use of a regular sentence to make the request.

What are the options of viewing my search results?
There are options available under preferences (located in top right corner) as to how your results are displayed. In general, Westlaw provides the citation list along with highlighted key words. One can select to hide search terms in the result list that provides only citations to documents. And one can select the number of words to be displayed on either side of the highlighted terms.

How can I narrow my search results?
Use the Locate in Result link at top of page, which will then give you a query box to enter more specific words/terms to further limit your search. Or, you can change the connectors to narrow the search or use it in conjunction with date restrictors.

What does the 'Locate' function do?
The locate function lets one add additional words to further restrict a search and reduce the number of hits.

How can I expand the scope of a search?
Once you do a search in a selected database, an Expand Search template allows one to select a more comprehensive related database to expand your research, e.g., NY-CS will give you the expanded listing for Federal and State Cases or State and Federal Cases in the Second Circuit.

How can I change database and edit query?
Use the edit search link in the upper left hand corner or use the database drop down box and type in the database name or select one from the drop-down list.

What is Westclip?
Westclip provides the researcher with a research request by email notification that can be done on a daily or weekly basis.

What are the printing options available in Westlaw?
One can print to an attached printer, save searches to computer or disk, save searches to Westlaw, email documents as attachments or fax.

How do I sign-off?
There is a Sign Off button along the top next to the Help button.

CHAPTER 2

LEGAL CITATIONS

Introduction: All practitioners in legal research have to learn how to document sources properly. In the legal field, the Uniform System of Citations, commonly known as the Bluebook, is the standard source for citations and is now in its eighteenth edition. Legal research instructors in a growing number of law schools use the Association of Legal Writers Directory (ALWD) Citation Manual.

What is a legal citation?
In most professional fields, there is a standard method by which one cites to primary and secondary sources that makes it easier for the researcher to find documents cited in primary and secondary materials. The legal field has several different sources for legal citation styles.

Is it necessary to have a proper citation in legal documents?
In litigation, the courts require proper citing of sources to make it easier for the judiciary to locate documents under review.

How does one cite legal materials?
There are two standard sources used in American law schools.

The first one is the *Uniform System of Citation* (KF245 U55) published by the law reviews of Harvard Law School, Yale, Columbia and University of Pennsylvania.

The second one is *ALWD Citation Manual* (3d ed. 2005) (KF245 A45) published by the Association of Legal Writing Directors.

What is the nickname or short title for the *Uniform System of Citation*?
The short title is the Bluebook and it is sometimes referred to as the "Harvard citator."

How often are these works revised?
They are revised every few years when it is felt that there are enough revisions to warrant a new edition. The current edition of the *Bluebook* is the eighteenth edition published in 2005 and the current edition of the *ALWD Citation Manual* is the third edition published in 2006.

Are there any other sources for citing legal materials?
The University of Chicago Law School publishes the *Maroon Book*. In certain states, there may be a standard format for citing legal materials, e.g., the California Citation.

What is universal citation?
Universal citation is a method to cite court cases without using the West Publishing Company volume and page number references. The legal citation format is the name of the case, the year, the court of jurisdiction, a sequential number for the opinion, and a paragraph number for the text. Citation then is to the paragraph number and not the page number. For example, Jones v. Brown, 2008 5th Cir. 25, §3, 2008 Pa. Super. 240, §23.

What is the public domain legal citation?
The citation format is the same as the universal citation. Different jurisdictions may use the name either public domain legal citation or universal citation.

What are the two sets of instructions in the *Bluebook* citation manual?
The "Basic" citation rules are used in legal practice (briefs and memoranda) and the more complex rules are used for citation in law reviews.

Are there listings of the most frequently used materials in the *Bluebook*?
Yes, on the inside cover there are two pages dealing with the Style of Law Review Footnotes and on the back inside cover there is a Quick Reference: Court Documents and Legal Memoranda.

How is the *Bluebook* organized?
The book is divided into three parts. Part I contains the Blue Pages which provide a basic how-to-guide for legal citation. The second part is the Rules Section containing Rules 1 to 9 that deal with general standards of citation and style. Also Rules 10 to 21 for specific types of legal documents. The third part is the Tables Section containing a series of tables to be used in conjunction with the rules showing authority for citation and how to abbreviate citations.

How is the *ALWD Citation Manual* organized?
The book is divided into 7 parts.

Part 1: Introductory Material.
Part 2: Citation Basics.
Part 3: Citing Specific Print Sources
Part 4: Electronic Sources
Part 5: Incorporating Citations into Documents
Part 6: Quotations
Part 7: Appendices
Index

How can I find what I am looking for in the *Bluebook* & *ALWD Citation Manual?*
There is an index in the back of each volume.

Does the *Bluebook* & *ALWD Citation Manual* contain the names of the case reports for each state?
The *Bluebook* in Table 1 contains United States Jurisdictions. The *ALWD Citation Manual* has it in the Appendix 1 without the early state nominative reports (referred to Morris Cohen's *Handbook of Legal Research* (1989)).

What else is listed under United States Jurisdictions?
Each state's web site, public domain citation format, court cases, statutory compilations (chronological and code), administrative compilation (codes), and administrative and executive registers are cited.

Does the *Bluebook* & *ALWD Citation Manual* contain the names of the frequently used law reviews/periodicals?
The *Bluebook* Table 13 contains abbreviations for English language legal periodicals.

The *ALWD Citation Manual* Appendix 5 contains Abbreviations for Legal Periodicals.

Where can one find rules for primary materials?
In the *Bluebook*, the following rules can be used:

Rule 10 is Case law
Rule 11 is Constitutions
Rule 12 is Statutes
Rule 13 is Legislative Materials
Rule 14 is Administrative and Executive Materials

In the *ALWD Citation Manual*, the following rules can be used:
Rule 12 is Case law

Rule 13 is Constitutions
Rule 14 is Statutory Codes, Session Laws, and Slip Laws
Rule 15 is Other Federal Legislative Materials
Rule 16 is Other State Legislative Materials
Rule 19 Federal Administrative and Executive Materials
Rule 20 State Administrative and Executive Materials

Where can one find the short form citations for primary materials?
In the *Bluebook*, there is a standard method by going to section 9 of each rule to find the short term citations, e.g., Rule 10.9 is Short Forms for Cases, Rule 12.9 is Short Forms for Statutes.

ALWD Citation Manual also contains references under each rule for the short form, e.g., Rule 12.21(e) and (f) is Short Forms for Cases, Rule 14.6 for Statutes.

Where can one find rules for secondary materials?
In the *Bluebook*, secondary materials are listed:

Rule 15: Books, Reports, and Other Nonperiodic Materials
Rule 16: Periodicals
Rule 17: Unpublished and Forthcoming Sources
Rule 18: Electronic Media and Other Nonprint Resources
Rule 19: Services

In the *ALWD Citation Manual*, secondary materials are listed:
Rule 22: Books, Treatises, and Other Nonperiodic Materials
Rule 23: Legal and Other Periodicals
Rule 24: A.L.R. Annotations
Rule 25: Legal Dictionaries
Rule 26: Legal Encyclopedias
Rule 27: Restatements, Model Codes, Uniform Laws, and Sentencing Guidelines
Rule 28: Looseleaf Services and Reporters
Rule 29: Practitioner and Court Documents, Transcripts, and Appellate Records
Rule 30: Speeches, Addresses, and Other Oral Presentations
Rule 31: Interviews
Rule 32: Letters and Memoranda
Rule 33: Video and Visual Recordings and Broadcasts
Rule 34: Sound Recordings
Rule 35: Microformed Materials
Rule 36: Forthcoming Works
Rule 37: Unpublished Works and Working Papers

Where can one find rules for foreign and international materials?
In the *Bluebook*, foreign and international materials are:
Rule 20: Foreign Materials
Rule 21: International Materials

In the *ALWD Citation Manual*, foreign and international materials are:
Rule 21: Treaties and Conventions to Which the United States is a Party, International Sources, and Foreign Sources

Is there a web site that contains information on the Bluebook?
Peter Martin has an *Introduction to Basic Legal Citation* based on the Bluebook along with examples, at www.law.cornell.edu/citation.

Where does one find legal abbreviations used in the legal literature?
Prince's Dictionary of Legal Abbreviations (KF246 P73) and *World Dictionary of Legal Abbreviations* (K89 W67) provides the meaning of legal abbreviations commonly used in legal literature.

How many abbreviations are included in *Prince's Dictionary*?
There are more than 30,000 abbreviations and acronyms included.

Is there a companion book to the *Bluebook?*
Prince's Dictionary of Legal Citations (KF246 P73) is intended to assist the legal professional in citing legal authorities according to the rules given in the *Bluebook*.

Is there any book to help me abbreviate the titles of the legal information material used in the legal literature?
Bieber's Dictionary of Legal Abbreviations Reversed: A Dictionary of Terms and Titles With Their Abbreviations provide abbreviations to the titles of the legal information material such as reporters, legal periodicals, etc.

Where can I find the meaning of an abbreviation or an acronym used in a foreign country's legal literature?
The multi-volume work, *World Dictionary of Legal Abbreviations* provides the precise meaning of abbreviations and acronyms as they appear in the foreign legal literature.

What is CiteStation?
CiteStation is a series of online exercises available via The West Education Network (TWEN) that are designed to help make teaching legal citation more effective.

Each of the exercises is presented in the context of practical legal documents, such as contracts, memoranda, and pleadings, in both *Bluebook* and *ALWD Citation Manual* format. *(Westlaw handout)*

How does one cite court cases?
Case law is usually cited by the volume number, abbreviated name of the court report, and page number, with the date of the decision in parenthesis. In addition, the court is generally listed inside the parenthesis with the date.

BLUEBOOK
Foucha v. Louisiana, 504 U.S. 71 (2004), 118 L.Ed.2d 437, 112 S. Ct. 1780 (1992)

Ross v. Artuz, 150 F.3d 97 (2d Cir. 1998)

Graffam v. Town of Harpswell, 250 F.Supp.2d 1 (D.Me. 2003)

In re Jackson, 245 B.R. 23 (Bkrtcy. E.D.Pa. 2000)

Highland Ins. Group, Inc. v. Halliburton Co., 852 A.2d 1 (Del. Ch. 2003)

Storey v. State, 175 S.W.3d 116 (Mo. 2005)

Grossman v. Amalgamated Housing Corp., 298 A.D. 2d 224,750 N.Y.S.2d 1 (N.Y. A.D. Dept. 1, 2002)

ALWD
Foucha v. Louisiana, 504 U.S. 71 (2004), 118 L.Ed.2d 437, 112 S. Ct. 1780 (1992)

Ross v. Artuz, 150 F.3d 97 (2d Cir. 1998)

Graffam v. Town of Harpswell, 250 F.Supp.2d 1 (D.Me. 2003)

In re Jackson, 245 B.R. 23 (Bkrtcy. E.D.Pa. 2000)

Highland Ins. Group, Inc. v. Halliburton Co., 852 A.2d 1 (Del. Ch. 2003)

Storey v. State, 175 S.W.3d 116 (Mo. 2005)

Grossman v. Amalgamated Housing Corp., 298 A.D. 2d 224,750 N.Y.S.2d 1 . (1st Dept. 2002)

How does one cite constitutions?
BLUEBOOK
U.S. Const. art. IV, § 2, cl. 1

U. S. Const. amend. xiv, §3

Ga. Const. art 1, §2, 1

ALWD

U.S. Const. art. IV, § 2, cl. 1

U. S. Const. amend. XIV, § 3

Ga. Const. art. 1, § 2, 1

How does one cite statutory law?

BLUEBOOK

Chronological laws are cited by the public law number of Congress, the U.S. Statutes at Large, and the United States Code.

Pub. L. 106-210, 114 Stat. 321, 15 U.S.C. § 1601 (2000)

New York: N. Y. Laws, 2003, ch. 10

Pennsylvania: 2003 Pa. Laws 1

ALWD

Pub. L. 106-210, 114 Stat. 321, 15 U.S.C. §1601 (2000)

Pub. L. 106-210, 2000 U.S.C.C.A.N. (114 Stat.) 321.

New York: N. Y. Laws, 2003, ch. 10

Pennsylvania: 2003 Pa. Laws 1

How does one cite codified statutes?

BLUEBOOK

U. S. Code: 18 U.S.C. § 351 (2000)

U.S.C.A.: 18 U.S.C.A. § 351 (West Supp. 2007)

U.S.C.S.: 18 U.S.C.S. § 351 (LexisNexis 1995)

California Code: Cal. Prob. Code. § 101 (2005)

Pennsylvania Consolidated Statutes: 23 Pa.C.S. § 101 (2004)

ALWD

U. S. Code: 18 U.S.C. § 351 (2000)

U.S.C.A.: 18 U.S.C.A. § 351 (West Supp. 2007)

U.S.C.S.: 18 U.S.C.S. § 351 (Law Coop. & Lexis Supp. 2007)

California Code: Cal. Prob. Code. § 101 (2005)

Pennsylvania Consolidated Statutes: 23 Pa.C.S. § 101 (2004)

How does one cite legislative materials?

BLUEBOOK
Report: H.R. Rep. No. 106-200, at 2 (2000), as reprinted in 2000 U.S.C.C.A.N.
Hearing: 106th Congress (1999) (statement of)
Congressional Record: Cong. Rec. (2007)

How does one cite administrative law?
Citations are to the Federal Register and the Code of Federal Regulations.

BLUEBOOK
72 Fed .Reg. 44,367 (August 8, 2007)
11 C.F.R. § 4.2 (2007).

ALWD
72 Fed. Reg. 44367 (August 8, 2007)
11 C.F.R. § 4.2 (2007).

How are court rules cited?

BLUEBOOK

Federal Rules of Appellate Procedure	Fed. R. App. P 1924
Federal Rules of Civil Procedure	Fed. R. Civ. P. 4001
Federal Rules of Criminal Procedure	Fed. R. Crim. P. 32
Federal Rules of Evidence	Fed. R. E. 901
New Jersey Rules of Civil Procedure	N.J. R. Civ. P. 1.8

ALWD

Federal Rules of Appellate Procedure	Fed. R. App. P 1924
Federal Rules of Civil Procedure	Fed. R. Civ. P. 4001
Federal Rules of Criminal Procedure	Fed. R. Crim. P. 32
Federal Rules of Evidence	Fed. R. Evid. 901
New Jersey Rules of Civil Procedure	N.J. R. Civ. P. 1.8

How are books cited?

BLUEBOOK
Author:
Erwin C. Surrency, A History of American Law Publishing 25 (1990).

Editor:
Prestatehood Legal Materials (Michael Chiorazzi and Marguerite Most eds., 2005).

ALWD
Erwin C. Surrency. *A History of American Law Publishing* 25 (Oceana 1990).

Prestatehood Legal Materials (Michael Chiorazzi and Marguerite Most, eds., Haworth Press 2005).

How are legal periodicals cited?
They are cited by volume, name of journal, page number and date in parenthesis.

BLUEBOOK
Richard A. Nagareda, *Autonomy, Peace, and Put Options in the Mass Tort Class Action*, 115 Harv. L. Rev. 747 (2001-2002).

For periodicals that are published without continuous pagination, the citation includes the issue number and the page numbers.

Savage, David G. *Open for Business: The Concerns of Corporate America are Front and Center at the Supreme Court*, 92 no. 5 ABA J. 18 (May 2006).

ALWD
Richard A. Nagareda, *Autonomy, Peace, and Put Options in the Mass Tort Class Action*, 115 Harv. L. Rev. 747 (2001-2002).

For periodicals that are published without continuous pagination, the citation includes the issue number and the page numbers.

Savage, David G. *Open for Business: The Concerns of Corporate America are Front and Center at the Supreme Court*, 92 no. 5 ABA J. 18 (May 2006).

How are legal newspapers cited?

BLUEBOOK
Miriam Rozen, *Vinson & Elkins Settles Claim Over Enron*, NYLJ, June 5, 2006 at 1.

ALWD

Miriam Rozen, *Vinson & Elkins Settles Claim Over Enron*, NYLJ 1 (June 5, 2006)

How are encyclopedias cited?

BLUEBOOK

32B Am. Jur. 2d *Federal Courts* § 1909 (1996).

71 C.J.S. *Pleading* § 45 (2000).

ALWD

32B Am. Jur. 2d *Federal Courts* § 1909 (1996).

71 C.J.S. *Pleading* § 45 (2000).

How are *American Law Reports* (ALR) cited?

BLUEBOOK

Marjorie A. Shields, Annotation, *Excessive or Inadequacy of Damage Awards Against Drunken Drivers*, 14 A.L.R 6th 263 (2006).

ALWD

Marjorie A. Shields, *Excessive or Inadequacy of Damage Awards Against Drunken Drivers*, 14 A.L.R. 6th 263 (2006).

How are *Restatements of the Law* cited?

BLUEBOOK

Restatement (Second) of Torts § 85 (1965).

ALWD

Restatement (Second) of Torts § 85 (1965).

How are electronic media and other nonprint resources cited?

BLUEBOOK

Rule 18 of the Bluebook provides the method for citation based on whether it is a Lexis/Westlaw citation (Rule 18.1) or an Internet citation (Rule 18.2).

Cases

Slip Opinion on Internet

New Jersey Transit Corp. v. Harsco Corp., No. 06-3507 (3d Cir. Aug. 7, 2007),

available at http://www.ca3.uscourts.gov/opinarch/063507p.pdf

Case Published only in Lexis or Westlaw

Lopez v. Meluzio, No. CV 05-0009, 2006 U.S. Dist. LEXIS 93912 (E.D.N.Y. Dec. 29, 2006)

Lopez v. Meluzio, No. CV 05-0009, 2006 WL3833115 (E.D.N.Y. Dec. 29, 2006)

For Internet citations, generally cite to the specific web address or Uniform Resource Locator (URL); however, if the link is too long, it is permissible to cite to the root URL and give directions to reach the page under review.

The rule also states that given a choice between the HTML and PDF format of a document, one should always cite to the PDF document.

ALWD
Slip Opinion on Internet
New Jersey Transit Corp. v. Harsco Corp.,
http://www.ca3.uscourts.gov/opinarch/063507p.pdf (3d Cir. Aug. 7, 2007)
Case Published only in Lexis or Westlaw
Lopez v. Meluzio, 2006 U.S. Dist. LEXIS 93912 (Dec. 29, 2006)
Lopez v. Meluzio, 2006 WL3833115 (E.D.N.Y. Dec. 29, 2006)

How does one cite material repeated in a document?
Under other citation formats one usually uses Ibid., but in legal citations, it is not used. Instead one uses id. and supra.

What is *Id.*?
After a full citation is given, one uses *Id.* for consecutive references from the same source.

   If you are citing a different page, then the citation should be *Id.* at [page number].

What is a short citation?
In citing cases, articles, books, etc. a short citation is a succeeding citation after the first full citation is provided. The short citation for a court case is the name of the case, volume, abbreviation for the case, and exact page number, e.g., *Roe v. Wade*, 410 U.S. at 118.

When does one use *supra*?
After a full citation is given, *supra* is used after a citation is provided later in a document. One may cite an author's name and short title of a book or article, e.g., Levinson, Second Amendment, *supra*, at [page number].

When do you know when to stop the legal research process?
It is time to stop researching when you keep on finding the same answers from different sources.

CHAPTER 3

CASE LAW—REPORTERS

Introduction: This chapter covers General Information, Court systems, and Case law publications. General information provides some of the general terms associated with preparing documents for submission to the court as well as some terms in researching case law. The court system describes mainly the federal court system with some general questions concerning state courts. The case law publications deal with the individual reports published by the various jurisdictions of the federal courts including both official and unofficial reports. There is also coverage of basic Lexis, Westlaw, and Internet case law research.

I. MANUAL

A. CASE LAW —GENERAL INFORMATION

Why is case law so important?

The American legal system follows the pattern of the English common law system. The main principle of the common law system is *"stare decisis,"* which means "stand by the settled." If precedence is there, the precedent prevails.

Why is *stare decisis* essential to the American legal system?

Stare decisis provides stability to the law, predictability of the outcome of the case, and fairness.

What is the goal of case research?

To find cases on the specific issues to determine precedents for these cases.

What are the factors determining whether a case is a binding precedent?

  a. Jurisdiction
  b. Mandatory vs. Persuasive Precedent

    c.   Level of the Court
    d.   History and Treatment of a Case
    e.   Similarity of Facts and Legal issues

What is primary mandatory versus primary persuasive authority?

Primary mandatory authority are those statutes and decisions of the highest court of a jurisdiction that must be followed by all courts within a particular jurisdiction. Persuasive authority may be judicial decisions decided by one court that offer guidance to another court. Constitutions and statutes of other jurisdictions should not be considered either mandatory or persuasive.

What is the "Statement of Facts"?

The party's account of the events leading up to the lawsuit usually is found in the beginning of a brief.

What are the types of cases?

Civil and criminal cases.

What is a civil case?

Generally, a dispute between two private citizens.

What is a criminal case?

Criminal cases involve the state, city, county, or federal government proceeding against individuals.

What type of case contains an "In Re" at the beginning of the case?

"In Re" refers to In the matter of or In regard to. It is used in a non-adversary proceeding that deals with a particular thing or person, e.g., competency, guardianship, trust, or bankruptcy.

What is an indictment?

A criminal complaint issued by a grand jury charging a person with a crime.

What is the TARP Rule in researching case law?

Things: What are the things involved in this case?

Action: What legal action might be filed?

Relief: What legal relief is sought?

Parties: What people might be involved in the case?

What is the IRAC Rule in researching case law?

Issue: What facts and circumstances brought these parties to court?

Rule: What is the governing law for the issue?

Analysis: Does the rule apply to these unique facts?

Conclusion: How does the court's holding modify the rule of law?

What is the "Common Law" Rule?

Legal rules made by courts are called "Common Law" rules.

What are cases on point?

It is where cases contain the same fact situation as the case one is researching.

What is meant by 'case of first instance'?

Case of first instance is referred to a trial court where generally the cases are first heard. In states they are known as county courts, Courts of Common Pleas, etc. and at federal level they are known as United States District Courts.

What is meant by a case of first impression?

A case that presents the court with an issue of law that has not previously been decided by any controlling legal authority in that jurisdiction.

What is meant when a case is "on all fours?"

The case is on target for both law and fact.

What is meant by a "controlling case?"

A judge recognizes that a particular case is the main case cited for precedential value in a decision.

What is meant by pedestrian cases?

Cases that provide no new legal precedents but are easily decided based on earlier decisions.

B. COURT SYSTEM

Where do the cases originate from?

Cases are suits between at least two parties which are decided in the courts. Cases are also known as opinions or decisions.

How many court systems are in the United States?
There are fifty-two court systems in the United States consisting of the federal courts, District of Columbia, and fifty state court systems.

What is the court structure in the United States?
Generally it is a three-tier system. The highest court is the court of last resort, generally known as the Supreme Court. At the lower level, cases originate at trial courts. Between the trial courts and the highest court are the intermediate appellate court(s).

How many courts are in the United States?
There are close to 30,000 courts at different levels. There are 445 federal courts (9 types); 122 territories and possessive (10 types); 229 Native American tribes; 19,334 state and local courts (50 types).

What are the Federal courts?
The United States Supreme Court, Courts of Appeal (also known as circuit courts) and the district courts. There are 13 circuit courts and 94 district courts.

What are the appellate courts?
When cases are appealed from the lower courts to higher courts, the higher courts are know as appellate courts. Appellate courts deal only with error in the application of law in the lower court. Generally they don't revisit the facts of the case.

What are trial courts?
Trial courts are below the appellate courts in the hierarchy of court systems. Trial courts deal with facts and applicable laws. Federal courts on the trial court level are called United States District Courts.

What are constitutional courts?
These are courts that have been identified by name in the federal or state constitution, e.g., United States Supreme Court or Pennsylvania Supreme Court.

What are statutory courts?
These are courts not part of the constitutional framework and created through statutory law, e.g., Federal Circuit and District Courts.

What is the highest court in the country?
The Supreme Court of the United States is the highest court designated under Article III, Section 1 of the United States Constitution.

What types of cases come before the United States Supreme Court?
The Supreme Court has original jurisdiction dealing with all cases affecting ambassadors, public ministers, and consuls and disputes between states.

Appellate jurisdiction includes admiralty and maritime jurisdiction, controversies in which the United States is a party, between a state and citizens of another state, citizens of the same state claiming lands under grants of different states, and between states, citizens of the states and foreign States.

What are the circuit courts?
The United States Courts of Appeal for the _____ Circuit is the official name for the thirteen circuits. There are eleven numbered circuits that have multistate coverage, plus the District of Columbia and Federal Circuit Court. There are 179 judgeships.

What states and territories fall under the circuit courts?
1st Circuit: Maine, Massachusetts, Puerto Rico, Rhode Island
2d Circuit: New Hampshire, Vermont, New York
3d Circuit: Delaware, New Jersey, Pennsylvania, Virgin Islands
4th Circuit: Maryland, North Carolina, South Carolina, Virginia, West Virginia
5th Circuit: Louisiana, Mississippi, Texas
6th Circuit: Kentucky, Michigan, Ohio, Tennessee
7th Circuit: Illinois, Indiana, Wisconsin
8th Circuit: Arkansas, Iowa, Minnesota, Missouri, Nebraska, North Dakota, South Dakota
9th Circuit: Alaska, Arizona, California, Guam, Hawaii, Idaho, Montana, Nevada, Oregon, Washington
10th Circuit: Colorado, Kansas, New Mexico, Oklahoma, Utah, Wyoming
11th Circuit: Alabama, Florida, Georgia
D.C. Circuit
Federal Circuit

What are the district courts?
The district courts are the trial courts in the federal system. The United States is divided into 94 district courts for the fifty states, District of Columbia, and Puerto Rico for a total of 662 judges. Based on the population of the state, there may be from one to four district courts, e.g., N.Y. and California have four; Pennsylvania, three; and Montana, one.

The district courts for the states are:
Alabama: Middle, Northern, and Southern Districts
Alaska: District Court

Arizona: District Court
Arkansas: Eastern and Western Districts
California: Central, Northern, Southern Districts
Colorado: District Court
Connecticut: District Court
Delaware: District Court
District of Columbia: District Court
Florida: Middle, Northern, and Southern Districts
Georgia: Middle, Northern, and Southern Districts
Guam: District Court
Hawaii: District Court
Idaho: District Court
Illinois: Central, Northern, and Southern Districts
Indiana: Northern and Southern Districts
Iowa: Northern and Southern Districts
Kansas: District Court
Kentucky: Eastern and Western Districts
Louisiana: Eastern, Middle, and Western Districts
Maine: District Court
Maryland: District Court
Massachusetts: District Court
Michigan: Eastern and Western Districts
Minnesota: District Court
Mississippi: Northern and Southern Districts
Missouri: Eastern and Western Districts
Montana: District Court
Nebraska: District Court
Nevada: District Court
New Jersey: District Court
New Mexico: District Court
New York: Eastern, Northern, Southern, and Western Districts
North Carolina: Eastern, Middle, and Western Districts
North Dakota: District Court
Ohio: Northern and Southern Districts
Oklahoma: Eastern and Western Districts
Oregon: District Court
Pennsylvania: Eastern, Middle, and Western Districts
Puerto Rico: District Court
Rhode Island: District Court
South Carolina: District Court
South Dakota: District Court

Tennessee: Eastern, Middle, and Western Districts
Texas: Eastern, Northern, Southern, and Western Districts
Utah: District Court
Vermont: District Court
Virginia: Eastern and Western Districts
Washington: Eastern and Western Districts
West Virginia: Northern and Southern Districts
Wisconsin: Eastern and Western Districts
Wyoming: District Court

What are the bankruptcy courts?
Bankruptcy courts have similar jurisdictions as district courts but handle only bankruptcy cases. There are 350 bankruptcy judges who serve for fourteen-year terms and are appointed by the court of appeals of the jurisdiction.

How many justices sit on the United States Supreme Court?
There are nine justices on the U.S. Supreme Court. Congressional statutes determine how many members the court has.

How many justices have sat on the Court since its inception?
There have been a total of 109 justices, including 17 chief justices and 98 associate justices (5 associates became chiefs).

Who becomes Chief Justice of the United States?
The President of the United States appoints the Chief Justice with the consent of the Senate.

Where can I find the Chief Justice's Year-End Reports on the Federal Judiciary?
The reports can be found under Public Information on the U.S. Supreme Court website, at http://www.supremecourtus.gov/publicinfo/year-end/year-endreports.html.

How many cases does the United States Supreme Court receive and decide each year?
The United States Supreme Court receives approximately 10,000 cases every court term, but hears less than one hundred cases. In 2006 term, the court heard only 75 cases. In general, the Supreme Court hears anywhere from 80 to 85% of its cases from the Circuit Courts and 15 to 20% from the state courts.

How many judges sit on the circuit courts?
179 judges sit on the thirteen Circuit courts consisting of the following:

Circuit	Number of Judges
1st	6
2nd	13
3rd	14
4th	15
5th	17
6th	16
7th	11
8th	11
9th	28
10th	12
11th	12
D.C.	12
Federal	12

How many judges sit on the District Courts?
There are 94 district courts including the 50 states, the District of Columbia, Puerto Rico, Virgin Islands, Guam, and Northern Mariana Islands for a total of 663 judges.

Number of Judges by District

Alabama:		Georgia:		Louisiana:	
Northern	5	Northern	8	Eastern	2
Middle	2	Middle	2	Middle	1
Southern	2	Southern	2	Western	3
Alaska	2	Middle and		Maine	2
Arizona	7	Southern	1	Maryland	4
Arkansas:		Hawaii	1	Massachusetts	5
Eastern and		Idaho	2	Michigan:	
Western	3	Illinois:		Eastern	4
California:		Northern	1	Western	3
Northern	9	Central	3	Minnesota	4
Eastern	6	Southern	1	Mississippi:	
Central	21	Indiana:		Northern	1
Southern	4	Northern	3	Southern	2
Colorado	5	Southern	4	Missouri:	
Connecticut	3	Iowa:		Eastern	3
Delaware	1	Northern	2	Western	3
District of Columbia	1	Southern		Montana	1

Florida:		Kansas	4	Nebraska	2
Northern	1	Kentucky:		Nevada	3
Middle	8	Eastern	2	New Hampshire	1
Southern	5	Western	3	New Jersey	8
New Mexico	2	Oregon	5	Utah	3
New York:		Pennsylvania:		Vermont	1
Northern	2	Eastern	5	Virginia:	
Southern	9	Middle	2	Eastern	5
Eastern	6	Western	4	Western	3
Western	3	Puerto Rico	2	Washington:	
North Carolina:		Rhode Island	1	Eastern	2
Eastern	2	South Carolina	2	Western	5
Middle	2	South Dakota	2	West Virginia:	
Western	2	Tennessee:		Northern	1
North Dakota	1	Eastern	3	Southern	1
Ohio:		Middle	3	Wisconsin:	
Northern	8	Western	4	Eastern	4
Southern	7	Texas:		Western	2
Oklahoma:		Northern	6	Wyoming	1.
Northern	2	Eastern	2		
Eastern	1	Southern	6		
Western	3	Western	4		

How many judges sit on the Bankruptcy Courts?
There are 352 bankruptcy judges.

Are federal judges appointed or elected?
Federal judges are appointed by the President with the consent of the Senate.

What is the term of office for a federal judge?
Federal judges have lifetime appointments.

Are bankruptcy judges appointed or elected?
Bankruptcy judges are appointed for a fourteen year term of office by the Circuit Court of Appeals in which the bankruptcy court sits. They can be reappointed.

What is the role of federal magistrates?
Magistrate judges are officers of a district court who conduct initial proceedings in felony cases, decide misdemeanor cases, conduct many pretrial civil and criminal matters, and decide civil cases with the parties' consent.

What is the term of office for federal district magistrates?
A district court for the jurisdiction appoints magistrates for an eight-year term. There are 532 full-time and part-time magistrates.

What are the state courts?
State courts have their own structure and jurisdiction based on each state's constitution and statutory law.

Generally, the highest court is the supreme court. The names of the intermediary courts and trial courts differ from state to state. In Pennsylvania, the intermediary courts are the Superior Court and Commonwealth Court; the trial courts (county courts) are known as Courts of Common Pleas.

What is the highest court of a state court system?
The highest court is an appellate court that is the court of the last resort in the state. Its jurisdiction may be determined by the state's constitution or statutory law. The name for the highest court varies from state to state, but is usually called Supreme Court. In New York, for instance, the highest court is the Court of Appeals and the New York trial courts are called the Supreme Courts.

For a listing of court structures, see Table 1, United States Jurisdictions in the *Uniform System of Citation* (Bluebook) or Appendix 1, Primary Sources by Jurisdiction, in the *ALWD Citation Manual*.

What are the intermediate courts in the state system?
The intermediate appellate courts were created to relieve the burden on the state supreme courts. Today, they may be constitutional and/or statutory courts. In Pennsylvania, there are two intermediate courts, the Superior Court and the Commonwealth Court.

What are the trial courts or county courts?
The trial courts in the judicial system hear all types of cases either by judge or by jury. Each state has the trial courts usually divided into districts based on the county government within the state. The county court name will differ from state to state, e.g., in Pennsylvania it is known as "Courts of Common Pleas."

What is the minor judiciary?
The minor judiciary commonly known as justices of the peace, district magistrates or district justices, serve as judges in small claims courts, neighborhood courts, or district magistrate courts. It varies from state to state whether the minor judiciary is elected or appointed and length of term of office may vary as well.

What are small claims courts?
Small claims court is the court not of record, that hears disputes, usually of fairly small sums, that involve local disputes.

What does court "not of record" mean?
A lower court below the trial court level, e.g., district magistrate or justice of the peace level.

How are judges selected for the state courts?
In some states judges are appointed by the governor, while in others the position is elected. New York has merit selection for the high court and city courts, but others are elected. Pennsylvania elects all justices and judges for a ten-year period. California has judicial nominations for its two highest courts, followed by retention election, while lower court judges are elected.

What is the term of office for a state judge?
The term of office varies from state to state. California appellate judges serve for twelve years and lower court judges for six. All Pennsylvania judges sit for ten years, while Texas judges serve for six years.

Who is the plaintiff?
The plaintiff is the person who brings the case into the trial court.

Who is the defendant?
The defendant is the person against whom the case is brought in the trial court.

Who is the appellant?
The person in a case who takes an appeal from the trial court. The appellant wants the trial-court opinion reversed.

Who is the appellee?
The person in a case against whom an appeal is taken. The appellee does not want the trial-court opinion reversed.

Who is the petitioner?
The petitioner is the plaintiff in the case. It is the name used in the United States Supreme Court for the person taking the appeal from the lower courts.

Who is the respondent?
The defendant in the case. It is the name used in the United States Supreme Court for the person who does not want the appeals court ruling reversed.

Who is the movant?

A party filing the motion is called the movant.

What is the caption in the case?

The caption includes the names of the parties and the court.

C. COURT REPORTS

How are court cases published?

First they are published as slip opinions that contain the text of the opinion without any editorial comments and a citation. Then they are published in advance sheets and finally in bound volumes known as reporters.

Are all court cases published?

No. The United States Supreme Court publishes all of their opinions, but the majority of lower federal court cases are not published. On the state level, the supreme court cases are generally published, but it will vary from state to state how many intermediate appellate court cases and trial court cases are published.

Who decides what cases are published in the court reports?

The judges decide which cases are published in the court reports published by West. For trial court level publications, the bar association of the publication may have committees who review the cases for publication.

What are the reasons court cases are not published?

If the cases have little precedential value with no new legal principles involved, then the cases may not be published nor considered binding if rules prohibit their citation.

What is a slip opinion?

This is the individual decision handed down by the court that is now published on the Internet at the court's website or may be published in Lexis or Westlaw.

The slip opinion online is no different from a paper version. Slip opinions have no extra editorial materials added to the opinion. One needs to follow the court rules to cite a slip opinion in a particular jurisdiction. Lexis and Westlaw add their own online citation to the slip opinion citation. Slip opinion citations are replaced with name of reporter, volume and page number when the advance sheet is published.

What is an advance sheet?
This is a group of slip opinions brought together into a pamphlet that contains both a title with a volume and page numbers. The number of advance sheets varies from title to title, e.g., a weekly *Federal Supplement* may be the equivalent of one bound volume, three-to-eight advance sheets equal one bound volume of a regional reporter. Citations can be made to advance sheets.

What is a bound volume reporter?
This is the collection of advance sheets with cases, tables, and subject indexes in the front of each volume. The cases can cover various time periods from a couple of weeks or months (*Federal Reporter*, regional reporter), or year/years (county court reports).

Where are the U.S. Supreme Court's cases published?
The United States Supreme Court's cases are published officially in the *United States Reports* which are published by the Government Printing Office and commercially published in the *Supreme Court Reporter* by West Publishing Company and in the *United States Supreme Court Reports, Lawyers Edition* by Lexis Publishing Company.

How are these reporters cited in the legal research publications?
The official *U.S. Reports* is cited as 500 U.S. 1; *West's Supreme Court Reporter* is cited as 123 S. Ct. 1 ; and the *United States Supreme Court Reports, Lawyers Edition* is cited as 100 L. Ed 1 (second series is cited as 147 L. Ed. 2d 1).

Where are Federal Circuit court cases published?
Federal circuit cases are published in the *Federal Reporter*, 1st, 2nd, and 3d series. Only about 25% of all circuit cases are published today. The bound volumes are updated weekly with advance sheets.

Where are the United States District Court's cases published?
District cases are published in the *Federal Supplement*, 1st and 2d series. Only about 15%-20% of cases are published. The bound volumes are updated with weekly advance sheets.

What are unpublished cases?
The judges of each court determine if a case should be published in one of the reporters.

Where can one find unpublished opinions?
Unpublished opinions are published selectively on the court's web site and also in Lexis and Westlaw.

Starting in 2001, West Group began to publish *West's Federal Appendix* that contains unpublished opinions not selected for the *Federal Reporter*. The set is published with weekly advance sheets and bound volumes like the *Federal Reporter*.

How do I obtain a copy of unpublished cases?
The case may be obtained from the clerk of the court or may be published in one of the full-text databases like Lexis and Westlaw.

What is precedent?
A court decision that serves as the basis for future cases dealing with the same point of law.

Do trial court cases have any precedential value?
Yes, they are useful to cite when future cases deal with the same subject in the same jurisdiction. They do not have precedent over appellate court cases.

Do unpublished cases have any precedential value?
Generally, unpublished cases do not have precedential value. The court will usually make a policy statement establishing whether unpublished cases may be cited or not.

Can federal courts cite to unpublished cases?
Yes, the United States Supreme Court in May, 2006, approved the citation to unpublished cases beginning in 2007 under Federal Rules of Appellate Procedure Rule 32.1.

How does one cite a court case?
In case law, a citation contains the volume number, abbreviated name of the reporter, and the page number where the first page of the case appears; e.g. 291 U.S. 301. In this example 291 is the volume number that is on the spine, U. S. means the *United States Reports* and 301 means the page number on which the case begins.

What are the types of opinions issued by a court?
There are three types of opinions: full-text, *per curiam*, and memorandum opinions.

What is a full-text opinion?

The court issues an opinion with the reasoning for its decision. The opinion is written by one judge and may have unanimous approval or have concurring and/or dissenting opinions too.

What is a *per curiam* opinion?

Per curiam means "by the court." It is an opinion given by the court with no individual judge's name assigned to the opinion.

What is a memorandum opinion?

A memorandum opinion is a unanimous opinion that reports the court's conclusion without elaboration. U.S. Supreme Court cases usually refer to the lower court's opinion when it is affirming the case.

What are advisory opinions in case law?

Opinions that do not involve a live case or controversy (*Understanding Law School*, LexisNexis)

What is the majority opinion?

The majority members of the court vote on which side is going to win the case. In the written opinion the judge's name who writes the opinion is given at the beginning of the opinion. In opinions, there is a list of judges who participate in the case with the judges listed for the majority or dissenting opinions.

What is the dissenting opinion?

The minority member(s) of the court provide an opinion that supports the losing side in the case.

What is the concurring opinion?

A judge can agree with either the majority or minority decision but for different reasons.

What is a concurring/dissenting opinion?

A judge may agree with one part of the decision but disagree on the reasons and at the same time offer a dissent on a portion of the decision as well.

What is a plurality opinion?

An opinion lacking enough votes for a majority, but receiving more votes than any other opinion, e.g., 4-1-4 opinion is a plurality opinion with one concurring and four dissenting opinions.

What is meant by a panel?
Generally appeals are heard by a group of judges (three judges) who are known as panels.

What does en banc mean?
In some courts, panels of three judges hear cases and provide the decision in the case. En banc is when the entire court or a majority of the court hears and determines the decision in the case. In Pennsylvania, the Superior Court of 15 judges considers 9 judges as en banc.

What are the parts of the case?

Name/Title/Caption of the Case

Docket Number

Argued Date

Filed Date

Syllabus

Headnotes

Synopsis

Judges

Attorneys

Opinion

What is the name/caption of the case?
The caption provides the names of the parties involved in the case.

What is the docket number?
The docket number is the number assigned to each case as it is filed into the clerk's office of the court. Most docket numbers begin with the year and the sequential number of the case docketed.

What is the argued date?
This is the date that the judges heard the case in court.

What is the filed date?
This is the date the court gave its opinion in the case.

What is the syllabus in the court opinion?
The syllabus is the summary of the case produced by the official court reporter. The syllabus is not considered part of the case in all jurisdictions, except Ohio where it is prepared by the Supreme Court as the official statement of law of the case. (Cohen, *How to Find the Law* 24n.12)

What is the synopsis in the court opinion?
The synopsis is the summary of the case produced by the lawyers-editors who work for the commercial vendor as in *United States Supreme Court Reports, L.Ed.* (Lexis) and *Supreme Court Reporter* (West).

Can I find the name of the judge who wrote the opinion?
The judges who participated in the case are listed before the opinion text with identification of the judge who wrote the opinion followed by those who concurred and/or dissented.

What is the holding or "ratio decidendi" in an opinion?
This is the court's decision in the case: which side has won or lost. In an appellate case, the decision approves or reverses the lower opinion.

What is the obiter dicta/dictum in an opinion?
The obiter dicta/dictum is the statement or observation of the judge that is not part of the decision of the case.

What is a brief?
A brief is the written arguments presented by each side to the court in defense of each position. There are several types of briefs that may be submitted, for instance, a plaintiff's brief, defendant's brief, an answer to a ....

What is a friend of the court brief?
It is the same as an *amicus curiae* brief.

What is an *amicus curiae* brief?
Amicus curiae means friend of the court. These are briefs submitted by individuals or groups supporting one position or the other of the case. Only a limited number of cases contain these briefs.

Are there rules for writing briefs?
Yes, court rules contain information on how to prepare briefs, e.g., U. S. Supreme Court Rule 3 provides instructions as to the format and number of words.

Are there any standard works on writing briefs?

There are several books that deal with the writing of briefs including various continuing legal education publications. One of the standard works is Edward Re and Joseph Re, *Brief Writing & Oral Argument* (KF251 R4).

What are the types of reports?

Reports can cover a jurisdiction, a chronological period, or a specialty topic. Reports can also be considered official or unofficial reports. Commercial publications are usually called reporters.

How are reports published?

The reports are chronologically published and sequentially numbered. All federal and state reports are published chronologically; however, there are some titles that publish cases by topic, e.g., *Federal Rules Decisions*, *Federal Rules Service*, *American Maritime Cases*.

What is a nominative reporter?

Nominative reports began in England in the sixteenth century and continued until the mid-nineteenth century. In the United States, judges and lawyers in the late eighteenth and nineteenth centuries published court reports as commercial ventures before courts designated official court reporters and/or official reports.

What is an official reporter?

The reports designated by statute or court rule as the official reports for the court. The United States Supreme Court has its *United States Reports* as the official reports; New Jersey has *New Jersey Reports*, Pennsylvania has *Pennsylvania State Reports*.

What is an unofficial report?

An unofficial report is usually published by a commercial vendor and adds information to each case to assist the researcher. The seven regional reporters are mostly unofficial reports except for those states that have adopted them as official. In Pennsylvania, the *Atlantic Reporter* is unofficial for Supreme Court cases; in Texas, *South Western Reporter* is the official report for Texas Civil and Criminal Courts (its highest appellate courts).

What is the commercial reporter?

These are reports published by commercial vendors who usually add additional information to assist those researching case law, e.g., digest references, encyclopedias, annotations, periodicals, etc., for instance, *United States Supreme Court Reports, L.Ed.2d* (Lexis) and *Supreme Court Reporter* (West)

Where can I find a listing of all published court reports by jurisdiction?
See Table 1, United States Jurisdictions in the *Uniform System of Citation*, 18th ed. (also known as the Bluebook) and Appendix 1, Primary Sources by Jurisdiction, in the *ALWD Citation Manual*.

Who are the popular publishers publishing commercial reporters?
Thomson-West (formerly West Publishing Co., Lawyers Cooperative Publishing Co., and Callaghan Co.), Reed-Elsevier (Lexis, Matthew Bender, and Shepard's Citations), Wolters-Kluwer (Aspen, CCH, Kluwer, Little Brown, and Wiley).

What are the parts of a case volume in a West Reporter?
Title page
   List of judges by jurisdiction: list of judges by jurisdiction providing starting date of term of office.
   Table of Cases Reported alphabetically in order
   Table of Cases Reported by Circuit/District/State
   Table of Statutes Construed: list of federal and state constitutions and statutory law usually by code title and section cited in text of cases.
   Table of Rules Construed: list of federal and state court rules cited in the text of cases.
   Table of Words and Phrases: list of words and phrases defined in the court cases of the volume.
   Cases Reported
   West Digest System Found in Volume: list of digest topics and key-numbers cumulated from all cases reported in the volume.

What are the official reports for the Supreme Court of the United States?
United States Reports published by the Government Printing Office.

What are the unofficial reports for the Supreme Court of the United States?
United States Supreme Court Reports, L.Ed. (Lexis)

Supreme Court Reporter (West)

United States Law Week (BNA)

Which one of the unofficial reports for the United States Supreme Court should one use?
L.Ed. (Lexis) and *Supreme Court Reporter* (West) both provide additional information to the text of the opinion. L.Ed. is useful if you are interested in secondary sources cross-referenced to other L.Ed. publications (*Am. Jur. 2d, U.S.C.S., A.L.R.* etc.). It also has its own Digest system headnotes. The publisher's

summary has a more detailed summary than the West version. The *Supreme Court Reporter* provides a syllabus of the case and West Digest key number topics.

What are the nominative reports for the *United States Reports*?
The first 90 volumes are cited sometimes by the name of the reporter who compiled the reports, e.g., Dallas, Cranch, Black, or Wallace.

Nominative Reports	No. of Vols.	Dates of Coverage	U.S. Reports Volume Nos.
Dallas	1-4	(1789-1800)	1-4
Cranch	1-9	(1801-1815)	5-13
Wheaton	1-12	(1816-1827)	14-25
Peters	1-16	(1828-1842)	26-41
Howard	1-24	(1843-1861)	42-65
Black	1-2	(1861-1863)	65-66
Wallace	1-23	(1863-1875)	68-90

How does one cite these nominative reports?
Marbury v. Madison, 5 U.S. (1 Cranch) 137 (1803).

Are there state nominative reports too?
Yes, many states have nominative reports in their beginning decades. In many states, the case reports are individually cited; in other states, they may have been renumbered into a chronologically numbered set. For example, in Pennsylvania, the early Supreme Court reports (60 volumes) are cited by the name of the reporter, but in Virginia they are sequentially numbered in one series of reports.

Is there a difference in coverage between the two sets and the official reports?
Yes. *L.Ed.* is published in two series covering the U.S. Supreme Court from its beginnings in 1789. The first series contains 100 volumes covering from 1789 to 1955; the second series covers from 1956 to present. The current session is updated by biweekly advance sheets.

Supreme Court Reporter begins in 1881 with volume 106 of the *U. S. Reports*. The current session is covered by biweekly advance sheets.

L.Ed.2d publishes three to four volumes for the court year; *Supreme Court Reporter* publishes two or three volumes with one volume number and consecutive pagination throughout the volumes. For instance, volumes 153 to 156 L.Ed.2d is the equivalent of coverage in volume 123 of the *Supreme Court Reporter*.

What is *United States Law Week*?

U. S. Law Week is a Bureau of National Affairs looseleaf publication that is kept up to date on a weekly basis. It is divided into two volumes. One volume (entitled Supreme Court on the binder) contains all United States Supreme Court cases, weekly actions, and articles, e.g., annual reviews of the court's previous term. Abstracts of each case with the main questions presented before the court are provided. The second volume (entitled General Law on the binder) contains a survey summary of federal and state appellate cases, a legal news section of general legal news of pre-decisional and non-judicial developments, and special articles. In legal citations, it is cited as __ U.S.L.W. __ (date).

What are the reports for the Federal Circuit Courts?

West publishes the *Federal Reporter* 1st series (1880-1928), 2nd series (1928-1993), 3rd series (1993 to present). Only about 20% to 25% of federal circuit court cases are published currently in this reporter.

What are the reports for the Federal District Courts?

West publishes the *Federal Supplement* 1st series (1932-1999), 2nd series (1999 to present). Only about 15% to 20% of the federal district court cases are published currently in this reporter.

What is the publication entitled *Federal Cases*?

Federal Cases is a collection of 18,000 Federal Circuit and District Court cases from 1789 to 1879 arranged alphabetically in order rather than chronologically. It is a compilation of individual nominative reports brought together and published by West Publishing Co. in the mid-1890s. The set has 30 volumes of cases and a one-volume Table of Cases.

It is the standard source to access these early federal cases. It can be cited by the Case number (Fed. Cases No. 12,500) or by volume, name of vol., page no.(1 Fed. Cases 1). It is the predecessor to the *Federal Reporter*.

What are the reports for the Federal Bankruptcy Courts?

West's Bankruptcy Reporter contains bankruptcy cases from the bankruptcy courts, the U.S. Circuit Courts, and the U.S. Supreme Court from 1978 to the present.

What are the reports for the Federal Rules of Civil and Criminal Procedure?

West's Federal Rules Decisions contains cases on the Federal Rules of Civil and Criminal Procedure.

Federal Rules Service contains civil procedure cases arranged by rule number

What is the National Reporter System?

This is the collection of all major court report titles published by West: *Supreme Court Reporter, Federal Reporter, Federal Supplement, Federal Appendix,* seven regional reporters, *California Reporter,* and *New York Supplement.* There are also specialty reporters.

What are the subject specialty reporters?

The specialty reporters include *American Tribal Reporter, Education Reporter, Federal Claims Reporter, Federal Rules Decisions, Federal Merit Systems Review Board Reporter, Military Justice Reporter, Social Security Law Reporting Service,* and *Veterans' Affairs Reporter.*

What are the regional reporters?

West Publishing Co. began publishing all states' appellate court reports in seven regional reporters: *Atlantic, North Eastern, North Western, Pacific, South Eastern, South Western,* and *Southern Reporters.* In addition, there are individual reports *California Reporter* 1st and 2nd Series and *New York Supplement* 1st and 2nd Series.

How many series are there in the regional reporters?

All seven series have one series from 200 to 300 volumes. Five of the series are published in their second series (up to 999 volumes); two, the *Pacific Reporter* and the *South Western Reporter,* are in their third series.

How does one know when a reporter goes into a new series?

The *Bluebook* Table 1 (United States Jurisdictions) p.193, contains a listing of the federal and state jurisdictions and their reports
    The *ALWD Manual* Appendix 1A, p.407 contains a list of regional reporters.

How do I know what states are included in each regional reporter?

The title page of each reporter identifies which states are parts of that reporter.

What states are included in each regional reporter?

Atlantic Reporter: Connecticut, Delaware, District of Columbia, Maine, Maryland, New Hampshire, New Jersey, Pennsylvania, Rhode Island, Vermont

North Eastern Reporter: Illinois, Indiana, Massachusetts, New York, Ohio

North Western Reporter: Iowa, Michigan, Minnesota, Nebraska, North Dakota, South Dakota, Wisconsin

Pacific Reporter: Alaska, Arizona, California, Colorado, Hawaii, Idaho, Kansas, Montana, Nevada, New Mexico, Oklahoma, Oregon, Utah, Washington, and Wyoming

South Eastern Reporter: Georgia, North Carolina, South Carolina, Virginia, West Virginia

South Western Reporter: Arkansas, Kentucky, Missouri, Tennessee, Texas

Southern Reporter: Alabama, Florida, Louisiana, Mississippi

What opinions are published in the regional reporters?
State appellate court decisions are published in the regional reporters. Federal and state trial court decisions are not published in the regional reporters.

Does *West's California Reporter* and *West's New York Supplement* include lower court opinions of those states?
Both sets contain state trial court opinions.

What is an offprint edition of the state regional reporters?
West reprints cases from the regional reporters for each state, e.g., *Pennsylvania Reporter* contains cases from the Pennsylvania Supreme, Superior, and Commonwealth Courts. These volumes contain only one state's cases with the same pagination as the regional reporter.

Can I cite to an offprint reporter?
No, citation is to the regional reporter with its volume and page numbers.

What does it mean when Rules, Inductions, Memorials of Judges are listed on the spine of the reporter?
The volumes contain text of new rules as well as induction and/or memorial ceremonies for judges.

What does it mean when "Tables" is listed on the spine of reporter?
The volume contains tables of citations to cases that are affirmed or reversed without written opinions. These opinions are cited as being in the table.

What are state reports?
All fifty states have had state reports usually published by the state government, but more recently by commercial vendors like West or Lexis. More than

twenty jurisdictions have given up their state reports to use the regional reporters instead.

Who is the state reporter?

The court appoints a court reporter who collects the cases, provides the syllabus for each case, and today works with West Group to submit cases for publication in the regional reporters.

What is meant by the official cite?

A statute or court rule declares a set of books as the official report for the jurisdiction. In New York, there are three official reports for the state courts, while Pennsylvania has only one for its Supreme Court.

Why does a researcher use one of the unofficial reports?

The reports are kept up-to-date with advance sheets and they are annotated by the publishers with citations to case digests, periodicals, encyclopedias, form books, ALR annotations, and treatises.

What is a parallel cite?

This is the publication of the same court case in at least two different books, usually an official report and an unofficial report. *People v. Ault* has the official citation as 33 Cal.4th 1250 and the unofficial citation is 95 P.3d 523 (2004)

Are there sources to locate parallel citations between state and regional reporters?

The *National Reporter Blue Book*, table of cases of state digests, and Shepard's citators for each state provide parallel citations.

What is the *National Reporter Blue Book*?

The *National Reporter Blue Book* (West Group) is a multivolume set containing the parallel citations for all of the regional reporters from the first series to present. The bound volume set is updated with an annual supplement that cumulates into a bound volume every ten years.

What is the running case name in a reporter?

This is the short title provided at the top of the page of the reporter.

What does the series mean in relation to a reporter?

Reports are published in series based on a certain number of volumes. At a specific point, the publisher decides to end one series and begin a new series. The number of volumes in a series will vary from series to series, e.g., *Federal Reporter*

1st series has 300 volumes, *Federal Reporter* 2d & *Federal Supplement* have 999 volumes.

What is the order of the cases published in a reporter?
Cases are published in chronological order. The time period covered will vary from title to title.

How many cases are published in each reporter?
The number published varies from volume to volume but generally at least 100 cases are published.

How can I find cases on a specific topic in a reporter?
There may be an index at the front or back of each volume. If there are digest topics, they may be cumulated at the end of the volume.

What is star pagination?
This method provides the citations of cases reported in the original official reports in the unofficial reports, e.g., *U.S. Reports* are referenced in West's *Supreme Court Reporter* and *L.Ed.*1st & 2d series.

Where can one find short names of court cases?
Popular short titles of cases can be found in *Shepard's Acts and Cases by Popular Names*.

II. INTERNET

Can I get the full text of cases from the Internet?
Full texts of the cases are available from the official court web sites.

Are slip opinions available?
The majority of courts, especially the highest courts, post opinions on their web sites on the same day they are issued.

How far back are cases available?
It varies from court to court. Generally cases are available for at least ten years. However, cases from the United States Supreme Court are available from the inception of the court. For example, the official United Supreme Court website (www.supremecourtus.gov) has PDF versions of decisions starting with vol. 502 U.S. (October 1991 term). The U.S. Department of Commerce website, Fedworld, has

ASCII versions of Supreme Court decisions from 1937 to 1975 at www.fedworld. gov/supcourt/index.htm. HeinOnline (www.heinonline.org) has a PDF archive of the U.S. Reports from 1754 (vol.1) to 2001 (vol. 534).

What are official web sites?

Official web sites are maintained by the court. On these web sites cases are posted on the same day they are decided.

How do I know the correct URL for each court web site?

You can obtain them from research guides or from court directories. General search engines such as Google or Yahoo will also help you to find the proper URL for court web sites. The best method is to use one of the comprehensive legal sites.

What are some of the comprehensive legal Internet sites for case law?

There are several comprehensive sites. Some of the popular sites are: Findlaw (www.findlaw.com), HeirosGamos (www.hg.org), Virtual Chase (www.virtualchase. com) and the Legal Information Institute (www.law.cornell.edu).

What fields (segments) are available for searching on a web site?

The majority of the comprehensive sites will allow one to retrieve cases by names of the parties, date, cite and topic.

Are general purpose search engines such as Google and Yahoo good sources to retrieve cases?

It is better to use either official court sites or comprehensive legal web sites. A general search engine may occasionally give you the full text of a case but it will often only give an abbreviated version of the case.

How reliable are cases found on the Internet?

Cases posted on the court web sites are one hundred percent reliable. Cases from the popular comprehensive sites such as Findlaw, Cornell, HeirosGamos are also reliable.

How do I get briefs and oral arguments from the Internet?

Court web sites and some private web sites offer briefs and oral arguments. For example, the U.S. Supreme Court web site (www.supremecourtus.gov) and private sites such as Oyez (www.oyez.org) and the Mayer, Brown, Rowe and Maws law firm site (www.appellate.net) offer briefs and oral arguments for the U.S. Supreme Court.

Are cases available in audio format?
Some commercial companies make cases available as audio files. For example audiocasefiles at www.audiocasefiles.com provides digitally recorded legal opinions, audio briefs, online opinions and case summaries. The cases are available under "Recently Popular", "Most Popular", "By Course" and "By Casebook" headings.

Are podcasts available for court cases?
Podcasts for the U.S. Supreme Court cases are available from the Oyez site (www. oyez.org/podcasts). The name of the site is The Oyez Supreme Court Podcasts.

Are cases available in video format?
CourttoomLive (www.courtroomlive.com) provides live streaming trial videos to the subscribers to their desk top directly.

What are the names of the official court sites for federal case law?
The United States Supreme Court cases are available on www.supremecourtus.gov and Circuit Court and District Court's cases are available from www.uscourts.gov

Where can I find official opinions of the U. S. Supreme Court?
The official web site is www.supremecourtus.gov.

Where can I find 'questions presented' for the U.S. Supreme Court cases online?
The official Supreme Court web site offers "questions presented" from the "Granted and Noted Lists" under Orders and Journal.

Is there any directory where I can get the names of the federal and state courts?
Most of the comprehensive legal sites such as Findlaw, Cornell, HeirosGamos, Law Guru, and Mega Law provide direct links to the courts' web sites.

Can I Shepardize cases from any Internet site?
You may find cases citing to your case but finding how other cases treated your case is rare. Once you retrieve a case from the United States Supreme Court, Findlaw provides the "Cases citing this case: Supreme Court" and the "Cases citing this case: Circuit Courts" links to find more cases citing to your case. Shepards on Lexis and KeyCite in Westlaw are the only sources to validate and find the treatment of your case. Loislaw offers Globalcite which only provides more cases citing to your case. Lexis offers a separate subscription to Shepards and Westlaw offers a separate subscription to its KeyCite service. Nowadays, most of the county or court

libraries and some academic libraries are offering Shepards on Lexis and KeyCite free of charge to the public.

Are there any web sites that help me know how to cite court cases and other Internet information in my legal documents?
You will find proper citation formats for Internet publications under rule 18.2 in the eighteenth edition of the Blue Book. The following is an example: Dittakavi Rao, Digests (last visited Sep.17, 1999) <http://www.pennsylvanialegalresearch.com>

Legal Information Institute site has a link to Peter W. Martin's "Introduction to Basic Legal Information (LII 2006) page (www.law.cornell.edu/citation) that provides citation examples.

CiteIt (www.citeit.com) is a computer software program designed specifically to assist in the legal research and writing process. It automatically formats legal citations according to *The Bluebook* or *The ALWD Citation Manual*.

How do I access Supreme Court cases of other countries?
Global Courts (www.globalcourts.com) provides links to supreme court decisions from more than 125 countries around the world.

III. LexisNexis

How can I retrieve a case if I have a citation to a case?
Select 'Get a Document' and then select by citation and enter the citation of the case and click on 'Get'.

How can I retrieve a case by party name?
You have an option of selecting party name tab under the 'Get a Document' template. For an efficient result select jurisdiction and date if you know.

Can I retrieve a case just by having a docket number?
Select docket number option under 'Get a Document' template and enter the docket number to retrieve a case.

Can I use the West's key numbers for my topic search?
No. West's key numbers work with Westlaw only. You simply enter your topic search either in words and or phrases in "Terms and Connectors" search method.

Search Advisor is similar to West's key number system. It is a topical index of legal issues and it is tied to the headnotes within each case.

Is there any other search method to retrieve cases for topic search?
You can also use "Natural Language" method or "Easy Search" method to express your topic in query formulation.

How can I find cases on a specific issue without entering any query?
Use Search Advisor feature to obtain cases by selecting a topic and a sub-topic.

How many topics are available in Search Advisor?
Currently there are more than 40 topics.

Do I get all cases on a particular topic when I use Search Advisor?
No. LexisNexis has more cases on its database when compared to search advisor topic.

What are the display options for my search results?
You have an option of viewing your search results as a cite list (by default), KWIC (key word in context), Full and Custom formats.

What is Custom format?
On selection of this format you will see a custom view options box where you can select all or few options for display. For example you can select you want the results should show only court or opinionby etc.

How does a displayed case look in Full format?
Along with the name, court, citation and date of the decision segments, you will also get subsequent history, prior history, disposition and case summary in full format. The cursor will also pop up the parallel citations to the case.

What is "More Like This"?
"More Like This" allows one to retrieve documents with similar citation patterns (Core Cites) or similar words taken from the document (Core Terms) to search in other libraries or files. One can add additional terms as well as mandatory terms that must be found in the retrieved documents. One can also place a date restriction on the search as well.

What is 'More Like Selected Text'?
The feature 'More Like Selected Text' allows you to highlight any part of a document you are reading and to create a search that will retrieve documents matching your selection.

What is TOA link?

TOA stands for Table of Authorities that provides a citation list of all citations cited in the case under review, for example, Roe v. Wade has 143 case citations. The citations are also listed with Shepard's signals to identify if they are still good law.

What is Copy W/ Cite?

Copy w/ Cite lets you select a portion of the document and place it in a popup box for export to be used in a word processing document (click on Copy to Clipboard to get to the word processing document). The hyperlinks in the original document are no longer present, though the star pagination is still in the document. The citation to the case is available at the end of the copied text with or without the hyperlink to the case.

What does one obtain when completing a search?

The results display the Source and Terms before providing all of the case law citations. Source is the hierarchy of the libraries and files that the research question is derived from. Terms are the words or phrases that you entered for your search. It is possible to change the search by using the Edit Search link following the terms used. Lexis also provides Search Terms for My Search link that provides suggested words and concepts.

What is Save as Alert link?

Save as Alert keeps you updated as new cases on your research topic becomes available in a monthly, weekly, or daily email.

What is Hide Hits link?

Hide Hits removes the highlighting of the search terms in the retrieved documents.

Is the case summary part of the court opinion?

No. The case summary is written by LexisNexis editors.

What type of information do I get from the case summary?

Case summary includes: procedural posture, overview, outcome and core terms.

Do I see the head notes of the print copy of the opinion in LexisNexis?

Headnotes appearing in LexisNexis are not similar to what you see in a print reporter. Instead these headnotes are LexisNexis headnotes.

What Segments are available for cases?

Cites

Concur

Concurby

Core Terms

Counsel

Court

Court-text

Decision

Disposition

Dissent

Dissentby

Writtenby

What is Procedural Posture?
Procedural posture describes the procedural history of the case to explain how it reached the current court.

What is the overview?
Overview is the summary paragraph of the court's holding on the legal issues raised.

What is outcome in a court case?
Outcome is the judicial decision that explains the procedural disposition of the case.

What are Core Concepts?
Core concepts are similar to digest headnotes created by the Lexis/Nexis editors along with the point of law derived from the court case taken in wording exactly from the case.

What does it mean when parallel citations at the top of the case have asterisks next to the citation?
The asterisk next to each citation identifies the pagination in the body of the text for each reporter citation. For a *U. S. Supreme Court* case that has been published in a bound volume, *U.S.* has one asterisk, *Supreme Court Reporter* has two asterisks, and *Lawyers Edition* has three asterisks.

   This process of identifying the exact page breaks between volumes is called Star paging or star pagination.

Does Lexis provide page numbers for parallel reporters?
Yes. Lexis provides parallel citations next to each case, if available, and the star pagination within the case.

What are the LexisNexis headnotes found in a case?
The headnotes are selected for the case by the editors of Lexis. The editors are creating a digest system similar to West's Digest System, but it is only in an electronic format.

How are the headnotes created?
The text for each headnote is copied from the case itself.

How can one retrieve additional cases using the headnotes?
There is an icon at the end of all headnotes that retrieves all headnotes and additional cases on this topic. One has to select the jurisdiction(s) to retrieve the headnotes and cases.

What happens when one clicks on the headnote topic itself?
The Topic will then be displayed with all of its subtopics that can be further divided down.

What is the link to Related Topics next to some headnote topics?
The link will take you to additional topics, e.g., Juvenile Offenders under Criminal Law & Procedure will take you to Family Law, Delinquency Proceedings.

What is the purpose of the headnote number with a green down arrow?
Click on the down arrow to go to the headnote in the text of the case.

What is LexisNexis Analyzer?
LexisNexis describes this new program as the ability to carry out "critical due diligence on key players in a case." It pulls information from all files within LexisNexis to obtain information on judges, attorneys, experts, arbitrators, or company profile that can be downloaded or printed.

IV. WESTLAW

Where can I find names of the case law databases?
Names of the case law databases are available form the Directory link on the home page.

What are the general case law databases?
Select ALLCASES database for all cases from federal and state jurisdictions; ALLFEDS for all federal cases; ALLSTATES for all cases from 50 state jurisdictions.

What are the state specific case law databases?
All state case law databases will have two letters (postal abbreviation) of a state and CS stands for the case law, e.g., PA-CS for all Pennsylvania cases and PA-CS-ALL for all Pennsylvania and federal cases coming out of Pennsylvania courts.

Can I get the trial court cases also from the state case law databases?
No. Only the cases from appellate courts are available from the state case law databases. You have to find out the database name for trial court cases from the Directory.

Is there any other way to find the case law other than searching through the case law databases?
KeySearch can also be used to retrieve cases on a particular subject matter.

What are the search methods available to retrieve cases by an issue?
You may use Terms and Connectors or Natural language methods in Standard Search mode or you can use key numbers through KeySearch.

Do I get the same number of results for my query using any search method?
No. The results are different from each search method. With a Terms and Connectors search, you will get all of the results that match your search and they will be listed in reverse chronological order. With a Natural Language search, you will get pre-determined (in your preferences) number of results ranked in order of statistical relevance.

Can I retrieve a case by citation?
Yes. If you know the citation to a case use "FIND" command and enter the citation. Do not worry about spacing or periods in the FIND box.

Can I retrieve a case by party name of the case?
Yes. Use the Find & Print feature and then Find by Party Name. You can also retrieve a brief by Party Name.

Can I retrieve cases by Key Numbers?
If you know the key number for your research issue use that key number in Terms and Connectors search method. For example you should enter 17k5 in the query box to retrieve cases related to persons who may be adopted.

Can I restrict my search results by using any specific field such as judge name or holding of a case etc.?
Westlaw provides several fields to restrict your search results. Fields are given under the query box.

Do I have to use one field at a time or can I use more than one field in my search query?
You may select any one or several at the same time to include in your query.

Can I restrict my search to a particular time period?
Yes. Under the query box you will find Dates tab. You may restrict your search results from unrestricted time period to today to last 10 years. Or, you may customize the dates between a certain period of time by putting in after and before dates.

What are the display choices for a retrieved search result?
Your search results appear as a cite list including highlighting the word you have entered in your query. Once you click any document for full text format it provides the KeyCite options along with ResultsPlus. You may change how your result is displayed in your preference settings, e.g., number of words shown on either side of the search term or number of citations shown at a time.

What is the purpose of ResultsPlus in the search results?
ResultsPlus provides secondary sources (treatises, encyclopedias, periodicals, and practitioner materials) related to a query. In obtaining a list of documents as a result of a search, ResultsPlus provides related documents for that search in the right column. Once a document is selected, ResultsPlus provides links to secondary sources in the left column that relate to that specific document.

Can I find petitions, briefs, or other documents filed in a particular case?
Once a case is opened for full-text format, the left-side column displays a link for Petitions, Briefs & Filings if any are available.

Where can I find 'Most Cited Cases' feature?
On the displayed results screen for the full text of a case you will see the 'Most Cited Cases' feature next to the headnotes.

What is the use of using the 'Most Cited Cases' feature?
You can use the 'Most Cited Cases' feature to create a custom digest that lists cases containing headnotes classified under that topic and key number.

Are trials available in the Westlaw database?
Under Legal Newsletters, Highlights, and Notable Trials, Notable Trials includes databases for the Clinton Impeachment (IMPEACH-TRANS), Libby CIA Trial (LIBBY INQUIRY), O.J. Simpson Trial (OJ-TRANS), etc.

CHAPTER 4

CASE LAW —DIGESTS

Introduction: Digests are a major tool in researching case law. Digests organize case law into subject classifications that bring all related cases under similar subjects. This chapter reviews what a digest is, the various types of digests as part of the West Digest System, and how to research the digest system. West's Digest System is the most comprehensive system available both in print and online; however, LexisNexis has developed its own online digest for its case law.

I. MANUAL

What is a digest?

A digest contains headnotes of court cases which are originally published in the reports. It is arranged under a subject classification provided by a commercial vendor. West's Digest System contains seven major categories divided into approximately 420 digest topics. Each topic is subdivided from 10 to more than 2,000 subtopics. The topics are arranged first by regulatory and substantive law and then by procedural law.

Where can one find a list of the Digest Topics under the West Digest System?

In every volume, there is an outline of the law followed by an alphabetical list of the Digest Topics. The complete list of Digest Topics can also be found in the pocket parts.

Where can one find a complete breakdown of all of the topics under the West Digest System?

West publishes *West's Analysis of American Law: Guide to the American Digest System* (KF240 W454) annually providing the complete breakdown of the entire digest system (1666 pages).

What are headnotes?
Headnotes are the points of law identified and written by the editors of the court reports. A headnote consists of a digest topic and key number of the subtopic, e.g., Criminal Law k400. Since the headnotes are not written by the judges and not part of the case, they cannot be cited. However, one can use the headnotes as a secondary source of information if it is needed.

How many West headnotes are there of cases?
There are more than 24 million headnotes of cases in the digest system.

How does one identify the headnotes in the text of a court opinion in the West reporters?
Headnote numbers are identified in the text of the opinion with the corresponding numbers within brackets in bold print.

Have the topics been revised over the decades?
Yes, they have. Older topics such as Employers' Liability, Labor Relations, and Master and Servant are all incorporated under the new topic of Labor & Employment and more recently, Consumer Protection can now be found under Antitrust Law.

Does West add new topics to the Digest System?
Yes, digest topics are infrequently added, such as Children Out-of-Wedlock.

Do the Key Numbers ever change?
The numbers change when older topics may be either renamed, e.g., Master and Servant as a topic name has been eliminated and included under Labor and Employment or periodically renumbered to expand the subtopics, e.g., constitutional law was recently updated in early 2007.

Where can one find the changes between the old and new key numbers?
Following the table of contents under the Topic, are two tables. Table 1 is the Key Number Translation Table providing the former key number to the present key number. Table 2 is the Key Number Translation Table providing the present key number to the former key number.

What are the key numbers?
Key numbers are actually the subtopics within each digest topic. For the research point of view, key numbers consist of the digest topic name and then the key number assigned to a subtopic under the main topic, e.g., Criminal Law k551 (Positive and negative evidence). In this example, k551 is the subtopic assigned to Positive and negative evidence under the Main Digest Topic of Criminal Law.

How many key numbers are there?
There are about 100,000 individual Key Numbers used in the digest system.

Where do I find the key numbers for my research?
One can use either the Descriptive Word Index or the topic outline at the beginning of each topic. One can also find key numbers from other West sources such as statutes, encyclopedias, texts, and practice books published by West.

Do the key numbers stay the same in all of the digests?
The key numbers in the digests remain the same in federal, regional, state, decennial and general digests.

The *Century Digest* (1656-1896) is arranged by topic and sections that are not key numbers. Consult the *Century Digest* Sections table in the 1906 Decennial Edition (pink pages).

Can one cite headnotes for points of law in a case?
No. Headnotes are not part of an opinion. They are added by the court reporter or by the commercial vendor.

What information can be found in the digest topic?
At the beginning of each topic is a listing of what subjects are included and excluded in the digest topic. An analysis section provides the broad categories broken down into parts. Next there is a complete breakdown of all digest topics in the table of contents.

What is meant by West's Key Number Digest System?
West Group publishes the most comprehensive collection of digests covering both federal and state cases back to the colonial period. The system provides the same digest topics and key numbers for all jurisdictions so, for example, one researching "products liability of lawnmowers" (313A K56) will find the information under the same Digest Key Number throughout all of the individual digest titles.

Lexis publishes a more limited number of digests for the United States Supreme Court and some states.

What digests are available for the United States Supreme Court?
West publishes the *United States Supreme Court Digest* (KF101.1 U55) and Lexis publishes the *Digest of the United States Supreme Court , L.Ed.* (KF101.1 D54).

Also, Supreme Court cases are found in the *Federal Practice Digests.*

What digest covers the federal courts?
The U.S. Supreme Court, U.S. Circuit Courts of Appeal and the U.S. District Courts are covered in five different series published by date of coverage: *Federal Digest*

(1789-1939), *Modern Federal Practice Digest* (1939-1961), *West's Federal Practice Digest 2d* (1962-1975), *West's Federal Practice Digest 3d* (1975-1985), and *West's Federal Practice Digest 4*[th] (1985 to present) (KF127 F43).

Where else are federal cases covered?

The individual state digests also cover federal cases within the jurisdiction, e.g., *West's Ohio Digest* covers U.S. Supreme Court cases, 6th Circuit cases, and cases from the U.S. District Courts within Ohio.

They are also covered in the *Decennial Digests* and *General Digest*.

Are cases organized by circuits (sequentially) in federal practice and decennial digests?

Circuit court cases are not organized sequentially by circuit number. Cases are listed from highest to lowest court (U.S. Supreme Court, Circuit Courts, District Courts) and then organized alphabetically by state. If there is more than one case under each jurisdiction, then they are listed in reverse chronological order.

What is a state digest?

A state digest covers federal cases from the state, state appellate, and trial court cases. The cases are arranged in order from highest court to lowest court and within each court in reverse chronological order. In some states there are more than one series, e.g., New York has four series, California three series, Pennsylvania and other states has two series, while some states only have one series (some in a revised edition).

Cases include the U.S. Supreme Court, Circuit Courts, District Courts, state appellate courts, and state trial courts. For instance, *West's Pennsylvania Digest 2d* cites to Pennsylvania cases from the U.S. Supreme Court, U.S. Court of Appeals for the Third Circuit, U.S. District Courts for Pennsylvania, Pennsylvania Supreme, Superior, and Commonwealth courts, and trial cases reported in the *Pa. District & County Reports* (1918 to present).

Does every state have an individual digest?

No. Utah and Delaware do not have digests. North Dakota and South Dakota are combined into one title; Virginia and West Virginia are combined into one title.

How do you find cases for Delaware and Utah?

Utah is included in the *Pacific Reporter Digest*; Delaware is included in the *Atlantic Reporter Digest*.

What is the regional digest?

There are four regional digests that correspond to the West regional reporters: *Atlantic, North Western, Pacific,* and *South Eastern Reporter Digests*. These digests cover only state appellate court cases. They do not cover federal and state trial court opinions.

If one is researching state cases, is it better to use the regional digest or the state digest?
Since state digests include lower court decisions of the state as well as federal cases originating from that state, the researcher obtains a broader selection of cases from the state digest. The regional is useful because of its showing similar cases in other jurisdictions surrounding your state.

What is the American Digest System?
This is West's cumulative sets of the *Century Digest*, the *Decennial Digest*, and the *General Digest*.

What is the *Century Digest*?
The *Century Digest* (KF139) is the first part of the West's American Digest System that contains all federal (U.S. Supreme Court, circuit and district court cases), and state appellate court cases from 1658 to 1896.

What are the *Decennial Digests*?
This is the second part of the American Digest System. The *Decennial Digest* (KF141) contains ten-year cumulative supplements of all federal and only state appellate court cases.

When did the first *Decennial Digest* start?
The first *Decennial Digest* started in the year 1897. Succeeding decennials are on the "six" year: 1906-1916, 1916-1926, etc.

When did the Decennial Digests begin to split into parts?
Since 1976 the Decennials have been divided into two five-year supplements: 9th Decennial, Part 1 (1976-1981), 9th Decennial, Part 2 (1981-1986), 10th Decennial, Part 1 (1986-1991), 10th Decennial, Part 2 (1991-1996), 11th Decennial, Part 1 (1996-2001), the 11th Decennial, Part 2 (2001-2004), and Part 3 (2004-2007).

What is the *General Digest*?
This is the third part of the American Digest System. The *General Digest* contains current volumes published monthly with the latest cumulative digest headnotes of all federal cases and state appellate court cases.

Are the volumes of the current *General Digest* cumulative?
No. Each volume stands on its own. After the set is completed, they are cumulated and published as the new Decennial set and the individual volumes are discarded.

How are current digests updated?
There are two methods of updating current sets. First, there are cumulative new volumes replacing older volumes as needed. Second, all digests have annual pocket parts and interim supplementary pamphlets. For the federal digests, there are bimonthly pamphlets, for regional and state digests, there are semi-annual pamphlets. These pamphlets are discarded as they are cumulated into the annual pocket parts.

What digests are not updated with pocket parts?
Decennial digests and the General Digest are not updated with pocket parts because they cover a specific time period. Decennial Digests cumulate cases for a specific time period from the General Digest. The General Digest is a non-cumulative collection of monthly volumes that cumulates at the end of a specific time period into a new Decennial.

Where can one find what volumes of the reporters are covered in the digests?
In each volume of the various digests, there is a listing called "Closing With Cases Reported In" on the back of the title page which provides the latest reporter volume information. This information can also be found in the pocket part and supplementary pamphlets.

How does one access the federal digests?
There are Tables of Cases, Descriptive-Word Indexes, and Words and Phrases volumes.

How does one access the state digests?
There are Tables of Cases, Descriptive-Word Indexes, and Words and Phrases volumes.

How does one access the Decennial Digests?
There are Table of Cases volumes and Descriptive-Word Indexes for each decennial digest. There are no Words and Phrases volumes.

Where can I find the Descriptive-Word Index table for the monthly *General Digest*?
Every tenth volume of the *General Digest* has a Descriptive-Word Index table covering the previous 10 volumes.

Where can I find a cumulative table of cases for the *General Digest*?
Every tenth volume of the *General Digest* has a cumulative list of cases covering the previous ten volumes.

Which digest is the best one to find state case law?
Use the state digest for your own state. It will cover federal, state appellate cases, and for some states, trial courts as well.

What is the Descriptive Word Index?
This is the cumulative index of multiple volumes found at the end of the set. One looks up a subject and locates the appropriate topic and key number associated with the topic.

Is the Descriptive Word Index available for each set in the digest system?
Yes, they are available for all federal, decennial, regional, and state digests except for the *General Digest* (only every 10th volume).

What are the Table of Cases volumes?
The Table of Cases contains the plaintiff-defendant and defendant-plaintiff names arranged alphabetically along with the history of the case.

Why are digest topics listed along with the case citation and history of the case in the Table of Cases volumes?
The digest topics provide the researcher with all of the digest key numbers for that case if you don't have the case in your hands. For instance, there are four key numbers (headnotes) for the following case of University of Washington, Harborview Medical Center v. Marengo, 95 P.3d 787 (Washington App. Div. 1 2004), Statutes 181(1), 209; Workers Comp. 750, 1939.11(7)

What is Words and Phrases?
The volumes contain the judicial definition of words and phrases cited in court cases. Current volumes provide the paragraph citation from the court case. Federal and state digests contain Words and Phrases volumes. There are no comparative volumes for the *Decennial Digest* or the *General Digest* series. There is a cumulative set called *Words and Phrases* (over 100 volumes) that lists definitions from all jurisdictions.

II. INTERNET

Are there digests available on the Internet?

There are no digests available on the Internet similar to those in LexisNexis and Westlaw.

III. LEXISNEXIS

Is the West Digest System available on LexisNexis?

The West Digest System is not available on LexisNexis. LexisNexis has created its own digest system. The headnotes found in the system are available only online and cannot be found in the various bound volume sets, e.g., *Lawyers Edition*, which contains a different set of topic and headnotes.

Where can one find the headnotes in the LexisNexis system?

Headnotes are found in the front of each case. (Older cases may not have headnotes.)

Under Search Tab on the home page, there is an option to select "by topic or headnote." Once selected, Option 1 lets you type in your term to retrieve several topics in which your search is part of; Option 2 allows one to select a topic and then run your search.

Research Litigator has the link for "Search by Topic or Headnote" under the category of Research, which will provide you with the same options as mentioned above. (Research Litigator is a separate subscription.)

How do the headnotes differ from West headnotes?

Lexis creates headnote topics and then takes direct quotes from the cases to demonstrate each topic.

IV. WESTLAW

Where can one find West digests in Westlaw?

West's digests in Westlaw are different from other titles since the individual books are not actually available like annotated statutes, encyclopedias, ALR, etc.

There are two methods of searching the Digest System.

The entire West Keynumber Digest (Custom Digest) is available under the Search Westlaw or Browse Westlaw categories under Site Map link.

There is also a link called Key Numbers that will provide key-word searching mechanism to find the key numbers for a specific word or phrase as well as browsing key numbers to access the digest topics.

The entire list of digest topics will then be shown for selection. Each topic is broken down into its subtopics. To retrieve cases, select the appropriate topic and then select jurisdiction and date.

Digest topic headnotes can be found in the front of each case that West has included in its database.

How can one use the headnotes in one case to locate cases in other jurisdictions?

Click on the reference More Like This next to the headnote you are interested in. It will take you to a query box to identify other jurisdictions.

How can one locate the state digests?

The digest is not available as the print version; however, one can retrieve the cases by key words under state specific headnote databases, such as AL-HN, CA-HN, etc.

CHAPTER 5

CITATORS

Introduction: Citators are an important tool in identifying whether primary sources (cases, constitutions, statutes, administrative law, and court rules) are good law or not. They also provide important references to secondary sources like periodicals, ALRs, and treatises. Citators include the manual Shepard's Citations and the two electronic versions of Shepard's on Lexis and West's KeyCite. This chapter reviews the three sources for citator research.

I. MANUAL

What is the purpose of Shepard's Citations?

It is necessary to check all primary sources to see if they are still good law. Citators assist the researcher in checking constitutions, statutes, cases, regulations, and court rules.

What topics does Shepard's Citations cover?

There are Shepard's for U. S. Supreme Court (1 set for each reporter), Federal lower courts (1 set for *Federal Reporter* and *Federal Supplement*), Federal Constitution and statutes (*Shepard's Federal Statutes Citations*), federal court rules (*Shepard's Federal Rules Citations*), and administrative law (*Shepard's C.F.R. Citations*).

There are Shepard's Citations for each state, and the seven regional reporters.

There are specialty subjects including administrative law, bankruptcy, employment, environmental law, labor, taxation, uniform commercial code, and model rules of professional conduct.

How are the bound volumes published?

Shepard's Citations publishes a bound volume set from one to 20+ volumes dealing with a specific jurisdiction in maroon, hard-cover bound volumes. There is a date on the spine of the book informing the reader of the coverage of the book, e.g., *Shepard's United States Reports* has a 2004 date on the spine.

How are the bound volumes updated?

There are advance sheets or supplementary pamphlets published first: monthly red issues, semiannual or annual yellow paperback books, and finally bound volume supplements.

Some sets have biweekly blue cover updates, e.g., U.S. Supreme Court.

Bound volumes have dates of coverage on their spines like the initial volumes.

Do you keep all advance sheets on the shelf as they come in?

No, the advance sheet pamphlets are cumulative and each new one replaces an older one. A February red issue would replace a January monthly red issue and a February blue biweekly issue.

How does the table "What your library should contain" help me in research?

On the front cover of the advance sheets is a box that tells the researcher what the contents of the particular title contains, e.g., main volumes, bound volume supplements, and advance sheets.

How do I know what the abbreviations mean in a citation?

There is a Table of Abbreviations in the introductory pages of the bound volume.

Are these citations the same as those found in the *Uniform System of Citation* (Harvard Bluebook)?

No, Shepard's compiles its own abbreviations used in its books, e.g., HLR for *Harvard Law Review*.

What is the cited case?

It is the case that one is looking up in the citators to determine if it is still good law.

What is the citing case?

This is the later case found in the citators that affects the case being looked up.

How do I begin to Shepardize cases?

Find the title that covers the reports that you need to research. Look up the citation by volume and page number. Under the citation, one will find the name of the case along with its date of publication. Below the citation, there are generally five different listings: parallel citation, history of the case, treatment of the case, periodicals, and ALR annotations.

Do I start Shepardizing with the most recent bound volumes or paperback supplements first?
One should always begin with the first time the case is being cited in the citator whether it is the original bound volumes, supplementary volumes, or supplementary pamphlets.

Is it enough to use the most recent pamphlets to determine whether the case is still good law?
It is necessary to check all volumes and supplementary pamphlets for citations to the case under review in order to determine that you have not missed a citation that affects the case.

How are cases (citations) organized in the Shepard's volumes?
Federal volumes cite to other federal cases first and then state citations.

A state citation will cite to cases within that state first, other states, and then federal citations.

What are the main functions of the Shepard's?
Shepard's provides primary source references through its history and treatment and secondary sources (periodicals and annotations).

1. Parallel Citation: cross listing from official citation to unofficial or unofficial back to official citation.
2. History of the Case: Provides the history of the case from the lowest court to the highest court or the highest court back to the lowest. The marginal notes to the left of the citations identify cases under this category. If there are no marginal notes, then the case listing is part of the treatment of the case.
3. Treatment of the Case: Provides what happened to the case when it is heard by a later court, cases from the federal, state, or trial level. Most cases cited are treatment. There are marginal notes to identify positive treatment (e.g., followed), negative ( ), or neutral (cited in dissenting or concurring opinion).
4. Periodicals: Generally, the top twenty law reviews are cited, e.g, Harvard, Yale, Columbia, U. of Pennsylvania, etc. For state digests, the law reviews of the state law reviews are also cited, e.g., in Pennsylvania, it includes Duquesne, Penn State, Temple, University of Pittsburgh, Villanova, and Widener Universities.
5. American Law Reports: Citation to all annotations from the American Law Reports.

How do I know if there is a parallel cite in Shepard's results?

The first time a citation is listed in Shepard's Citations, a parallel citation is identified by being placed in parenthesis underneath the title of the case. For example, in Shepard's Maryland Citations, Boyd v. State, 321 Md. 69 will have a parallel citation in parenthesis (581 A.2d 1); if you look up the case in Shepard's Atlantic Reporter Citations under 581 A.2d 1, the parallel citation to the official report will be in the parenthesis (321 Md. 69).

What is the history of the case?

The history of the case shows the rulings of the case from the lowest court to the highest court or from the highest court back to the lowest. The marginal notes to the left of the citations identify cases under this category. If there are no marginal notes, then the case listing is part of the treatment of the case.

How do I know that the case has been appealed to the higher court by looking at the citations?

The marginal note has to appear to the left of the citation identifying what happened to the case when it went to the higher court, e.g., if you see the letter "a" the case has been affirmed on appeal; if you see the letter "r," the case has been reversed on appeal.

Where can I find the marginal notes for history of the case?

The marginal notes are given on the inside cover of the book or advance sheet. There is also a table in the first introductory pages.

What are the marginal notes for the history of a case?

The following table is copied from McGraw-Hill, Shepard's Citations:

HISTORY OF CASES	ABBREVIATIONS
a (affirmed)	On appeal, reconsideration or rehearing, the citing case affirms or adheres to the case you are *Shepardizing*.
Alloc den (denied)	The citing order denies allocatur in the case you are *Shepardizing*.
Alloc gr (granted)	The citing order grants allocatur in the case you are *Shepardizing*.
cc (connected case)	The citing case is related to the case you are *Shepardizing*, arising out of the same subject matter or involving the same parties.
D (dismissed)	The citing case dismisses an appeal from the case you are *Shepardizing*.

DE/Cert den (denied)	The citing case has denied further appeal in the case you are *Shepardizing*.
Gr (granted)	The citing case has granted further appeal in the case you are *Shepardizing*.
m (modified)	On appeal, reconsideration or rehearing, the citing case modifies or changes in some way, including affirming in part and reversal in part, the case you are *Shepardizing*.
r (reversed)	On appeal, reconsideration or rehearing, the citing case reverses the case you are *Shepardizing*.
Reh den (Reh./recon. denied)	The citing order denies rehearing or reconsideration in the case you are *Shepardizing*.
Reh gran (reh./recon. granted)	The citing order grants rehearing or reconsideration in the case you are *Shepardizing*.
s (same case)	The citing case involves the same litigation as the case you are *Shepardizing*, but at a different stage of the proceedings.
S (superseded)	On appeal, reconsideration or rehearing, the citing case supersedes or is substituted for the case you are *Shepardizing*.
U.S. cert den	The citing order by the U.S. Supreme Court denies certiorari in the cases you are *Shepardizing*.
US cert dis	The citing order by the U.S. Supreme Court dismisses certiorari in the case you are *Shepardizing*.
US cert gran	The citing order by the U.S. Supreme Court grants certiorari in the case you are *Shepardizing*.
US reh den	The citing order by the U. S. Supreme Court denies rehearing in the case you are *Shepardizing*.
US reh dis	The citing order by the U. S. Supreme Court dismisses rehearing in the case you are *Shepardizing*.
v (vacated)	The citing case vacates or withdraws the case you are *Shepardizing*.
W (withdrawn)	The citing decision or opinion withdraws the decision or order you are *Shepardizing*.

What is the treatment of the case?

Treatment of the case provides what happened to the case when it is heard by a later court, cases from the federal, state, or trial level. Most cases cited are treatments. There are marginal notes to identify positive treatment (e.g., followed), negative (criticized, distinguished), or neutral (cited in dissenting or concurring opinion).

Where can one find the abbreviations for treatment of the case?
The marginal notes are given on the back cover of the book or advance sheet. There is also a table in the first introductory pages.

What are the marginal notes for treatment of a case?
The following table is copied from McGraw-Hill, Shepard's Citations:

TREATMENT OF CASES	ABBREVIATIONS
c (criticized)	The citing opinion disagrees with the reasoning/result of the case you are *Shepardizing,* although the citing court may not have the authority to materially affect its precedential value.
ca (conflicting authorities)	Among conflicting authorities as noted in cited case.
d (distinguished)	The citing case differs from the case you are *She pardizing,* either involving dissimilar facts or requiring a different application of the law.
e (explained)	The citing opinion interprets or clarifies the case you are *Shepardizing* in a significant way.
f (followed)	The citing opinion relies on the case you are *Shepardizing* as controlling or persuasive authority.
h (harmonized)	The citing case differs from the case you are *Shepardizing,* but the citing court reconciles the difference or inconsistency in reaching its decision.
j (dissenting opinion)	A dissenting opinion cites the case you are *Shepardizing.*
~ (concurring opinion)	A concurring opinion cites the case you are *Shepardizing.*
L (limited)	The citing opinion restricts the application of the case you are *Shepardizing,* finding its reasoning applies only in specific limited circumstances.
o (overruled)	The citing case expressly overrules or disapproves the case you are *Shepardizing.*
op (overruled in part)	Ruling in the cited case overruled partially or on other grounds or with other qualifications.
q (questioned)	The citing opinion questions the continuing validity or precedential value of the case you are *Shepar-*

dizing because of intervening circumstances, including judicial or legislative overruling.

su (superseded)   Superseded by statute as stated in cited case.

OTHER

The citing case is of questionable precedential value because review or rehearing has been granted by the California Supreme Court and/or the citing case has been ordered depublished pursuant to Rule 976 of the California Rules of Court. (Publication status should be verified before use of the citing case in California.)

What is positive treatment of a case?
Contains history or treatment of your case that has a positive impact on your case (e.g., affirmed or followed).

What is negative treatment of a case?
Contains history or treatment that may have a significant negative impact on your case (e.g., overruled or reversed).

What is neutral treatment of a case?
Neutral treatment contains treatment of your case that is neither positive or negative (e.g., explained, cited in a concurring or dissenting opinion).

What does the abbreviation analysis mean?
In the bound volumes, abbreviations can be found as marginal notes next to a citation. All cases that are part of history of the case have a citation next to it. Treatment, however, has citations only next to those cases that have positive, negative, or neutral citations. Most citations have no abbreviations and are probably string citations.

What is the superscript number found after the abbreviation for a citation, e.g., 350 F2d [3] 1240?
The superscript number 3 refers to the headnote in the original case. This helps the researcher in limiting one's research to just headnotes from the original case.

How do I know the cases I found are good cases?
There has to be no negative treatment of the case.

What does the 'n' and 's' mean at the end of an A.L.R. citation?
The 'n' stands for notes and the 's' stands for supplement.

When one has two citations for a state case (official and unofficial), which citation should I use to shepardize?
Official citations provide references to state appellate and county cases and federal citations, as well as, periodical literature limited to the published law reviews. The regional citators cite only to the regional reporters and omit federal and trial court cases and contain no periodicals.

II. INTERNET

Are there citators available on the Internet?

The internet does not provide citators similar to Shepard's or KeyCite.

Can I find Tables of Authorities for cases on the Internet?
The Internet does not contain cases for table of authorities.

III. SHEPARD's CITATIONS (LEXISNEXIS)

What are the advantages of using Shepard's Citations online rather than in print?
Online Shepard's Citations eliminates the need to go through multiple bound volumes and pamphlets to check for all citations. Instead of looking up parallel citations in different sets, the online system provides one listing of all citations. Online citations are also kept up to date daily. Online citators provide citations to more periodicals, not just a selected number of periodicals. The *ABA Journal* is included in citations. Citations to annotated codes are also listed. Treatises published by the same commercial vendor that publishes Shepard's are included in the citator. There is no need for marginal notes because all abbreviations are written out completely. It is possible to limit your searches by negative, positive, and Focus restricted by.

How do you know how many citations are provided for when using the citator?
At the top of the page, there is the number of citations listed for the cited reference, for instance for *Roe v. Wade*, 410 U.S. 113, there are over 14,500 citations listed.

Can one limit the viewing of the citations online?
On the top left side of the screen, there is the capability of selecting either KWIC or FULL view.

What is viewing a document in KWIC format?

The KWIC format gives the researcher only the citation in bold print that one is researching with up to 255 characters on either side of the citation.

What is viewing a document in Full format?

Full format gives the researcher the citation in bold print that is being researched within the complete document.

What are the Display Options under View?

Pinpoint pages, LexisNexis headnotes, Headnote Numbers, Citing Ref. Signals.

Shepard's lets one limit the types of information that one can view. One can see complete entries or limited to any or all of the four restrictions listed above.

Pinpoint pages are usually on to show the exact page on the citator.

LexisNexis headnotes show the new electronic headnotes available.

Headnote Numbers refers to the headnotes found in the bound volumes.

Citing Reference Signals provides the red, yellow, and green flags to identify if the cases are still good law.

What is Save as Shepard's Alert?

Save as Shepard's Alert provides an updating service to the researcher when a new citation is added to the citation under review.

What is the Shepard's Summary section at the top of a case citation?

Shepard's Summary provides all categories of citations listed in the citator for the history and treatment of the case as well as the secondary sources listed, e.g., law reviews, ALRs, annotated codes, treatises.

At the top of the box is a statement concerning whether the citing reference has been reversed or not, e.g., *Roe v. Wade*, 410 U.S. 113, says "No negative subsequent appellate history".

How does one limit searching when looking up citations?

Above the title of the case, there are four categories: Unrestrict, All Neg, All Pos, and Focus Retricted By.

How can one limit a search to just negative treatment?

Above the title of the case, is a link called "All Neg" to identify just negative treatment, e.g., distinguished and overruled.

How can one limit your searching to just positive treatment?

Above the top line is a link called "All Pos" to identify ALL POS just positive treatment, e.g., followed.

How does one limit searches to jurisdiction, individual federal circuit, or state courts?
Under the Focus Restrict By link, restrictions are provided for searching by jurisdiction, e.g., federal circuits or states.

How does one limit searches to secondary sources?
Under the Focus Restrict By link, searches can be limited to law reviews, statutes, and ALRs.

Can one limit searches to headnotes of the original case?
Under the Focus Restrict By, headnotes can be searched, including for L.Ed. and Supreme Court Reporter which have different headnote numbers.

Can one limit searches to Lexis electronic headnotes?
Under the Focus Restrict By, electronic headnotes can be found towards the bottom of the page.

How is parallel citation presented in the online version?
Parallel citation is provided under the title of the case.

How is the history of the case shown online?
Prior History is provided first with the case cited highlighted in gray with an arrow next to it. The citator also provides subsequent history too.

How is the treatment of the case shown online?
There is a line between the history and treatment of the case. Each citation is provided with the equivalent of the marginal note above the listing, e.g., Cited as; Followed by; Distinguished by; Cited in Dissenting Opinion; Cited in Concurring Opinion.

How does periodical coverage differ from manual citations?
Periodical coverage includes all legal periodicals available in Lexis. This includes hundreds more periodicals than what is available in the paper copy.

What other periodicals are covered in the online services?
Under Secondary Sources, Lexis provides citations to the *American Bar Association (ABA) Journal*.

What statutory sources are listed?
Online citators cite to the federal and state annotated codes.

What other citations are provided online?

Shepard's also cites to statutory law under the annotated codes on the federal level (*U.S.C.A.* or *U.S.C.A.*) and state codes.

What treatises are cited online?

Unlike the paper Shepard's that did not contain treatises, the online service provides citations to hundreds of treatises on general and state-related topics published by Lexis. When Shepard's cites to a standard treatise published by West, it provides only the citation, no hyperlink to the document.

What are Shepard's Signal Indicators?

Red stop sign Warning —Negative treatment indicated.

Orange square surrounding the letter "Q" in a box Warning —Questioned by the citing court

Green Diamond with a "+" in the center: Positive treatment indicated.

Yellow triangle: Caution: possible negative treatment

Blue circle surrounding the letter "A" –Citing references with analysis available

Blue circle surrounding the letter "I" —Citation information available

What is (TOA) next to the citation of the case?

TOA stands for Table of Authorities that provides a citation list of all citations cited in the case under review, for example, Roe v. Wade has 143 case citations. The citations are also listed with Shepard's signals to identify if they are still good law.

What are the options in printing or saving the results of the search?

On the right hand corner of the screen there are the options to print, download, fax, or email the documents.

What does it mean by "Text Only" on the top right corner?

Text Only provides the citation list in text format without hyperlinks for the documents. This might be useful for copying citations into a word processor without worrying about hyperlinks.

III. KEYCITE (WESTLAW)

What is KeyCite?

In the mid-1990s, Reed Elsevier purchased Shepard's Citations Company and added it to its other major legal publishing companies like Lexis and Matthew Bender. For a short period of time, Shepard's citators were available through Westlaw.

Thomson Corporation realized that it was necessary for it to develop its own citing system and developed Keycite to compete against Shepard's Citations. The addition of a second citator system is a major development in the history of electronic legal publishing.

What are similar features between the two systems?

KeyCite provides the means to check all primary sources similar to Shepard's, e.g. cases, constitutions, statutes, court rules, and administrative regulations. It provides the same types of references, such as parallel citations, history, treatment, along with citations to ALRs, periodicals, and treatises. It also identifies negative and positive treatment of cases and the history of statutory law.

What are the differences between the two systems?

KeyCite is incorporated into the West caselaw system by having its KC symbol next to all cases in Westaw. KC history provides a direct impact on the case's validity, while KC Citing Reference provides a full listing of all citing cases.

What is the easiest way of using KeyCite?

There are two methods of accessing KeyCite on a page. Along the top line is a KeyCite link. Click on KeyCite and an explanation of KeyCite will appear along with a "KeyCite text box" on the left side of the page to type in your citation.

On the left side of the search panel is "KeyCite this citation" which lets one enter case, statute, constitution, rule, law review, ALR citation, etc.

What does Citing References mean on the left hand side of the screen?

It is the link to the entire citation list for the cited reference.

What is the Publications List?

This is a list of more than 4400 titles with their abbreviations.

What is KeyCite Tips?

This is the information page on how to use KeyCite:

Accessing KeyCite

KeyCite Coverage

KeyCite Status Flags

KeyCite Quotation Marks

Viewing and Printing the History of a Case

Displaying the Direct History of a Case in Graphical View

Viewing and Printing Citing References for a Case

Restricting Citing References for a Case

Using KeyCite Notes to View Citing References for a Case

Viewing and Printing the History of a Statute

Viewing and Printing Citing References for a Statute

Restricting Citing References for a Statute

How is parallel citation presented in the online version?
Parallel citation is provided under the title of the case.

How is the history of the case shown online?
Under history, there is the number of citations divided into two sections: Direct history and Negative Citing References. Direct history presents the history of the case as it went through the court system; Negative Citing References provides citations to all cases giving negative analysis. Negative Citing References is followed by Related References and Court Documents?

What are Court Documents?
This is a listing of court briefs submitted for the case including the appellate briefs, related briefs, and possibly the transcripts of oral arguments before the U.S. Supreme Court, and docket entries.

What are the links on the left hand panel of the page?
Full history, Direct History (Graphical View), Citing References, Monitor with KeyCite Alert, Full-Text Document, Petitions, Briefs, & Filings, Results Plus, Table of Authorities, and West Key Numbers.

What is Full History under the Result List?
Full History provides all citations listed for the citation under review.

What is meant by Direct History (Graphical View)?
KeyCite provides a graphical view of the history of the cited case as it went through the court system from lowest to highest court. *Roe v. Wade*, for instance, shows how two connected cases, *Roe* and *Doe v. Bolton*, rose together through the federal system to reach the U.S. Supreme Court and have a single opinion issued on both cases.

What does the shading mean in the graphical view?
KeyCite identifies the levels of the courts by going from a darker to lighter shade of blue.

What are State Court Org Charts?
Click on this link in order to get a listing of all 50 states. Select a state and get a listing of the court structure in that state.

What is Monitor With KeyCite Alert?
KeyCite Alert is like Shepard's Alert notifying one of any new cases added to Key-Cite for the citation that one has entered for review.

What is Citing References?
This is the link to the complete list of history and treatment of the case as well as secondary sources and court documents.

What is Full-Text Document, Case Outline?
This provides the various segments for the case:

Synopsis
Headnote(s)
Opinion(s)
Concurring Opinion(s)
Dissenting Opinions(s)

If there is more than one concurring or dissenting opinion, additional hyperlinks are provided for them.

What is the link to Petitions, Briefs, & Filings?
This is a link to the petitions, briefs, and documents filed in the case. They come at the end of the citing list and so this provides a short-cut to that section.

What is Results Plus?
West provides links to at least three secondary sources (ALRs, *Am Jur 2d.*, *Corpus Juris Secundum*, *Am Jur Proof of Facts*, *Am Jur Trials*, and *Causes of Action*) depending on what the citation is.

What is the Table of Authorities on the left panel?
The Table of Authorities provides a list of all cases that derive from the case under review similar to the TOA in Shepard's Citations. KeyCite also identifies with its flags whether the underlying cases are still good law or not.

What are the West Key Numbers on the left panel?
The West Digest Key numbers for the case under review are listed here.

How is history of the case shown online?

Under the citation for the case, Direct History is shown including preceding and subsequent history. The cited case has an arrow and is in grey shading to identify the cited case. Negative Citing References are also provided.

How is the treatment of the case shown online?

Following Negative References, Positive References are provided broken down into depth of treatment identified by using a star system from four to one star.

What does the star system stand for?

It stands for depth of treatment:

4 stars means an extended discussion of the cited case, usually more than a printed page of text.

3 stars means a discussion of the cited case, usually more than a paragraph but less than a printed page.

2 stars means a discussion of less than a paragraph.

1 star means a string citation.

One can select any level of cases to show by placing a check in the box next to the stars.

What does it mean when the listing of HN: 9, 24 follows the star treatment in a citation?

The HN: 9, 24 refers to the specific headnotes of the cited case being referenced in the later citing cases. This is one method by which to limit one's searching for later cases by headnote number.

What are KeyCite Notes next to the Key Numbers within each case?

KeyCite Notes retrieves a listing of citing references that discuss legal issues similar to the one summarized in that headnote. The list includes cases, Administrative Decisions, Administrative Registers, Treatises & Encyclopedias, and Law Reviews & Journals.

How does one limit the number of documents looked at (similar to Shepard's Summary)?

KeyCite limits searches by a box at the bottom of the page, Limit KeyCite Display. KeyCite can be limited to Headnotes, Locate, Jurisdiction, Date, Document Type, and Depth of Treatment.

What does one find under Headnotes?

Headnotes provide a listing of all the headnotes found in the case.

Why does one use the Locate feature?
Locate allows one to search the list of cases and secondary sources for specific terms using terms and connectors with Boolean search terms and segment searching.

Why does one use the Jurisdiction feature?
Jurisdiction limits the search to individual federal circuits and/or state courts.

Why does one use the Date feature?
The drop down box under Date of Document lets one use standard dates —unrestricted, last month, three months, six months, last one year, last two years, or last three years) or specific dates selected to limit the search.
   Date added after provides the same listing of dates.

Why does one use Document type?
Document type limits the search to Cases (Highest court and Other courts); Secondary Sources (ALR annotations, Law Reviews, Andrews Litigation Reporters, Others); Administrative Materials (Administrative Decisions, Federal Register); Court Documents (Verdicts & Settlements, Appellate Petitions, Appellate Briefs, Joint Appendices, Oral Arguments, Trial Pleadings, Expert Testimony, Trial Depositions & Discovery, Trial Motions, Memoranda & Affidavits, Trial Transcripts, Trial Filings, Jury Instructions, Proposed Orders, Agreements & Settlements, Verdicts, Agreements & Settlements).

How does periodical coverage compare to Shepard's online?
Periodical coverage is similar to Shepard's coverage in Lexis as it provides hundreds of legal periodicals. Coverage may vary by date of individual periodical. Most periodicals will have selective inclusion from the 1980s and full-text from the 1990s.

What statutory sources are listed?
KeyCite provides citations to *U.S.C.A.* and state annotated codes.

What treatises are cited online?
KeyCite provides citations to hundreds of treatises on general and state-related topics that are published by West. For citations to Lexis treatises, there are no hyperlinks to the documents.

What are KeyCite indicators?
Red flag warning — A red flag warns that a case is no longer good law for at least on of the points of law it contains.

Yellow flag warning —A yellow flag warns that the case has some negative history but has not been reversed or overruled

H —A blue H indicates that the case has some history.

C —A green C indicates that the case has some citing references but no direct history or negative citing references.

CHAPTER 6

CONSTITUTIONS

Introduction: The constitution is the main primary written document that provides the organizational structure of the government of the jurisdiction that it is written for. The Constitution of the United States is still the same document written in 1787 with an additional twenty-seven amendments that affect the original document. State constitutions, however, are different, since the people of each state have revised their constitutions from two to more than eleven times. State constitutions also provide for more detailed restrictions upon their local government. Local or municipal constitutions are called charters.

I. MANUAL

What are the organic laws of the United States?

The Declaration of Independence of 1776, Articles of Confederation of 1777, and the Ordinance of 1787 (Northwest Territorial Government)

When was the Constitution of the United States adopted?

The Constitution was adopted in 1787 by the Constitutional Convention. It was ratified by the required nine states by 1789.

What is federalism?

"Federalism is the theory or advocacy of federal political orders, where final authority is divided between sub-units and a center. Unlike a unitary state, sovereignty is constitutionally split between at least two territorial levels so that units at each level have final authority and can act independently of the others in some areas. Citizens thus have political obligations to two authorities." (*Stanford Encyclopedia of Philosophy*, http://plato.stanford.edu)

What is separation of powers?
Separation of powers refers to the policy by which the three branches of government each have their own powers, e.g., President as head of the military, Congress creates law, Judiciary interprets law.

How many times has the Constitution been rewritten?
None.

How many articles are there in the Constitution of the United States?
Seven articles.

What is the outline of the Articles of the Constitution of the United States?
Preamble ["We the people"]

Article I [The Legislative Branch]

Section 1. [Legislative Power Vested]

Section 2. [House of Representatives]

Section 3. [Senate]

Section 4. [Elections of Senators and Representatives]

Section 5. [Rules of House and Senate]

Section 6. [Compensation and Privileges of Members]

Section 7. [Passage of Bills]

Section 8. [Scope of Legislative Power]

Section 9. [Limits on Legislative Power]

Section 10. [Limits on States]

Article II [The Presidency]

Section 1. [Election, Installation, Removal]

Section 2. [Presidential Power]

Section 3. [State of the Union, Receive Ambassadors, Laws Faithfully Executed, Commission Officers]

Section 4. [Impeachment]

Article III [The Judiciary]

Section 1. [Judicial Power Vested]

Section 2. [Scope of Judicial Power]

Section 3. [Treason]

Article IV [The States]

Section 1. [Full Faith and Credit]

Section 2. [Privileges and Immunities, Extradiction, Fugitive Slaves]

Section 3. [Admission of States]

Section 4. [Guarantees to States]

Article V [The Amendment Process]

Article VI [Legal Status of the Constitution]

Article VII [Ratification]

Signers

How does one change the Constitution?

Amendments provide the method by which the Constitution is updated.

Article V of the U.S. Constitution provides for the amendment process:

The Congress, whenever two thirds of both houses shall deem it necessary, shall propose amendments to this Constitution, or, on the application of the legislatures of two thirds of the several states, shall call a convention for proposing amendments, which, in either case, shall be valid to all intents and purposes, as part of this Constitution, when ratified by the legislatures of three fourths of the several states, or by conventions in three fourths thereof, as the one or the other mode of ratification may be proposed by the Congress; provided that no amendment which may be made prior to the year one thousand eight hundred and eight shall in any manner affect the first and fourth clauses in the ninth section of the first article; and that no state, without its consent, shall be deprived of its equal suffrage in the Senate.

How many amendments are there?

There are twenty-seven amendments to the Constitution.

What are the first ten amendments to the Constitution called?

The Bill of Rights. Originally, there were twelve amendments, but the first two were not approved by Congress and so ten amendments were adopted.

When was the Bill of Rights passed into law?

In 1791 after eleven states had ratified the passage of the Bill of Rights

What are the amendments under the Bill of Rights?

Amendment I

Congress shall make no law respecting an establishment of religion, or prohibiting the free exercise thereof; or abridging the freedom of speech, or of the press; or the right of the people peaceably to assemble, and to petition the government for a redress of grievances.

Amendment II

A well regulated militia, being necessary to the security of a free state, the right of the people to keep and bear arms, shall not be infringed.

Amendment III

No soldier shall, in time of peace be quartered in any house, without the consent of the owner, nor in time of war, but in a manner to be prescribed by law.

Amendment IV

The right of the people to be secure in their persons, houses, papers, and effects, against unreasonable searches and seizures, shall not be violated, and no warrants shall issue, but upon probable cause, supported by oath or affirmation, and particularly describing the place to be searched, and the persons or things to be seized.

Amendment V

No person shall be held to answer for a capital, or otherwise infamous crime, unless on a presentment or indictment of a grand jury, except in cases arising in the land or naval forces, or in the militia, when in actual service in time of war or public danger; nor shall any person be subject for the same offense to be twice put in jeopardy of life or limb; nor shall be compelled in any criminal case to be a witness against himself, nor be deprived of life, liberty, or property, without due process of law; nor shall private property be taken for public use, without just compensation.

Amendment VI

In all criminal prosecutions, the accused shall enjoy the right to a speedy and public trial, by an impartial jury of the state and district wherein the crime shall have been committed, which district shall have been previously ascertained by law, and to be informed of the nature and cause of the accusation; to be confronted with the witnesses against him; to have compulsory process for obtaining witnesses in his favor, and to have the assistance of counsel for his defense.

Amendment VII

In suits at common law, where the value in controversy shall exceed twenty dollars, the right of trial by jury shall be preserved, and no fact tried by a jury, shall be otherwise reexamined in any court of the United States, than according to the rules of the common law.

Amendment VIII

Excessive bail shall not be required, nor excessive fines imposed, nor cruel and unusual punishments inflicted.

Amendment IX

The enumeration in the Constitution, of certain rights, shall not be construed to deny or disparage others retained by the people.

Amendment X

The powers not delegated to the United States by the Constitution, nor prohibited by it to the states, are reserved to the states respectively, or to the people.

What are the Amendments XI to XXVII?

Amendment XI [Suits Against a State (1795)]

Amendment XII [Election of President and Vice-President (1804)]

Amendment XIII [Abolition of Slavery (1865)]

Amendment XIV [Privileges and Immunities, Due Process, Equal Protection, Apportionment of Representatives, Civil War Disqualification and Debt (1868)]

Amendment XV [Rights Not to Be Denied on Account of Race (1870)]

Amendment XVI [Income Tax (1913)]

Amendment XVII [Election of Senators (1913)]

Amendment XVIII [Prohibition (1919)]

Amendment XIX [Women's Right to Vote (1920)

Amendment XX [Presidential Term and Succession (1933)]

Amendment XXI [Repeal of Prohibition (1933)]

Amendment XXII [Two Term Limit on President (1951)]

Amendment XXIII [Presidential Vote in D.C. (1961)]

Amendment XXIV [Poll Tax (1964)]

Amendment XXV [Presidential Succession (1967)]

Amendment XXVI [Right to Vote at Age 18 (1971)]

Amendment XXVII [Compensation of Members of Congress (1992)]

Who did the Bill of Rights apply to?

The Bill of Rights was at first a limitation only upon the federal government. It did not affect state or local governments.

When was the Bill of Rights incorporated into state law?

It was not until 1868 with the ratification of the 14th Amendment that the Bill of Rights was incorporated into state law.

What is the Magna Carta?

Magna Carta, also called "the Great Writ," is a medieval legal document providing for the settlement of disputes between King John and his feudal lords in 1215. The document was reissued several times during medieval times. It was used by Edward Coke in the early seventeenth century as a statutory law against King James I and King Charles I in their disputes with parliament. From this document are derived the due process clause and trial by jury in the United States Constitution.

What is the due process clause?

The due process clause falls under the Fifth and Fourteenth Amendments which prohibit deprivation of "life, liberty or property" without due process of law. The clause in English law equates to "law of the land" which derives from ch. 39 of Magna Carta (1215).

What is procedural due process?

This term relates to certain rights primarily in criminal law that falls under the various sections of the Bill of Rights, e.g., Fifth, Sixth, and Eighth Amendments. Besides rights due under these amendments extended to both federal and state courts, people are due "fundamental fairness" in criminal proceedings, e.g., standard of proof applicable in criminal cases, right to an impartial decision-maker. In addition, most state constitutions contain similar clauses.

Civil aspects of due process may apply in administrative agency hearings, expansion of the ideas of "liberty" and "property" in modern society.

What is substantive due process?

Substantive due process limits the states to regulate certain areas of economic and non-economic life. From late nineteenth century to the mid-1930s, the courts regulated private contracts (Munn v. Illinois, 1877) and liberty of contract (Lochner v. N.Y., 1905). From 1937, the U.S. Supreme Court has stopped reviewing state legislation for substantive due process violations. In recent decades, non-economic rights include birth control, abortion, sexual practices, privacy, and personal appearance.

What is a good source for the Constitution?
The Constitution of the United States of America (Library of Congress ed., 2006) (KF4527 U54). It is a single volume published as a Senate document. It is available online at http://www.gpoaccess.gov/constitution/index.html.

Where else can one find an annotated edition of the Constitution?
Both *United States Code Annotated* (West) (KF62.5 W45) and *United States Code Service* (Lexis) (KF62.5 L38) contain multiple volumes of the Constitution and its amendments.

What is the main source to find the debates of the Constitutional Convention of 1787?
Max Farrand, ed. *Records of the Constitutional Convention of 1787*. Rev. ed. New Haven: Yale University Press, 1966. 4 vols. (KF4510 U547)

What is the main source to find the state debates ratifying the Constitutional Convention of 1787?
The Documentary History of the Ratification of the Constitution (State Historical Society of Wisconsin, 1976-). 21 vols. so far. This is a recent scholarly edition of the ratification by the states. Merrill Jensen was the first editor, followed by John P. Kaminski and Gaspare J. Saladino. (KF4502 D63) It replaces the earlier title dealing with the ratification, Jonathan Elliot, ed. *The Debates in the Several State Conventions on the Adoption of the Federal Constitution as Recommended by the General Convention at Philadelphia in 1787* .... 1827-1830. 4 vols. Updated in various editions. (KF4502 E5)

What is a sourcebook for background materials on the Constitution?
Philip Kurland, ed. *The Founders' Constitution*. University of Chicago Press, 1987 (KF4502 F68). It is available on the internet at http://press-pubs.uchicago.edu/founders/.

What is a sourcebook for background materials on the Bill of Rights?
Cogan, Neil H., ed. *The Complete Bill of Rights: The Drafts, Debates, Sources, and Origins* (1997). (KF4744 1997)
   Schwartz, Bernard, ed. *The Bill of Rights: A Documentary History* (1971). (KF4744 S3 1971)

How many constitutions can be found under each state?
Each state has revised its constitution at least twice since their creation, Pennsylvania has five and Georgia has eleven.

The political, social, and economic conditions that led to state constitution revisions are different from federal constitutional law.

Where can one find annotated versions of the state constitutions?
The annotated codes of each state have at least one volume containing the state's constitutions.

How are state constitutions created?
They can be created by constitutional conventions and be amended by procedures usually provided for in the state constitutions.

How else can one research state constitutions?
One can use Shepard's Citations and/or KeyCite for state constitutional law research.

Are there constitutions for local government, e.g., counties, municipalities?
Local constitutions can be found in municipal charters for counties, cities, boroughs, towns, etc. They may be found online or within various publications, e.g., *Pennsylvania Code* contains home rule charters for all counties and its subdivisions.

II. INTERNET

Where can I find the full text of the United States Constitution?
There are several online sources to obtain the full text of the United States Constitution. Many comprehensive legal web sites such as Findlaw, Cornell, Heiros Gamos provide links to the U.S. Constitution.

Are there any free web sites that provide annotations (case law) to the U.S. Constitution?
In addition to LexisNexis and Westlaw, Findlaw provides annotations to the articles of the constitution.
   The Constitution of the United States of America, Library of Congress edition, is an annotated edition of the Constitution, at
   http://www.gpoaccess.gov/constitution/index.html.

Where can I find the debates of the constitutional convention and ratification by the states?
The Library of Congress Century of Lawmaking, at

http://memory.loc.gov/ammem/amlaw/, contains Journals *of the Continental Congress, Letters of Delegates to the Congress, Farrand's Records,* and *Elliott's Debates.*

Where can I get a copy of the original images of the articles of the constitution?

U.S. government official web site (www.firstgov.gov) provides a link to the "Law & Regulations". Click on that link and then click on "constitution of the United States" to find the images for the articles of the U.S. constitution under "Charters of Freedom" (www.nara.gov/national-archives-experience/charters/ constitution. html) title.

Where do I get the transcript of the Bill of Rights of 1791?

The full text of the Bill of Rights 1791 and many documents related to freedom and the constitution are available from 'Our Documents' site (www.ourdocuments. gov). You also can get several important documents from the Thomas (Thomas. loc.gov) site. Look for a list of the documents under the heading "Learn" from the home page.

Also visit Prof. Douglas Linder's site exploring constitutional law (http://www. law.umkc.edu/faculty/projects/ftrials/conlaw/home.html) which provides links to several important documents such as the Bill of Rights, History of the Constitution, First Amendment etc.

Where do I get a copy of the Magna Carta?

Yale's Avalon project site (http://www.yale.edu/lawweb/avalon/constpap.htm) provides a copy of the Magna Carta (1215) and several other documents such as Mayflower Compact (1620), Fundamental Orders of 1639, etc.

Where do I get information about U.S. constitutional conventions?

Several sites provide information on U.S. constitutional conventions. You can obtain a copy of the 1787 constitutional convention from www.usconstitution.net site. The contents of this site include the Annapolis Plan, Madison's Notes, and Virginia plan, etc. Roger Sherman Hoar's *Constitutional Convention: Their Nature, Powers, and Limitations* (1917) provides detailed information about constitutional conventions (available through Google Books project). Constitution Society site (www.constitution.org) and a constitutional blog (http://constitutionalism.blog-spot.com) are also good sources.

Where can I find state constitutions?

Most of the comprehensive legal websites such as Findlaw, Heiros Gamos, Cornell, LawGuru, Megalaw have links to state constitution pages. The best way is to go to the states' official websites which you can find in several websites including

State Local Government site (www.statelocalgov.net) and find a link for the constitution.

How do I get annotations (cases) to state constitutions?

In addition to LexisNexis and Westlaw you may get annotations to the state constitutions from sites developed by the individuals such as law school faculty members or practicing attorneys. For example, in Pennsylvania, Prof. Bruce Ledewitz and Dr. Joel Fishman maintain a Pennsylvania Constitution web site (www.duq.edu/law/pa-constitution) which provides case law, a comprehensive collection of constitutions and constitutional conventions, and other related information to the Pennsylvania constitution.

III. LEXISNEXIS

Where can one find the U. S. Constitution in Lexis?

The annotated edition can be found as part of the *United States Code Service* (U.S.C.S.). It is either part of the complete collection or as an individual file under *United States Code Service* (U.S.C.S.) Materials.

Where can one find individual state constitutions?

Under each state's "Statutes and Regulations," the state constitution is part of the annotated code or is listed as an individual file.

IV. WESTLAW

Where can one find the U.S. Constitution in Westlaw?

The annotated edition can be found in *United States Code Annotated* (U.S.C.A.). Under the Table of Contents, the Constitution is listed after Organic Law of the United States. It is available in an unannotated or annotated version.

Where can one find state constitutions?

Under each state's "Statutes and Regulations," the state constitution is part of the state's annotated code, [state abbreviation]-st-all, for example, for the Pennsylvania State, it is pa-st-all.

CHAPTER 7

STATUTES

Introduction: Legislative bodies create legislation by enacting bills into law through a standard procedure. Statutes created by the U.S. Congress or a state or a local legislature are published first chronologically and then compiled into a subject classification that may or may not be codified with or without annotations. This chapter reviews the various types of statutes and the publications used for researching chronological and codified laws.

I. MANUAL

What are statutes?

Statutes are one of the four primary sources of law. These are the laws that are passed by Congress on the federal level, the state legislature on the state level, and municipal governments (county commissioners, councils) on the local level.

What does the legislative branch consist of?

Congress consists of two houses consisting of a senate and house of representatives. There are 100 members in the Senate with two senators per state. There are 435 members in the House of Representatives with a different number of members in each state based on population. The number of assigned representatives change after the decennial census.

How often does the Congress meet?

Each congress meets for two years beginning the first Tuesday in January in the odd year until December 31 of the even year.

How many years does a member of the House of Representatives serve?

A representative of the House serves for two years and has to be elected for each new Congress.

How many years does a member of the Senate serve?
A senator serves for a six-year staggered term of office.

What are the enumerated powers of Congress?
Under Article I, section 8 the enumerated powers of Congress include:

The Congress shall have power to lay and collect taxes, duties, imposts and excises, to pay the debts and provide for the common defense and general welfare of the United States; but all duties, imposts and excises shall be uniform throughout the United States;

- To borrow money on the credit of the United States;
- To regulate commerce with foreign nations, and among the several states, and with the Indian tribes;
- To establish a uniform rule of naturalization, and uniform laws on the subject of bankruptcy throughout the United States;
- To coin money, regulate the value thereof, and of foreign coin, and fix the standard of weights and measures;
- To provide for the punishment of counterfeiting the securities and current coin of the United States;
- To establish post offices and post roads;
- To promote the progress of science and useful arts, by securing for limited times to authors and inventors the exclusive right to their respective writings and discoveries;
- To constitute tribunals inferior to the Supreme Court;
- To define and punish piracies and felonies committed on the high seas, and offenses against the law of nations;
- To declare war, grant letters of marque and reprisal, and make rules concerning captures on land and water;
- To raise and support armies, but no appropriation of money to that use shall be for a longer term than two years;
- To provide and maintain a navy;
- To make rules for the government and regulation of the land and naval forces;
- To provide for calling forth the militia to execute the laws of the union, suppress insurrections and repel invasions;

- To provide for organizing, arming, and disciplining, the militia, and for governing such part of them as may be employed in the service of the United States, reserving to the states respectively, the appointment of the officers, and the authority of training the militia according to the discipline prescribed by Congress;

- To exercise exclusive legislation in all cases whatsoever, over such District (not exceeding ten miles (16 km) square) as may, by cession of particular states, and the acceptance of Congress, become the seat of the government of the United States, and to exercise like authority over all places purchased by the consent of the legislature of the state in which the same shall be, for the erection of forts, magazines, arsenals, dockyards, and other needful buildings.

What are the implied powers of Congress?

Congress also has implied powers derived from the necessary-and-proper clause of the Constitution which permits Congress "To make all laws which shall be necessary and proper for carrying into execution the foregoing powers, and all other powers vested by this Constitution in the government of the United States, or in any department or officer thereof" The Supreme Court has interpreted the necessary-and-proper clause broadly, to recognize the Congress has all the power and delegates it rather than being burdened with a separation of powers.

Where can one find biographical information on the members of Congress?

The *Biographical Directory of the United States Congress (1774-2005)* contains biographical information on all members of Congress.

What is the relationship between statutes and case law?
A. Statutes create new areas of law not covered in case law.
B. Some statutes codify, clarify or supplement case law.
C. Some statutes overturn the case law.
D. Statutes usually take precedence over case law that conflicts with statutory provisions.
E. The constitution grants the legislative branch broad powers to create legal rules to govern society.
F. The legislature's exclusive authority to enact statutes is balanced by the court's authority to apply those statutes and other laws, to assess the constitutionality of the statutes, and to make case law.

What is the relationship between case law and statutory law?
Statutes usually state a general rule of law and usually operate prospectively, whereas judicial rulings usually state more particularized rules of law and usually operate retroactively. Courts do not make law, but simply declare law. (Bodenheimer, Edgar, Oakley John B and Love, Jean C. An *Introduction to the Anglo-American Legal System*, 2001)

What are treaties?
Treaties are formal agreements made between two or more sovereign counties. In the United States, the Senate has to approve all treaties by a two-thirds vote of its membership before the United States can participate in them. The Treaty of Versailles following World War I is an example of a failed treaty not confirmed by the Senate.

What are interstate compacts?
An interstate compact is an agreement between at least two states adopted through legislation by both states. Under Article I, Section 10 of the United States Constitution "no state shall enter into an agreement or compact with another state without the consent of Congress." There are over fifty different compacts in existence.

Can case law be superseded by statute?
Yes, a statute can be passed by a legislative body to overrule a judicial decision. However, the new legislation can be found unconstitutional by a subsequent judicial opinion.

What documents are not included in the codified statute books?
Codified statutes may not contain all sections of the acts and private laws that deal with single individuals.

What is conventional legislation?
Conventional legislation includes both federal and state statutory law passed by the Congress or state legislatures. It may also include constitutions.

What is subordinate legislation?
Subordinate legislation refers usually to legislative powers being conferred on an executive branch department or agency to create administrative regulations. The executive's proclamations and executive orders fall under this category. In some states, municipal ordinances may be considered conventional or subordinate legislation

What types of conventional legislation have force of law?
There are five types of legislation that have the force of law:

Acts of Congress

Joint Resolutions

Treaties

Interstate Compacts

Reorganization Plans

What types of conventional legislation do not have force of law?
There are four types of legislation that do not have the force of law:
Simple Resolutions
Concurrent Resolutions
Pre-constitutional period federal legislation (Articles of Confederation period from 1784 to 1788).
Confederate States of America legislation, 1861-65.

What is a simple resolution?
Simple resolutions relate to the operations of a single chamber or express the collective opinion of that chamber on public policy issues.

What is a concurrent resolution?
Concurrent resolutions relate to the operations of Congress, including both chambers, or express the collective opinion of both chambers on public policy issues.

What is a joint resolution?
Joint resolutions are the same as legislation. They may originate in one house and go through the same legislative procedure as a regular bill. The joint resolution has to be signed by the President to become law. A constitutional amendment, however, can be passed by the two houses only and does not require the signature of the President. Instead it is sent to the Archivist of the United States to be sent to the states for their ratification.

What are the exclusive powers of the House of Representatives (Congress)?
The House has certain exclusive powers such as the power to impeach (bring up on charges) the President and other federal officers and federal judges. In addition, spending legislation must be initiated in the House. (Toni M. Fine: *American Legal System: A Resource and Reference Guide*, 2008)

What are the exclusive powers of the senate (Congress)?
Senators have certain powers that the members of the House do not have. For instance, the Senate ratifies treaties, confirms major presidential appointees, and tries impeached parties. (Toni M. Fine: *American Legal System: A Resource and Reference Guide*, 2008)

What is a rider in legislation?
Specific type of amendment: generally attached to a bill or resolution with the specific purpose of coercing opponents to favor passage of the bill or resolution. (Toni M. Fine: *American Legal System: A Resource and Reference Guide*, 2008)

How many bills are enacted into law every year in Congress?
Several thousand bills are introduced into Congress, but only less than six hundred are enacted into laws.

How many new statutes are enacted each year?
A little more than 15,000 new laws are passed together in the U.S. Congress and state legislatures each year.

How are statutes made?
Legislatures pass statutes through the legislative process. On the federal level, Congress passes laws; on the state level, state legislatures pass laws; and on the local level, county governments or municipal councils pass ordinances.

How are amendments made to statutes?
Statutes are amended by the passage of new statutes that have their own public law number. The amendment may only extend the enforcement of a statute by providing only a later date change; or, the new law may extensively revise the earlier statute in the form of additions or deletions.

What is a slip law?
This is the individual law published by the U.S. Congress or state legislatures.

What is a public law?
These are general laws passed by the Congress that affect everyone in the country. They are published in sequential order chronologically by date.

What is a private law?
A private law deals with only one person. Generally, there are fewer private laws passed today by Congress than in the past, e.g., an act providing for the immigration of a person.

What does the public law number mean?
The public law is the law passed by Congress that has the number of the Congress and the sequential number of the law passed in the legislature that year, e.g., Pub. L. 105-100 is the 105th Congress and the 100th law passed during the session of the Congress.

Who publishes the Congressional laws?
The Government Printing Office.

What is the popular name or short title of the statute?
The popular name or short title is the abbreviated title of the official name of the statute. It is usually found in section one of the statute, e.g., Muhammad Ali Boxing Reform Act.

Is there a directory of popular names?
Shepard's Acts and Cases by Popular Name include both federal and state names of the acts. The *U. S. Code*, *U.S.C.A.* and *U.S.C.S.* all provide popular names tables for federal statutes.

The last volume of the *U. S. Code* has in it the statutes; in both the current edition and supplements.

U.S.C.A. (West) publishes a separate volume for only federal statutes. *U.S.C.S.* has a separate bound volume as part of its Tables volumes.

For state statutes, popular names can be found in the general index of the annotated code.

What are session laws?
Session laws are the chronological laws passed by the legislature during a single year. These laws are published annually in bound volumes on the federal, state, and local levels. Each calendar year is considered a session whether it is on the federal or state level.

Are the slip law, public law and the session law the same?
Yes, they can be the same act depending on how they are published and cited.

What is the *United States Statutes at Large*?
The *United States Statutes at Large* (KF50 U5) is the official set of the chronological laws passed by Congress. They are in multiple volumes each year. The laws are first published in slip law format and then rebound into bound volumes.

How is the *United States Statutes at Large* cited in legal literature?
Citation is generally to the Public Law, .e.g, Pub. L. 106-210, 114 Stat. 321.

What is the *United States Statutes at Large* citation that has a year and chapter number (c.) rather than a Public Law Number?

- From 1789 to 1901 (Volume 1 to 31), public laws were assigned chapter numbers,
- From 1901 to 1956 (Volume 32 to 70), public laws were assigned chapter numbers and public resolution numbers, e.g., e.g., August 25, 1949, c. 512, 63 Stat. 665.
- From 1957 to present (Volume 71 to present), public laws are assigned public law numbers.

Is the volume number on the spine of the *United States Statutes at Large* the same as the Congressional session found in the public law number of the acts found inside the book?
No, the volume number of the book has no relationship to the Congressional session number found in the Public Law number.

How are laws arranged in the volumes of the *United States Statutes at Large*?
The laws are divided into public and private laws. The laws are then arranged chronologically.

Can I find federal statutory information by topic in *United States Statutes at Large*?
There is a cumulative index at the end of each session's volumes.

What are the unofficial sources for the federal chronological laws?
West publishes the *United States Code Congressional and Administrative News* (U.S.C.C.A.N.) (KF48 U55) for each Congress since 1941. This is a monthly paperback publication that is cumulated into bound volumes at the end of each Congressional session. This is a separate subscription from the *U.S.C.A.* Lexis publishes monthly advance sheets of the chronological laws as part of a subscription to the *U.S.C.S.*

What is contained in the *United States Code Congressional and Administrative News* (U.S.C.C.A.N.)?
U.S.C.C.A.N. contains the annual chronological laws of the Congress in the first volumes followed by the full text/abridged versions of House and Senate Reports (separately paginated). The last volume of each year contains Presidential proclamations and executive orders arranged chronologically in order. There are multiple tables dealing with the statutes, and a cumulative index.

How can one find where the *United States Statutes at Large* appear in the *United States Code*?
Tables in the back of the *U. S. Statutes at Large*, *Unites States Code Congressional and Administrative News* (Table 2), and *U. S. Code* provide a cross reference between the *Statutes at Large* and the *U.S. Code*.

How can one find whether the recent statute is affected by amendments?
Table 3 (*U. S. Code* and *U. S. Code Annotated* Sections Amended, Repealed, News, etc.) of *U.S.C.C.A.N.* contains cross references from *U. S. Code* citations to page numbers in the *Statutes at Large*.

What other tables can be found in *United States Code Congressional & Administrative News* (U.S.C.CA.N.)?
Table 4 deals with the legislative history of each law as reported in *U.S.C.C.A.N.* Table 4A lists Signing Statements of the President. Table 5 lists Bills and Joint Resolutions Enacted; Table 7 lists Proclamations chronologically. Table 8 lists Executive Orders chronologically. Table 9 lists Major Bills Pending During the Session. Table 10 lists Popular Names Acts.

What are compiled statutes?
Compiled statutes take the chronological laws and bring them together into an organized subject arrangement without revision or any re-enactment of the laws by the legislature.

What are revised statutes?
Revised statutes are the product of a revision, collection, and arrangement of the statutory law, and a reenactment of the whole by act of the legislature. (*Legal Research Primer*, Lawyers Co-op).

What does the term consolidation mean?
Consolidation is the process of revising and restating the general and permanent public statutes into a concise code of laws that is clear, consistent and organized. The law on related subjects is placed together and the language is simplified and put into a more understandable and consistent format. (Lawrence G. Feinberg, Consolidation and the Consolidation Counsel, *Legislative Process, Statutory Drafting, Regulatory Process & Update*, PBI, 2008).

What does the term codification mean?
Codification is the process by which the legislature (federal, state, or local) organizes the chronological laws for the jurisdiction into a subject approach. The

legislature repeals older laws no longer in force and brings all similar laws together under a single topic, e.g., adoption, children, divorce, husband and wife, marriage under a new topic called domestic relations.

What is the official federal statutory code?
Congress has designated by statute the *United States Code* (U.S.C.) as the primary source of the codification of the chronological statutes.

What is the *United States Code* (U.S.C.)?
The *United States Code* is the official, unannotated edition of the codified statutes of the United States arranged under 50 different topics/subjects.

When did the *United States Code* begin?
The *United States Code* began in 1926.

Before the publication of *United States Code* was there any attempt to codify the federal laws?
In the 1860s Congress ordered the revision of all federal statutes. All statutes were divided into 74 classifications called 'titles.' The *Revised Statutes of 1873* was the official publication. The Statutes were revised in 1878, but did not pass Congress.

Who is the publisher for *United States Code*?
The Government Printing Office (GPO) is the official printer for the *United States Code*.

How many topics / titles are in *United States Code*?
There are fifty titles in the *United States Code* with the addition of a new 51st title now being introduced into Congress.

Title 1 General Provisions
Title 2 The Congress
Title 3 The President
Title 4 Flag and Seal, Seat Of Government, and the States
Title 5 Government Organization and Employees
Appendix to Title 5
Title 6 Domestic Security
Title 7 Agriculture
Title 8 Aliens and Nationality
Title 9 Arbitration
Title 10 Armed Forces
Appendix to Title 10 (Rules of Court of Appeals for the Armed Forces)

Appendix to Title 46
Title 47 Telegraphs, Telephones, and Radiotelegraphs
Title 48 Territories and Insular Possessions
Title 49 Transportation
Title 50 War and National Defense
Appendix to Title 50
Title 51: National and Commercial Space Programs

What are the contents of the *United States Code*?

The *U. S. Code* provides 50 titles broken down into sections that contain the text of the current law along with the citations to the *Statutes At Large* for where the statutory law derives from. There is a Historical and Statutory Notes section added at the end of each section.

What does it mean when there are multiple listings of Public Laws under each section?

The original act is listed first followed by all amendments to the act.

Where do I get information concerning how a specific amendment affects the text of the code section?

Following the references to the Public Laws, there is usually a Historical and Statutory Notes Section that provides a listing of each amendment and how it affected the code section.

How is the *United States Code* updated?

The *United States Code* is published in a new edition every six years. The last complete edition was in 2000. There is an annual cumulative supplement for each of the years from 2001 to 2005. The 2006 edition of the *United States Code* will cumulate the 2000 edition and the five-year supplement. The new edition will be published over a period of a year and a half.

What is positive law?

Positive law is the adoption of a title into law by the Congress. Once the Congress has approved the title, it is no longer necessary to refer back to the *U.S. Statutes at Large* for the text of the Code.
The Code Titles are listed in 1 U.S.C. §204:
Title 1 General Provisions
Title 3 The President
Title 4 Flag and Seal, Seat Of Government, and the States
Title 5 Government Organization and Employees

Appendix to Title 5
Title 6 Domestic Security
Title 9 Arbitration
Title 10 Armed Forces
Appendix to Title 10 (Rules of Court of Appeals for the Armed Forces)
Title 11 Bankruptcy
Appendix to Title 11
Title 13 Census
Title 14 Coast Guard
Title 17 Copyrights
Title 18 Crimes and Criminal Procedure
Title 23 Highways
Title 26 Internal Revenue Code
Title 28 Judiciary and Judicial Procedure
Title 31 Money and Finance
Title 32 National Guard
Title 34 Navy (repealed)
Title 35 Patents
Title 36 Patriotic Societies and Observances
Title 37 Pay and Allowances Of the Uniformed Services
Title 38 Veterans' Benefits
Appendix to Title 38 (Rules of Court of Appeals for Veterans Claims()
Title 39 Postal Service
Title 44 Public Printing and Documents
Title 49 Transportation

What is the *"prima facie* evidence of law"?
Laws not part of the positive law are *prima facie* evidence of law. Proof that something is true unless shown to be false by further evidence.

Does it make any difference if the researcher finds a discrepancy in the text of the non-positive law and the statutory law?
Sometimes a word may be changed between the text of the code title (*U. S. Code*) and the statutory law (*United States Statutes at Large*). If it is one of the titles that have not been adopted as positive law, then the text of the *Statutes at Large* is the correct text to use.

Where can I find cases pertaining to the federal statutes?
The annotated codes provide case digests under each title and section of the code.

What are annotated codes?
Annotated codes are published by commercial vendors to provide more up-to-date information than what the official code offers by using pocket parts and advance sheets to update the codes on an annual basis. The vendors annotate the codes by adding references to court cases, West and/or LexisNexis digest system headnotes and key numbers, encyclopedias, form books, periodical articles, and treatises. This is done both on the federal and state levels.

What are the names of the annotated codes?
The two annotated codes are *United States Code Annotated* (West) and the *United States Code Service* (Lexis). On the state level, there are various names, e.g., *McKinney's New York* (West), *Consolidated Statutes of New York* (Lexis), *Purdon's Pennsylvania Statutes Annotated*, *West's California Codes*, etc.

When did the annotated codes begin?
United States Code Annotated began in 1927; *Federal Code Annotated*, the predecessor to *United States Code Service* began in 1936 and became the *U.S.C.S.* in 1972.

Who publishes these annotated codes?
West Group publishes the *United States Code Annotated* (*U.S.C.A.*) and Lexis publishes the *United States Code Service* (*U.S.C.S.*).

Are there any differences between *United States Code Annotated* and *United States Code Service*?
There used to be differences in coverage between the two sets. West cited to more caselaw, while Lawyers Co-op (the original publisher of *U.S.C.S.*), cited to limited cases but provided more references to the primary and secondary sources of the Total-Client Library. Currently, West still provides more caselaw citations, but both companies provide references to their own publications. West now includes A.L.R. annotations and other former Lawyers Co-op publications that it did not cite to before the mid-1990s.

Are private laws codified?
Private laws deal with an individual or a group but not the public at large. Only laws which are permanent in nature and effect the general public are codified, not the private laws.

Are appropriation acts codified?
Appropriation laws are temporary in nature and consequently are not codified.

What other information can be found in addition to statutory law in *United States Code Annotated* and *United States Code Service* books?
Both sets of books contain annotated editions of the U. S. Constitution, Federal Rules of Procedure (Appellate, Bankruptcy, Civil, Criminal, and Evidence) and the rules for specific courts: United States Supreme Court, the thirteen United States Courts of Appeal, and the Court of International Trade. There are tables volumes providing cross-references from the *Statutes at Large* to the *United States Code* and a Popular Names Table for statutory law. There are multivolume, paper bound, annual indexes to each set.

Since *U.S.C.A.* and *U.S.C.S.* are published by commercial publishers, is the information found in those books reliable?
The text of the annotated codes should match the official code. Once in awhile a word may be changed and there may be a need to check the original Statutes at Large. Generally, the books are reliable for text. At the beginning of the codification process, West Publishing Company assisted in compiling the official code.

When I am looking only for the text of a particular statutory section what books can I use?
One can use *U.S.C.*, *U.S.C.A.*, or *U.S.C.S.* for the text of the section. It is the annotations that will differ only between the latter two sets.

How do I research *U.S.C.*, *U.S.C.A.*, and *U.S.C.S.*?
All three sets have multivolume general indexes at the end of each set to locate information in each set. In *U.S.C.A.* and *U.S.C.S.* each title has its own subject index as well, as do the Constitution volumes and Rules volumes.

What are the other research methods to conduct federal statutory research?
One can use the Popular Name Table. In addition, one can use the topic outline at the front of each title.

What are Popular Name Tables?
Popular name tables provides the popular name or short title to a statute that is usually found in section one of the act. *U.S.C.*, *U.S.C.A.* and *U.S.C.S.*, as well as state codes, provide an index to all acts that have popular names/ short titles.

What is the most comprehensive source for popular names?
Shepard's Acts and Cases by Popular Name, (KF90.S52) published by Lexis, is a three-volume work covering both Federal and State popular names

What are uniform laws?

The National Conference of Commissioners on Uniform State Laws (NCCUSL) is a non-profit organization created to draw up well-written, clarified laws. It is up to each state to adopt the law, e.g., Uniform Commercial Code adopted by all 50 states; other acts may have just one.

The list of uniform laws includes:

Adoption Act
Anatomical Gift Act
Apportionment of Tort Responsibility Act
Arbitration Act
Assignment of Rents Act
Athlete Agents Act
Cert. Of Questions of Law
Certificate of Title Act
Child Custody Jurisdiction and Enforcement Act
Child Witness Testimony by Alternative Methods Act
Common Interest Ownership Act
Comparative Fault Act
Computer Information Transactions Act
Condominium Act
Conflicts of Laws - Limitations Act
Conservation Easement Act
Consumer Leases Act
Controlled Substances Act
Correction or Clarification of Defamation Act
Custodial Trust Act
Debt-Management Services Act
Declaratory Judgments Act
Determination of Death Act
Disclaimer of Property Interests Act
Disposition of Community Property Rights at Death
Division of Income for Tax Purposes
Durable Power of Attorney
Electronic Transactions Act
Enf. of Foreign Judgments Act
Entity Transactions Act
Environmental Covenants Act
Estate Tax Apportionment & Probate Code 3-916
Federal Lien Registration Act
Foreign Money Claims Act

Foreign Money Judgments Recognition Act
Foreign-Country Money Judgments Recognition Act
Fraudulent Transfer Act
Guardianship & Protective Proceedings Act
Health-Care Decisions Act
Health-Care Information Act
International Wills Act
Interstate Arbitration of Death Taxes Act
Interstate Compromise of Death Taxes Act
Interstate Enforcement of Domestic Violence Protection Orders Act
Interstate Family Support Act
Intestacy, Wills, and Donative Transfers Act
Limited Liability Company Act
Limited Partnership Act
Management of Institutional Funds Act
Management of Public Employee Retirement Systems Act
Mediation Act
Money Services Act
Multiple-Person Accounts
Nonjudicial Foreclosure Act
Nonprobate Transfers on Death Act
Notarial Acts
Parentage Act
Partnership Act
Periodic Payment of Judgments Act
Photographic Copies as Evidence Act
Planned Community Act
Premarital Agreement Act
Principal and Income Act
Probate Code
Prudent Investor Act
Real Property Electronic Recording Act
Residential Landlord and Tenant Act
Residential Mortgage Satisfaction Act
Rules of Evidence
Securities Act
Simultaneous Death Act
Status of Children of Assisted Conception Act
Statute and Rule Construction Act
Statutory Form Power of Attorney Act
Statutory Rule Against Perpetuities

Supervision of Trustees for Charitable Purposes Act
Testamentary Add. to Trusts Act
TOD Security Registration Act
Trade Secrets Act
Transfer of Litigation Act
Transfers to Minors Act
Trust Code
UCC Article 1, General Provisions
UCC Article 2A (1987) (1990)
UCC Article 5, Letters of Credit
UCC Article 6 (Repeal)
UCC Article 6 (Revise)
UCC Article 7 (2003)
UCC Article 8, Investment Securities
UCC Article 9 Amendments
UCC Article 9, Secured Transactions
UCC Articles 2 and 2A (2003)
UCC Articles 3 and 4
Unclaimed Property Act
Unincorporated Nonprofit Association Act
UPC Amendments
Wage Withholding and Unemployment Insurance Procedure Act

Where can one find the uniform laws?
West Group publishes *Uniform Laws Annotated* (KF165 A5). This is a multivolume annotated set containing annotations to court cases under each law.

For most laws, the following elements are provided:

Table of Jurisdictions Wherein the Act Has Been Adopted
Historical Notes
Commissioner's Prefatory Notes
General Statutory Notes
Jurisdictions Adopting Uniform Act in Manner Precluding Comparative Notes
Outline of Act

For each section of a uniform law, these elements are usually provided:
Text
Official Comment
Action in Adopting Jurisdictions
Law Review Commentaries

Library References
Annotations or Notes of Decisions

Is there a directory or index to the *Uniform Laws Annotated*?
There is a *Directory of Uniform Acts and Codes Tables—Index* that is published annually with the pocket parts. It contains the list of uniform laws adopted by the states followed by a subject index.

What are model laws?
The NCCUSL also composes model laws that are not expected to be passed by most of the states but may be partially adopted. The two main examples are the Model Penal Code and the Model Business Corporation Act.

The list of model laws:

Model Business Corporation Act
Model Construction Lien Act
Model Consumer Credit Code
Model Dormant Mineral Interests Act
Model Employment Termination Act
Model Exemptions Act
Model Extradition and Rendition Act
Model Mandatory Disposition of Detainers Act
Model Marital Property Act
Model Marketable Title Act
Model Marriage and Divorce Act
Model Penal Code
Model Post-Conviction Procedure Act
Model Punitive Damages Act
Model Real Estate Time-Share Act
Model Rules of Criminal Procedure
Model State Administrative Procedure Act
Model Surface Use and Mineral Development Accommodation Act
Model Transboundary Pollution Reciprocal Access Act
Model Tribal Secured Transactions Act
Model Victims of Crime Act

II. INTERNET

Where can one find biographical information on the members of Congress?
The *Biographical Directory of the United States Congress*,

http://bioguide.congress.gov/biosearch/biosearch.asp, contains biographical information on all members of Congress through the current Congress. One can search by individual's name, Congress, or by state.

Are federal and state statutes available on the Internet?

Federal statutes and congressional information are available from the Thomas site (thomas.loc.gov) and state statutes are available from official state government web sites. Another good site is StateNet (www.statenet.com).

Do comprehensive sites provide statutory information?

Comprehensive sites such as Findlaw, Legal Information Institute (Cornell), HeirosGamos, MegaLaw, LawGuru, Virtual Chase provide links to official and private sites.

Where can one find federal historical legislation?

The Century of Lawmaking (1774-1873) at the Library of Congress, http://memory.loc.gov/ammem/amlaw/lawhome.html, provides full text of the federal statutes from 1789 to 1873, House and Senate Journals, congressional debates, and other documents dealing with this time period. It also includes *Farrand's Records of the Constitutional Convention* and *Elliott's Debates* on the ratification by the states.

There are additional files available on the web site as well:

Journal of William Maclay United States Senator from Pennsylvania, 1789 to 1791

This journal gives a graphic description of the debates, ceremonies, and social life of that important period of our national history.

Diplomatic Correspondence of the American Revolution; Being the Letters of Benjamin Franklin, Silas Deane, John Adams ... Concerning the Foreign Relations of the United States During the Whole Revolution; Together with the Letters in Reply....

Both the first edition, a 12-volume set published in 1818, and the second edition, a 6-volume set published in 1857, were added to the U.S. Congressional Documents Collection. These sets contain the correspondence between the old Congress and the American agents, commissioners, and ministers in foreign countries during the American Revolution.

Bills

Are Senate and House bills available in full text format?

The full text of Senate and House bills are available from the Thomas web site.

How far back are the bills available?
The bills from the 101st Congress (1989) are available from the Thomas site. All published versions of bills from the 103rd (1993-1994) Congress onward are available from the Government Printing Office's site (www.gpoaccess.gov)

Committee Reports

If I am doing legislative history research, where can I find House and Senate Committee Reports?
House and Senate committee reports, joint reports, and conference reports are available in full text from the Thomas site.

How far back are the House and Senate committee reports available?
Both the House and Senate committee reports are available from the 104th congress (1995 to the present) on the Thomas site.

What is Congressional Universe?
Congressional Universe is a product of LexisNexis that provides a complete listing of all documents that comprise a legislative history. It provides access to the CIS (Congressional Information Service) Index which indexes and abstracts congressional publications and CIS legislative histories as well as provides access to the full text of congressional reports, documents, prints, bills and *Congressional Record*, public laws, and the *United States Code Service*.

United States Code **(U.S.C.)**

Where can I get information regarding all 50 titles of the *United States Code***?**
The *United States Code* is available in an official version from the House of Representatives web site (www.house.gov) with a link from the Thomas web site, GPO Access, and also from comprehensive legal sites such as Findlaw and Cornell.

Are there any differences in regard to access to the *United States Code* **from different sites?**
The House of Representatives web site provides both browsing and searching capability. Searching can retrieve information by key word using Boolean and proximity connectors. You also can retrieve a document by using the proper citation to the code. One can search all fifty titles or a single title.
 The Cornell web site provides both browsing and searching capability. Searching can retrieve information by key word using Boolean connectors. Each title has an update feature called "How Current is this?" that provides how the statute has

been amended with cross references from the Code to the session year, public law number and Statute-at-Large citations.

In addition, there is a RSS feed available for every title if anyone is interested to subscribe.

When searching the *United States Code* from the 1994 edition to the current 2006 edition, including all supplements available from Government Printing Office site, you may retrieve information by citation e.g. 7 USC 511, by Popular Name, e.g. "popular name" AND bonds, by public law number, e.g. "pub.l. 103-40", and by Statutes At Large citation, e.g. "107 stat 112".

Public Laws

Are public and private laws available?

Public and private laws, including amendments, are available from the 101st Congress (1989) from Thomas site and from the 104th Congress (1995) from the Government Printing Office site.

What are the research methods (access points) available to retrieve public and private laws?

You may retrieve the full text of laws by a key word, by the name of a senator or representative, and also by the name of the committee. You also can retrieve laws by the House or Senate bill and joint resolution numbers from the Thomas site.

Public and private laws are available from the 104th Congress (1995) forward from the Government Printing Office web site. You may retrieve laws by key word, by Public Law number, e.g. "public law 105-198", by Statutes At Large citation, e.g. "112 stat 3280", by United State Code citation, e.g. "31 USC 5112", and by bill number, e.g. "h.r. 765".

United States Statutes at Large

What are the sources for the *United States Statutes at Large* research?

Volumes 117 onwards is available from the Government Printing Office web site.

What are the research methods (access points) to retrieve information from the *United States Statutes at Large*?

You may retrieve information by key word, by citation, e.g. "117 stat. 1209", by Public Law Number, e.g. "public law 108-11", by USC citation, e.g. "22 USC 2151",

By Proclamation Number, e.g. "Proclamation 7661", by Concurrent Resolution cite, e.g. "H.Com.Res. 8", by Popular Name, e.g. "Museum and Library Services Act of 2003", and by Bill Number, e.g. "H.R. 11".

What other sources are available which contain information published in the *United States Statutes at Large*?

The Library of Congress web site (http://memory.loc.gov/ammem/amlaw/ lwsl. html) contains information related to the *Statutes At Large*. Information from the first through the Forty-Third Congress dating from 1789-1875 (volumes 1 to 18) is available from this site. You will also find a general index to volumes 1 to 18 and an alphabetical list of page headlines.

Are there any web sites where the information published in all the volumes of the *United States Statutes at Large* can be found?

At present, only HeinOnline (www.heinonline.org) provides volume 1 (1789-1789) to volume 120 (2006) of the *United States Statutes At Large*. You may retrieve information by key word, by Public Law Number, e.g. public_law_number: "64-100", by title of the public law, by date, e.g. date: "Sep. 2, 1945", by tribe name, by resolution number, by congress, e.g. congress: 16.

On the main page it also has tabs for Public Law Popular Name, Indian Treatises, and Other Treatises in addition to search.

Congressional Record

Is the *Congressional Record* available on the web?

The *Congressional Record* is available from the 101st Congress through the current congress from the Thomas site. Once you select a congress, you will have three options of searching: "Latest Daily Digest," "Browse Daily Issues," and "Browse the Key Word Index."

Once you enter a key word or phrase, you are also provided with other selections such as Session (first/second), Section of the *Congressional Record* (Senate/House), and Member of the Congress.

The *Congressional Record* from volume 140 (1994) through the current volume is available from the Government Printing Office site. You may retrieve information by keyword, by the names of the members of congress, e.g. Chenoweth AND ("national parks" OR "public lands"), by Bill Number, e.g. "h.r. 856", by Roll-Call Vote, e.g. "roll call vote no "AND defense, by page number, e.g. "page S821". The page number search method is available from 1995 forward.

Are there any other sources available for congressional information?
Use official sites for White House (www.whitehouse.gov), Senate (www.senate.gov), and House of Representatives (www.house.gov) for more congressional information.

Are there any commercial sites providing congressional information?
GalleryWatch (www.gallerywatch.com) provides current information about congress. It also sends email regarding the status of bills and other time-sensitive information to the subscribers on a daily basis.

Model Acts and Uniform Acts

Where do I get the full text of the model and uniform acts?
The full text of the model and uniform acts are available from the National Conference of Commissioners on Uniform State Laws Web site (www.nccusl.org/update) You can retrieve the full text of the act by first selecting the act by title and then the desired state. You also can obtain current state legislative information related to a particular act by selecting "Legislation report by Act 2006" and/or "Legislation report by state 2006."

How do I know if a particular state adopted a uniform act?
From the home page of the National Conference of Commissioners on Uniform State Laws Web site (www.nccusl.org/update) select "NCCUSL Acts-List" button from the menu bar, select the act and then click on Legislative fact sheet to obtain a list of the states adopted.

Where do I get the copies of the reports produced by the Congressional Reference Service (CRS)?
Some of the reports obtained from the members of the congress are available through Open CRS (www.opencrs.com): Congressional Research Reports for the People's Project.

Where do I get county, township and borough codes?
If the codes are available online by respective counties and boroughs, they are available from General Code web site (www.generalcode.com). Click on 'e-code online library' link to select a state and counties, boroughs, and townships in the state.

III. LEXISNEXIS

Can I retrieve statutes by citation?

Under the Get a Document tab, use Get by Citation a *United States Code* citation, e.g., 42 U.S.C.S.. @ 2000e. (Spaces are important to retrieve the document.)

Can I retrieve a public law or session law?

Click on a 'Get a Document' and select by citation function and enter the *Statutes at Large* citation, e.g. 104 stat 327 to retrieve Americans with Disabilities Act.

Are there other methods of retrieving documents from *United States Code Service*?

Under Federal Legal-U.S., there is the *United States Code Service* (*U.S.C.S.*) Titles 1 through 50 file. The *U. S. Code* can be either searched in full text of all 50 titles at one time or just the table of contents only. Or one can select an individual title and search the whole title or select individual sections within the title to search.

In addition, each title can be broken down into its individual sections for retrieval.

What is the *U.S.C.S.* Revised Title Table?

When you click on this table it lists Go to Table of Contents and Continue with Your Search. Under Table of Contents, the revised tables provide a cross reference from titles and sections that have been revised, renumbered and enacted into positive law.

Continue with Your Search will provide a query box to search the title table. One can search by citation or by word(s) or phrase(s).

Can I retrieve a table of the *United States Statutes at Large*?

Lexis provides a link to the Statutes at Large Table under *U.S.C.S.* Materials. There are three methods of searching: full text, Table of Contents only, and chronologically from the 1st Congress to the current Congress (110th).

Full text searching will give you the citation and link to the full text in pdf. format.

The Table of Contents

Chronological listing takes one to the individual chapter numbers (before the 57th Congress public laws were cited by year and chapter number) or public law numbers (congress and sequential number of act).

Can I retrieve an act by public law number?
Enter 101 pl 336 to retrieve the public law number 101-336.

Can I retrieve a session law by the name of the act?
Select the Find a Source tab and type 'popular name table' (make sure the radio button is selected for Match Terms in long names) and then click on *U.S.C.S.* – Popular Names Table. Click on New Search and enter American /2 disabilities to retrieve the text of the act.

Can I retrieve an act by name?
An act can be retrieved under the Table of Acts by Popular Name. The short title name or popular name can usually be found in section one of the act.

One can search for popular name using the query box or alphabetically under the Table of Acts by Popular Names.

Is Table of Contents available for all 50 titles of *United States Code Service*?
Select *United States Code Service* (*U.S.C.S.*) Materials from the directory and click on U.S.C.S. – Table of Contents.

Can I use 'Search Advisor' to retrieve relevant statutes?
Yes.

When I retrieve a statute what other types of materials do I get?
In addition to the full text of the statute, you will also obtain historical notes, research guide (legal encyclopedia, practitioner aides, *A.L.R.* annotations and law review articles), references to *C.F.R.* and Interpretive Notes and Decisions (cases).

Is 'More Like Selected Text' feature available for statutes?
From the full text of the statute highlight the text and click on More Like Selected Text.

Is there a General Index for all 50 titles?
There is a cumulative index.

How far back is the *United States Code Service* available?
The *U.S.C.S.* is available starting from 1992.

How do I move onto the next section from the retrieved document?
Select 'Book Browser' function from the menu bar and then select 'next section' button next to the citation.

Does Lexis provide additional commentary to its statutory law?

The National Institute for Trial Advocacy provides commentaries upon individual statutes within *U.S.C.S.* The materials are available in the USNITA file or individually preceding a specific statute.

STATE STATUTORY LAW

Can I obtain a single state statute by citation?

One can use LEXSEE to retrieve individual state statutes, e.g., 2005 ca ch 100, 2005 pa act 3.

Are state un-annotated and annotated statutes available?

The database for all fifty states is STCODE which covers mostly annotated state codes, but there are some unannotated state codes in this database. The database can be found under State Codes, Constitutions, Courts Rules, ALS, Combined under Legislation & Politics —U.S. & U.K.

The larger database ALLCODES contains annotated constitutions, state codes, and court rules of fifty states.

How do I search individual state statutes?

The database for individual state statutes can be found in each state's annotated set of constitutions, code, rules, and advance legislative codes that can be retrieved by each state's postal abbreviation along with CODE, e.g. CACODE, NJCODE, etc.

Can I retrieve State Session laws?

Session laws passed by the legislative bodies of the states and laws proposed by initiation or proposition can be found in the multi-state Advance Legislative Service database (ALLALS) or the individual state legislative service database using the state's two-letter postal abbreviation followed by ALS, e.g., ALALS, CAALS, etc.

Each state also has a full-text of state legislative bills for the current session, e.g., CATEXT.

It can also be accessible along with Bill Tracking files combined, e.g., CABILL.

Can I retrieve historical state laws?

The historical laws can be searched in a combined fifty-state database (TXTARCH) or by individual years back to 1991, e.g., TXT91, TXT92, etc.

The historical laws for each state back to 2002 can be found in the State Next Full Text of Bills —Current Term (STTEXT).

Is archival / historical legislative information available?
Historical legislative information is available regarding bills that were never enacted and laws that have been repealed. Use database BILLTRK-OLD and US-PL-OLD.

Can I retrieve the full text of the state bills?
The State Net Bill Tracking file provides access to all state bills from 2002 to present. Use the database STTRK for current legislation.

Use two-letter postal abbreviation along with TEXT, e.g., PATEXT, includes full text of the bills along with summaries and status of the current legislative bills.

How do I know the status of pending Senate and House bills?
Legislative tracking database provides status information regarding currently pending or bills from recent sessions. Current legislation from all fifty states is available (STTRCK). Use two-letter postal abbreviation for individual state's status information on current legislature, e.g. NYTRCK, PATRCK, etc.

IV. WESTLAW

Can I use the Find command to locate statutes?
One can use the Find command to locate a statute.

Do I have access to both unannotated code *U.S.C.* and annotated code *U.S.C.A.*?
The database for un-annotated code is USC. The annotated database U.S.C.A. provides references to cases, regulations and secondary materials pertaining to the statutes.

How does the official print version vary from the online Westlaw version?
The official version currently is the 2006 edition with one supplement. The Westlaw version incorporates all new laws from 2006 to present.

What documents can one find in *United States Code Annotated*?
U.S.C.A. database contains annotated editions of the Constitution of the United States, 50 titles of the *United States Code*, Federal court rules (both individual courts and procedural rules), Federal Sentencing Guidelines, and appendices.

To find more information concerning the database, click on the I button next to *United States Code Annotated* above the query box.

What do you find in an annotated edition of the *United States Code Annotated*?

The annotated edition contains case summaries, cross references to the *Code of Federal Regulations*, and references to secondary materials (encyclopedias, periodicals, ALR annotations, form books, treatises, etc.),

Can I use certain fields to retrieve statutory information?

Select fields from the query box. Useful fields for statutory information are: prelim (contains title, sub-title, chapter, and sub-chapter headings); caption (contains the section number followed by a few terms that describe the contents of the section), citation (ci), prelim (pr), caption (ca), text (te), statutory credits (cr), words and phrases (wp), historical notes (hn), and annotations (an).

Can I retrieve historical federal statutes?

Annotated federal statutes are available starting with 1990. The database is U.S.C.A.90, U.S.C.A.91, U.S.C.A.92, etc.

If you know the year and have the citation to a statute, for example, select appropriate database (U.S.C.A.90) and enter the citation (e.g. 42 +5 2000e).

Are there any exclusive databases within *United States Code Annotated* for subject research?

On the menu under Federal Statutes, there is a link for *U.S.C.A.* Organized by Area of Practice that lists more than twenty individual areas, such as bankruptcy (FBKR-U.S.C.A.), Environmental Law (FENV-U.S.C.A.), Family Law (FFL-U.S.C.A.).

Are the Tables and Index volumes of *United States Code* available in Westlaw?

The Tables and Index volumes are available as part of the *U.S.C.A.* database and can be used to conduct research in U.S.C. also.

Can you use a template to use the Tables?

U.S.C.A.-Tables database provides a template for the Statutes at Large to be able to cite by Public Law, Statute at Large, and Acts prior to 1957. In addition, there are four additional tables at the bottom of the template that can be accessed as well: Revised Statutes of 1878, Executive Orders, Proclamations, and Reorganization Plans.

Once you type a citation into the template, it will take you to the table where the link can be found to take you to the document. For example, typing in Pub. L.

89-185 into the template takes you to P.L.89-185 in a table that provides for each section of the law, the *Statutes-at-Large* cite, a *U.S.C.A.* cite, and current status. The *U.S.C.A.* cite and status cite provides links to the full text in *U.S.C.A.*

Are the Popular Name Tables available?

The Popular Name Table (U.S.C.A.-POP) database provides the list of the acts alphabetically by popular name.

Is there a general index available to *United States Code Annotated*?

There is a separate database (U.S.C.A.-IDX) that can be used to retrieve documents by citation, prelim, title, or index.

If you type in a search word or phrase, the database will retrieve all categories which contain the word or phrase being entered. One has to then click on the selected topic to find the detailed list of subtopics along with a link to the *U.S.C.A.* citation(s).

While reviewing a document is there any way that I can move into the next section of the retrieved document?

Click on the next section button (arrow), appears to the right side of the citation of the retrieved document, to move to the next section. For example, when you are viewing 42 U.S.C.A. 12201 click on next section to move to section 12202. Similarly you may select previous section button (arrow) to move to previous sections.

Are Federal Public Laws available?

Public laws passed by the U.S. Congress during the current term are available in US-PL database. Public Laws are also available in the U. S. Public Laws database (USCCAN-PL) that is under the *United States Code Congressional & Administrative News* database (link under Federal Statutes). The coverage begins with 1973 to present.

Are older Federal Public Laws available?

Public laws from 1973 to 2006 are available in US-PL-OLD.

Can I retrieve a particular year from the US-PL-OLD database?

As a combined database, one can run a query to find the public law which will retrieve the documents between 1973 and 2006.

However, a public law can be retrieved using the Find command by the congressional session and public law, e.g., us pl 106-210; or by citation, e.g., ci(106-210).

Are the *United States Statutes at Large* available in *United States Code Annotated*?

The *United States Statutes at Large* database (US-STATLRG) contains the statutes from 1789 to 1972 (92nd Congress). Only public laws are available in the database; private laws, treaties, and resolutions are not included.

    After completing your search in the query box, the documents will be available in pdf format.

Can one use the statutory citation as a query to find court cases?

If you perform a citation search, e.g., "42 U.S.C.A. 2000" you will retrieve cases on the topic.

STATE STATUTORY LAW

Are state un-annotated and annotated statutes available?

The database for all fifty states' un-annotated statutes is STAT-ALL and for annotated statutes is ST-ANN-ALL

How do I search individual state statutes?

The database for individual state statutes uses the two-letter postal abbreviation, e.g., CA-ST.

Can I retrieve State Session laws?

Session laws passed by the legislative bodies of the states and laws proposed by initiation or proposition can be found in the multi-state legislative service database (LEGIS-ALL) or the individual state legislative service database using state's two-letter postal abbreviation. E.g. PA-LEGIS.

Can I retrieve historical state laws?

The Multistate Legislative Service —Historical (LEGIS-OLD) provides access to a query box for searching. If you click on the I for database information, a listing of each state's database is then available, e.g., AL-LEGIS-OLD, CA-LEGIS-OLD, NY-LEGIS-OLD.

Can I retrieve archival / historical legislative information?

Historical legislative information is available regarding bills that were never enacted and laws that have been repealed. Use database BILLTRK-OLD and US-PL-OLD

Can I retrieve the full text of the state bills?

Databases that use two-letter postal abbreviation, such as PA-Bills includes full text of the bills along with summaries and status of the bills.

How do I know the status of pending Senate and House bills?

Legislative tracking database provides status information regarding currently pending or bills from recent sessions. Database ST-BILLTRK provides status information on current legislation from all 50 states. Use two-letter postal abbreviation for individual state's status information on current legislature. e.g., PA_BILLTRK.

How can one find statutory law on a specific topic for all fifty states?

Westlaw has a 50 State Surveys database (SURVEYS) which can be searched by topic and provides the links to all state legislation.

Are city administrative codes available on the web?

Many cities post their administrative code on their official web sites. Muni Code (www.municode.com) provides city codes for many cities. Once you are on the cite click on 'ONLINE LIBRARY' and select a particular state (click on map) and find what city codes are available.

CHAPTER 8

LEGISLATIVE HISTORY

Introduction: Legislative history provides the detailed information concerning how the bill goes through the legislative process on federal, state, or local levels. On the federal level, the government publishes an extensive amount of information on the passage of each bill that helps the researcher better understand why a bill has been enacted into law. At each step of the procedure there is a corresponding published document(s). The availability of documents for state legislative history varies from state to state, but will include at least the different versions of the bill and debates. The availability of legislative materials on the Internet differs from jurisdiction to jurisdiction. In general, both LexisNexis and Westlaw have been increasing the amount of state legislative history documents.

I. MANUAL

What is a legislative history?

A legislative history provides the documents produced as a bill goes through the procedure to become a law.

Is legislative history considered primary authority?

The materials located in a legislative history are not considered primary authority, though they are documents produced by the Congress and President. They are useful to help find the meaning of difficult or ambiguous terms found in the statutory law. It is not a secondary source either, since it has more persuasive weight than a commentary by a secondary treatise author.

Do the courts use legislative history in deciding their cases?

Courts will on occasion use legislative history to provide greater understanding of the legislative intent of the Congress and/or state legislatures in deciding their cases.

What is bill tracking?
Bill tracking follows the bill through all of the steps from its introduction to passage into law.

How often does Congress meet?
Congress meets for a two-year period beginning in January of the odd year and ending in December of the even year.

What are sessions of Congress?
A session of Congress is for one year.

What is the process for a bill to become law?
A legislator gives a first reading that introduces the bill.
The bill is assigned to a committee.
The subcommittee creates prints and documents.
The subcommittee holds hearings on the bill.
The full committee writes a report in support of the bill.
The second reading of the bill provides for debates and amendments to the bill.
The third reading of the bill provides for debates and a vote upon the bill. If the bill passes, it is then sent to the other Congressional chamber.
In the second house, the same steps are taken as in the previous house.
If the bill is approved by both houses, the enrolled bill goes to the President for his signature.
If the one house makes amendments, they have to be agreed upon by the other house before it can go to the President for his signature.
If the two houses cannot agree upon the text of the bill, a conference committee meets to create a compromise bill (called a conference report), for both houses to agree to before it can go to the President for his signature.
If the President signs the bill, he also may provide a message explaining his approval of the bill.
If the President rejects the bill, he can veto the bill.
The two houses of Congress can override a presidential veto with a two-thirds vote of both houses.

Are there any sources to read further on legislative histories?
Charles W. Johnson, *How Our Laws Are Made* (2003) (KF4945 Z9J64) and Robert B. Dove, *Enactment of a Law* (1997) (KF4945 A35). Both are available at the Thomas website, http://thomas.loc.gov.

How is procedure determined in each house?
Both houses have procedural manuals for their rules that are adopted at the beginning of each congress. *Jefferson's Manual*, written while Thomas

Jefferson was the head of the Senate from 1797 to 1801, is still used for procedure. Other books dealing with parliamentary precedents are *Hind's Precedents* and *Canon's Precedents of the House of Representatives* (1789-1935) and *Deschler-Brown Precedents of the House of Representatives* (1936 to present). (KF4992 H55)

Where can one find the debates of the Congress?
Congressional debates are currently found in the *Congressional Record* (KF35).

How often is the *Congressional Record* published?
It has been published daily from Monday to Friday since 1873 when Congress is in session.

What are the previous publications for Congressional debates?

Annals of Congress (1789-1824) (KF35)

Register of Debates (1824-1837) (KF35)

Congressional Globe (1833-1873) (KF35)

What are House and Senate committee reports?
A committee report describes the purpose and scope of the bill with reasons for its recommendation. A section-by-section analysis is provided as well. Changes in existing law and text of laws being repealed must be included. Committee amendments are given in the beginning of the report. It also includes the votes by the committee members.

In the printed version, committee amendments are shown in italics and deleted matters in line-through type.

What are House and Senate documents?
They contain various other materials ordered printed by both chambers of Congress. Documents can include reports of executive departments and agencies, some of which are submitted in accordance with Federal law, then later are ordered printed as documents. Sometimes committee prints are ordered printed as documents also, if the information they contain is in demand. Documents have a larger distribution than committee prints.

What are House and Senate prints?
These reports contain studies and research materials prepared by legislative staff or outside consultants to assist members of Congress in evaluating proposed legislation.

What are House and Senate hearings?

Bills are sent to a committee which holds hearings for those interested in the bill can speak for or against it. The statements are collected and published in as many volumes necessary.

What are Senate Executive Documents?

They contain the text of a Treaty as it is submitted to the U.S. Senate for ratification by the President of the United States. Beginning with the 97th Congress in 1981, Executive Documents became known as Treaty Documents, and they are now numbered instead of lettered alphabetically.

What are Senate Treaty Documents?

They contain the text of a Treaty as it is submitted to the U.S. Senate for ratification by the President of the United States. They were numbered consecutively from the 1st Session through the 2d Session of a Congress. Prior to the 97th Congress, they were known as Executive (Lettered) Documents, and identified by letters of the alphabet.

What are the House and Senate committees?

The House of Representatives has the following committees:
Committee on Agriculture
Committee on Appropriations
Committee on Armed Services
Committee on the Budget
Committee on Education and the Workforce
Committee on Energy and Commerce
Committee on Financial Services
Committee on Government Reform
Committee on Homeland Security
Committee on House Administration
Committee on International Relations
Committee on the Judiciary
Committee on Resources
Committee on Rules
Committee on Science
Committee on Small Business
Committee on Standards of Official Conduct
Committee on Transportation and Infrastructure
Committee on Veterans' Affairs
Committee on Ways and Means
Joint Economic Committee

Joint Committee on Printing
Joint Committee on Taxation
House Permanent Select Committee on Intelligence

The Senate has the following committees:
Standing Committees
Agriculture, Nutrition, and Forestry
Appropriations
Armed Services
Banking, Housing, and Urban Affairs
Budget
Commerce, Science, and Transportation
Energy and Natural Resources
Environment and Public Works
Finance
Foreign Relations
Health, Education, Labor, and Pensions
Homeland Security and Governmental Affairs
Judiciary
Rules and Administration
Small Business and Entrepreneurship
Veterans' Affairs

Special, Select, and Other
Indian Affairs
Select Committee on Ethics
Select Committee on Intelligence
Special Committee on Aging

Standing Joint Committees
Joint Committee on Printing
Joint Committee on Taxation
Joint Committee on the Library
Joint Economic Committee

How does one get appointed to a committee?
Both parties have members on a committee, but the proportion of majority members to minority members is determined by the majority party.

House members can serve on only two committees and four subcommittees. The chairperson of the committee is the longest serving member of the majority party.

How is a public hearing conducted?

The committee chairman is required to make a public announcement of the date, place, and subject matter of the hearing at least one week previous to the hearing date. Meetings are open to the public. Hearings may be closed if dealing with national security.

What is a bill?

Bills are introduced into the house (H.R.1) or senate (S.1) as a beginning step in the passage of legislation. All appropriation bills have to be introduced first in the House of Representatives.

What is a companion bill?

It is when bills on the same subject are introduced into both houses at the same time.

Is there a difference between a bill and a resolution?

A bill and a joint resolution are used interchangeably.

What are the types of resolutions?

There are three types of resolutions: simple, concurrent, and joint resolutions. Simple resolutions (H. Res. and S. Res.) passed by one house deals with procedures within that house. Concurrent resolutions (H. Con. Res. and S. Con. Res.) affect both houses. Simple and concurrent resolutions are not considered legislation, since they are not approved by the President.

Joint resolutions of both houses (H. J. Res. and S. J. Res.) can be the equivalent of a law and are usually considered interchangeably.

Who is a sponsor of a bill?

Any member of the House or Senate can sponsor a bill by having his/her name attached to a bill introduced into the legislature.

How many sponsors can be on a bill?

There has to be at least one sponsor for a bill. In the House, there can be only one sponsor and unlimited co-sponsors. In the Senate, an unlimited number of sponsors is permitted.

What is done on the first reading of the bill?

The first reading introduces the bill into the legislature. It is then sent to a committee of the House or Senate for review. In the Senate, a member presents the bill to the clerk at the Presiding Officer's desk without making a statement on the floor. A senator can make a formal introduction on the floor with a statement. In the House, it is no longer customary to read bills, instead the bills are entered into the *Journal* and printed in the *Congressional Record*.

What is done on the second reading of the bill?
The second reading provides for debates on the floor and amendments can be made to the bill.

What is the "germaneness rule"?
Amendments are prohibited to be on a subject different from subject matter of the bill. It is considered one of the most important House rules to keep everyone focused on a bill's subject.

What is done on the third reading of the bill?
The bill is debated and voted upon for passage. If it passes a majority vote, then it is sent to the other house for its consideration.

What is a roll call vote?
Roll call votes are recorded votes taken in both houses of Congress.

What is the marked-up version of the bill?
The subcommittee reviews the bill and reports it with or without amendments to the full committee.

How does the full committee determine whether to pass a bill?
The full committee reviews the subcommittee's actions. The committee can vote in favor, adversely, or without recommendation.

What is a "clean bill?"
The full committee takes the bill with all previous and new amendments and incorporates them into a new bill which is then published.

What are the calendars in the House of Representatives?
The two principal calendars are the Union Calendar and House Calendar. The Union Calendar lists the majority of public bills and resolutions reported in the House. The House Calendar contains bills not involving a cost to the government and resolutions providing special orders of business.

A Private Calendar lists all private bills heard by the House. The Corrections Calendar may have noncontroversial bills on the Union and House Calendars transferred to this Calendar for speedier action. The Calendar of Motions to Discharge Committees sets when to discharge a committee from consideration of a public bill or resolution. If adopted by the House then members vote upon its consideration immediately. If the members do not agree to vote upon the bill, then the bill is put back on the regular calendar.

What are the calendars in the Senate?
In the Senate, there are two calendars, the Calendar of Business and the Executive Calendar. The Calendar of Business contains all legislation; while the Executive Calendar contains treaties and nominations.

What is an engrossed bill?
An engrossed bill is a bill ready for passage in one chamber of the legislature.

What is an enrolled bill?
This is near the end of the legislative process after a bill has been approved by both houses and signed by the leaders of each house.

What is the presidential message?
The President's signing of the bill completes the process by which a bill is enacted into law. The presidential message is the statement made upon the signing of the act.

What is a Committee of the Whole House?
The parliamentary procedure of considering a bill as the committee of the whole house lets the quorum be only 100 members rather than the regular 218. All measures on the Union Calendar involve a tax, making appropriations, authorizing payments out of appropriations already made, or disposing of property.

What is a filibuster?
In the Senate, a senator or several can provide lengthy speeches in debates to prevent or defeat action on the bill.

What is cloture?
Debate can be closed by a vote of sixteen senators who sign a petition and then have it voted upon by three-fifths of the senators duly chosen and sworn. In 1986, "post-cloture" debate was limited to 30 hours or more if voted upon by three-fifths of the senators duly chosen and sworn.

What is a pocket veto?
This is when the President refuses to sign a bill into law within ten days after the Congress has stopped meeting.

What vote is needed to overturn a presidential veto?
Two-thirds vote of both the Senate and House of Representatives.

What is meant by logrolling?
Logrolling refers to the practice of inducing the passage of legislation by the addition of "goodies" that do not relate to the main bulk of the statute, so that policies that are not supported by a majority can be enacted through subtle bribery (for example, a bill to increase the income tax that also authorize highway or bridge projects within the districts of one or more key lawmakers). (Lawrence G. Feinberg, Consolidation and the Consolidation Counsel, *Legislative Process, Statutory Drafting, Regulatory Process & Update*, PBI, 2008).

What is meant by pork barrel?
Pork barrel refers to spending of money allocated through legislation to an individual or group by a politician in return for personal favors and contributions to the legislator's campaign.

How do I compile a legislative history?
The best source to use is *CIS Index and Abstracts, Public Legislative History* (KF49 C62) volumes from 1983 to present.

Are there any published compiled legislative histories?
The federal government publishes legislative histories for some acts, e.g., tax acts are published in the *Internal Revenue Cumulative Bulletin*. (KF6282 A2I495).

Commercial vendors publish legislative histories of major acts, e.g., the William S. Hein Co. has multiple titles and the Bureau of National Affairs has *Tax Management, Primary Sources* series (KF6365 B87) for tax legislative histories.

Are there any sources to find compilations of legislative histories?
Nancy P. Johnson, *Sources of Compiled Legislative Histories: A Bibliography of Government Documents* (1979-) (KF42.2 1979) and Bernard D. Reams, Jr., *Federal Legislative Histories: An Annotated Bibliography And Index to Officially Published Sources* (1994). (KF42.2 1994)

What does the *United States Statutes at Large* contain for legislative history?
At the end of each act is a listing of the House and Senate dates for passage of the bill.

What does the *United States Code Congressional and Administrative News* (U.S.C.C.A.N.) contain for legislative history?

The major acts contain all or part of the House and/or Senate Reports and the presidential message upon signing a bill into law. The reports have separate pagination from the session laws. The presidential messages can also be found here.

What is *CIS Index and Abstracts*?

Since 1970, the Congressional Information Service (CIS) has published the *Index and Abstracts* which are published monthly with quarterly supplements and annual volumes (one for index and one for abstracts).

Does *CIS Index and Abstracts* cover earlier Congresses?

CIS published an historical set of House and Senate reports from 1789 to 1969 in ten series of volumes providing chronological and subject indexes for each period. The documents are available in microfiche.

What does the Abstracts volume contain?

CIS abstracts all documents published by Congress. Each title has a breakdown of its contents, e.g. lists all speakers in a hearing.

What documents are indexed in the Abstracts?

Under each committee listing in the House of Representatives and Senate are bills. Then there are hearings, prints, reports, and documents.

What is the annual *Legislative Histories to the Public Laws*?

Beginning in 1983, this single volume lists each public law for a Congressional session listing all of the documents from the annual Abstract volumes needed to compile the legislative history.

What is Congressional Universe?

This is the online version of the *CIS Index and Abstracts*. It gives the researcher the ability to find documents for the legislative history.

Where do I find the actual publication?

Each document listed in *CIS Index and Abstracts* or Congressional Universe has a CIS number identifying the document and a Superintendent of Document classification number assigned to the document.

For instance, the Paperwork Reduction Act of 1995 has a Senate Report 101-487. It has a CIS no. : CIS90:S403-12 and Superintendent of Documents classification number of Y1.1/5:101-487.

What is the *Congressional Index*?

The *Congressional Index*, published by the Commerce Clearing House, is a weekly looseleaf service containing information about the Congress and the passage of bills into law.

Can I Shepardize statutory law?

Yes. One can shepardize the federal *U. S. Code* (by date of edition) and the chronological laws not published in the *Code*. On the state level, the codified statutes and the chronological laws can also be found in the Statute Ed.

In the Shepard's Citations volumes for the individual states, the Statute Edition contains citations to the federal Constitution, *U. S. Code*, and *Statutes at Large* cited in state cases, the current constitution, code, and chronological laws.

II. INTERNET

What are the databases available to locate federal legislative histories?

The two most comprehensive are gpoaccess.gov and thomas.loc.gov.

If I am doing legislative history research, where can I find House and Senate Committee Reports?

House and Senate committee reports, joint reports, and conference reports are available in full text from the Thomas site.

How far back are the House and Senate committee reports available?

Both the House and Senate committee reports are available from the 104th Congress (1995 to the present) on the Thomas site.

Where do I get Congressional committee prints?

House and Senate committee prints are available from the 105th Congress (1997) to date from the GPO web site (www.gpoaccess.gov/cprints). You can retrieve documents by committee print number and also by subject.

What is Congressional Universe?

Congressional Universe is a product of LexisNexis that provides a complete listing of all documents that comprise a legislative history. It provides access to the CIS (congressional information service) Index which indexes and abstracts congressional publications and CIS legislative histories as well as provides access to the full text of congressional reports, documents, prints, bills and *Congressional Record*, public laws, and the *United States Code Service*.

What is available under www.gpoaccess.gov?
Gpoaccess.gov has extensive coverage dealing with legislation and congressional documents.

Legislative Process

History of Bills: Bill summaries and status with links to the Congressional Record.

Conference Reports: Links to active ("unofficial") and archived ("official") conference reports.

Congressional Bills: Full-text of each bill version (e.g. introduced, engrossed, enrolled).

Congressional Record and House Journal: Debates on issues and legislation.

Congressional Record, Bound

Congressional Record Index: Index to the Congressional Record

Public and Private Laws: Full-text versions of all signed bills.

United States Statutes at Large

United States Code: The codification of laws.

Congressional Materials

Committees, Calendars, & Procedures

Congressional Calendars: The agenda for each chamber of Congress.

    House Calendars

    Senate Calendar of Business

Congressional Committees

    Congressional Committee Materials Online via GPO Access: Locate

    Publications by House or Senate Committee or by GPO Access Resource

        Congressional Hearings

        Congressional Committee Prints

        Congressional Executive Commission on the People's Republic of China

        Economic Indicators: Released by the Joint Economic Committee

        House Committee on Ways and Means Committee Prints

        House Committee on Ways and Means: Green Book

        Plum Book —United States Government Policy and Supporting Positions

        Selected Congressional Hearings and Reports from the Challenger Space Shuttle Accident

Congressional Rules and Procedures:

    Rules and Precedents that Govern the U.S. House of Representatives

        Cannon's Precedents of the House of Representatives

        Deschler's Precedents of the House of Representatives

        Hind's Precedents of the House of Representatives

        House Practice: A Guide to the Rules, Precedents and Procedures of the House

House Rules and Manual
  Riddick's Senate Procedure
  Senate Manual
Congressional Serial Set
  Congressional Documents
  Congressional Reports
Independent Counsel Reports
Featured Documents of the House and Senate
United States Constitution

What does Thomas.loc.gov have for legislative histories?

Thomas.loc.gov contains bills and resolutions (1973 to present), committee reports (1993 to present), and *Congressional Record* (1989 to present).

III. LEXISNEXIS

What are the different databases to locate federal legislative histories?

Under Federal Legal, there are databases for *United States Code Service (U.S.C.S.)* Materials, Legislative Histories & Materials, and Individual Congressional Record Materials

What are the sources available under *United States Code Service* materials?

There are databases for *United States Code* citations and individual statutes cited to Public Laws.

How does an individual Public Law provide for legislative history?

Under a Public Law, there are links to the individual bill for Bill Tracking Report, to the Full Text Version(s) of the Bill, and to the CIS Legislative History Document. For example, Public Law 109-100 contains:

BILL TRACKING REPORT: 109 Bill Tracking S. 37
FULL TEXT VERSION(S) OF BILL: 109 S. 37
CIS LEGIS. HISTORY DOCUMENT: 109 CIS Legis. Hist. P.L. 100

What does Bill Tracking Report provide?

SPONSOR: The first sponsor for the bill.

DATE-INTRO: Date the bill was introduced

LAST-ACTION-DATE: The date the bill was enacted into law.

STATUS: What public law the bill became and the enacted date.

TOTAL COSPONSORS: The number of cosponsors broken down by the number of Democrats and Republicans.

SYNOPSIS: A short summary of the purpose of the bill.

ACTIONS: Committee referrals followed by legislative activity by date with references to the *Congressional Record*.

BILL-DIGEST: Congressional Research Service provides a detailed paragraph digest summary of the bill.

CO-SPONSORS: Can be listed by date or by political party.

SUBJECT: Key terms for accessing the document.

LOAD DATE: Date the information is placed into Lexis.

What is Full-Text Versions of the Bill?
This link provides a link to the different versions of the bill from both the House of Representatives and Senate.

What is a CIS Legislative History Document?
This is a link to the CIS Legislative History Index for statutory law. The public law is cited by year and public law number, e.g., 2000 CIS PL 106210; 106 CIS Legis. Hist. P.L. 210 for the Muhammad Ali Boxing Reform Act, Pub. Law 106-210.

What information is found under the CIS Legislative History?
Under the heading is listed
LEGISLATIVE HISTORY OF: Public Law by Number
Title: Short Title or Popular Name title of the act.
CIS-NO: The CIS number designation for the act by year and public law number.
   DOC-TYPE: Legislative History
DATE: Date of Enactment of the act
LENGTH: The number of pages of the printed act.
ENACTED-BILL: The final version of the bill with links to the bill and the bill tracking report.
Stat: The U.S. Statutes at Large citation for the act.
CONG-SESS: The Congressional session listed by Congress and first or second session. ITEM-NO:
SUMMARY: Official title of the act with a short summary of the act.
CONTENT NOTATION: Key words for the act.
BILLS: List of the bills from both houses for this act.
DESCRIPTORS: Key words to identify subjects of act.

REFERENCES: Provide listings with links to Debates in the Congressional Record, Reports of the House and Senate, and Hearings.

What is the information provided for each document?

CIS NUMBER: This is the number assigned by CIS to identify this single document.

LENGTH: This is the number of pages for the document.

SUDOC NUMBER: All Congressional publications have Superintendent of Documents Classification System numbers assigned to each document (like Library of Congress Subject Classification system for books in the library). Congressional publications have a Y letter designation.

Where are there individual legislative histories available in Lexis?

Under Federal Legal, View More, Legislative Histories and Materials in the lower-right hand column provides a wide range of legislative histories, e.g., bankruptcy, environmental law, taxation, etc.

What is the *CIS Historical Index*?

This library provides CIS information for Congressional materials from 1789 to 1970 when the current set begins.

The materials included in the database includes:

U.S. Serial Set, including Reported Bill Numbers (1789-1969)
Senate Executive Documents and Reports (1817-1969)
U.S. Congressional Committee Hearings (1833-1969)
Unpublished U.S. Senate Committee Hearings (1823-1972)
Unpublished U.S. House Committee Hearings (1833-1958)
U.S. Congressional Committee Prints (1830-1969)

IV. WESTLAW

What are the different databases to locate federal legislative histories.

Legislative History —U. S. Code (LH), provides legislative history from 1948 to 1989 published in *U. S. Code Congressional & Administrative News*; all Congressional committee reports from 1990 to present;

Congressional Record (CR), Begins in 1985 to present.

Congressional Testimony (CONGTMY) begins in November 2004 contains documents from testimony presented before Congress.

U. S. Congressional Testimony (US Testimony) provides full text from January 1996 to present; select testimony from 1993 to 1996

U. S. Political Transcripts (USPOLTRANS) contains transcripts from the news conferences, press briefings, political speeches, and oral testimony from congressional committee meetings (February 1994 to present).

There are also databases for immigration (FIM-LH), securities and blue sky laws (FSEC-LH), and tax (FTX-LH).

United States Code Congressional & Administrative News, United States Code Annotated

Is there a graphical illustration for the federal legislative history process?

Under the Add/Remove Tabs, there is a Legislative History-Federal tab under Jurisdictional-Federal heading that provides an illustration of the legislative process.

What are the sources available under *United States Code Annotated* Materials?

There are databases for *United States Code* citations and individual statutes cited to Public Laws.

How does an individual Public Law provide for legislative history?

The testimony present at hearings, *Congressional Record*, and House and Senate Reports are available.

Where can one find complete legislative histories for individual acts?

Arnold & Porter Collection —Legislative Histories library contains thirty completed legislative histories including Americans With Disabilities Act of 1991, Bankruptcy Code of 1978 and 1994, Sarbanes-Oxley Act of 2002, and U.S. Patriot Act of 2002.

What libraries are available under Bill Tracking?

Westlaw provides federal and state bill tracking information.

Bill Tracking Federal (US-BILLTRK) for current federal legislation.

Bill Tracking (BILLTRK) contains summaries and status information for all fifty states and federal legislation.

Bill Tracking Old (BILLTRK-OLD) contains an historical database of all 50 states and U.S. Congress back to 1991.

Where can one find Presidential signing statements?

Presidential Messages and Signing Statements (USCCAN-MSG)

What congressional reports are available in Westlaw?

USCCAN-REP library contains all reports since 1990; all reports for bills enacted into law from 1948 to 1989, and all securities law reports since 1933.

CHAPTER 9

ADMINISTRATIVE LAW

Introduction: Administrative law is the fourth area of primary law dealing with departments and agencies of the federal, state, and local governments. These department/agencies provide regulations over particular industries, issue licenses for businesses to operate, and issue administrative agency decisions. These administrative law documents can be found in a specific type of legal publication called looseleaf services that contain primary sources of legislative, judicial, and administrative law materials. These services may contain federal and/or state documents. The major publishers of looseleaf services today —BNA, CCH, RIA —are available in print and as online subscriptions from the companies or in LexisNexis, Westlaw, and Loislaw.

I. MANUAL

What is administrative law?
Administrative law is part of primary law that deals with departments and independent administrative agencies on the federal and state levels.

What is included in administrative law?
Administrative law includes regulations, licensing, and court cases dealing with administrative law.

What is agency law?
The regulations created by each agency under federal legislation.

How many federal agencies are there?
There are more than 40 federal agencies.

What are the types of federal agencies?
There are two types of agencies, executive agencies and independent agencies.

What are the executive agencies?

Executive agencies are the departments that are part of the executive cabinet:
Department of Agriculture (USDA)
Department of Commerce (DOC)
Department of Defense (DOD)
Department of Education (ED)
Department of Energy (DOE)
Department of Health and Human Services (HHS)
Department of Homeland Security (DHS)
Department of Housing and Urban Development (HUD)
Department of Justice (DOJ)
Department of Labor (DOL)
Department of State (DOS)
Department of the Interior (DOI)
Department of the Treasury
Department of Transportation (DOT)
Department of Veterans' Affairs (VA)

What are the independent corporations and independent agencies?

African Development Foundation
Central Intelligence Agency (CIA)
Commission on Civil Rights
Commodity Futures Trading Commission
Consumer Product Safety Commission (CPSC)
Corporation for National and Community Service
Defense Nuclear Facilities Safety Board
Election Assistance Commission
Environmental Protection Agency (EPA)
Equal Employment Opportunity Commission (EEOC)
Export-Import Bank of the United States
Farm Credit Administration
Federal Communications Commission (FCC)
Federal Deposit Insurance Corporation (FDIC)
Federal Election Commission (FEC)
Federal Housing Finance Board
Federal Labor Relations Authority
Federal Maritime Commission
Federal Mediation and Conciliation Service
Federal Mine Safety and Health Review Commission
Federal Reserve System
Federal Retirement Thrift Investment Board

Federal Trade Commission (FTC)
General Services Administration (GSA)
Institute of Museum and Library Services
Inter-American Foundation
International Broadcasting Bureau (IBB)
Merit Systems Protection Board
National Aeronautics and Space Administration (NASA)
National Archives and Records Administration (NARA)
National Capital Planning Commission
National Council on Disability
National Credit Union Administration (NCUA)
National Endowment for the Arts
National Endowment for the Humanities
National Labor Relations Board (NLRB)
National Mediation Board
National Railroad Passenger Corporation (AMTRAK)
National Science Foundation (NSF)
National Transportation Safety Board
Nuclear Regulatory Commission (NRC)
Occupational Safety and Health Review Commission
Office of Compliance
Office of Government Ethics
Office of Personnel Management
Office of Special Counsel
Office of the National Counterintelligence Executive
Overseas Private Investment Corporation
Panama Canal Commission
Peace Corps
Pension Benefit Guaranty Corporation
Postal Rate Commission
Railroad Retirement Board
Securities and Exchange Commission (SEC)
Selective Service System
Small Business Administration (SBA)
Social Security Administration (SSA)
Tennessee Valley Authority
Trade and Development Agency
United States Agency for International Development
United States International Trade Commission
United States Postal Service (USPS)

How are executive agencies created?
Agencies are created by statutory law (organic laws) at the federal (Congress) and state (legislature) levels.

What is an organic act/statute?
An organic act/statute, sometimes referred to as "enabling legislation," establishes an administrative agency.

What was the first agency created?
The Interstate Commerce Commission was the first agency that was created in 1887 to help regulate the railroads.

What are some of the acts related to administrative law?
Administrative Procedural Act; *Federal Register* Act; Federal Registration Act; Privacy Act; Freedom of Information Act; Paper Reduction Act; Government in Sunshine Act.

Where are the administrative rules and regulations published?
Federal Register (F.R.) (KF70) and *Code of Federal Regulations (C.F.R.)* (KF70) and also in various looseleaf publications.

What is the *Federal Register*?
The *Federal Register* is the official publication for the administrative agencies of the United States Government published by the Office of the Federal Register, National Archives and Records Administration (NARA) that is published on a daily basis.

What type of information is published in the *Federal Register*?
The *Register* publishes all proposed and final regulations of the departments and agencies, notices of meetings, and grant applications. It also publishes Presidential Executive Documents, e.g., proclamations, executive orders, and reorganization plans.

What office of the federal government is responsible for creating the *Federal Register*, C.F.R., and LSA?
The National Archives and Records Administration (NARA) is the official publisher of the C.F.R., *Federal Register*, and *LSA*.

How often is the *Federal Register* published?
The *Federal Register* is published on a daily basis, on non-holidays, five days a week, but not on weekends. It is available on the Internet each morning after 6:00 a.m.

When was the *Federal Register* first published?
The first issue of the *Federal Register* was published on Saturday, March 14, 1936.

How is the material organized in the *Federal Register*?
The Register is arranged alphabetically by agency. Under each agency is listed proposed and final regulations, notices of meetings, etc.

What are the proposed rules?
Departments and agencies publish proposed administrative rules to regulate the business the department/agency is overseeing. Rules are published in the *Federal Register*, with a given period of time for commentary (30, 60, 90 days) before final approval is given to the regulation.

What are the procedures one should follow to send comments to the proposed rules?
It is possible to provide electronic submission to comment on proposed rules through the Regulations.gov web site, at www.regulations.gov. Comments can be sent by email or by regular mail submitting handwritten (original + 14 copies) on or before the due date published in the *Federal Register*.
   There are instructions for filing comments electronically under Frequently Asked Questions (FAQs) at http://www.regulations.gov/search/footer/faq.jsp#15.

What are the final or permanent rules?
The rules which have been adopted by the department or agency after review.

Are all proposed rules adopted into final rules?
No. It is possible that departments and agencies can withdraw the proposed regulation.

What are the notices of meetings?
Agencies have meetings concerning topics that fall under the agency's purview.

How can I find administrative law research information on a specific topic in the *Federal Register*?
One can go through the table of contents of each issue or the monthly index.

What is meant by regulatory history?
Regulatory history can be found in the summary, further information, and supplementary information found in the *Federal Register*.

What are 'summary', 'further information', and 'supplementary information' in the *Federal Register*?

Proposed rules provide a summary which is an explanation of the need for the proposed rule. There is a date for when comments can be received concerning the proposed rule. Supplementary information includes the names of contact persons at the agencies to obtain further information and how to be able to view public comments concerning the proposed rule. This is referred to as regulatory history.

What is 'unified agenda' in relation to federal regulatory research and where can I find the information?

Agencies publish semiannual regulatory agendas describing regulatory actions they are developing or have recently completed in the *Federal Register*, usually during April and October each year, as part of the Unified Agenda of Federal Regulatory and Deregulatory Actions. The Unified Agenda has appeared in the *Federal Register* twice each year since 1983 and is available electronically on *GPO Access* from 1994 forward.

What are Privacy Act Issuances?

According to the Privacy Act of 1974, the Office of the Federal Register (OFR) must biennially compile and publish (1) descriptions of system of records maintained on individuals by Federal agencies which were published in the *Federal Register*; and (2) rules of each agency which set out the procedures that agencies will follow in helping individuals who request information about their records. In addition, the Privacy Act of 1974 requires OFR to publish the compilation in a form available to the public at a low cost (www.gpoaccess.gov)

Is there an index to the *Federal Register*?

The *Federal Register* has a monthly index that cumulates into quarterly issues and then an annual index.

What is the *Code of Federal Regulations* (C.F.R.)?

This is the codification of all of the permanent (final) rules published in the *Federal Register*.

How many topics/titles are in the *C.F.R.*?

There are fifty topics/titles in the *Code of Federal Regulations*.

Are the titles of the *C.F.R.* and *United States Code* the same?

Yes, they have the same names for the fifty titles.

Where can I find a complete listing of the *C.F.R.* outline?

The *C.F.R. Index and Finding Aids* volume provides a List of C.F.R. Titles, Chapters, Subchapters, and Parts.

When was the first edition of the *C.F.R.* published?
The first edition of *C.F.R.* was published in 1939 containing the regulations in force as of June 1, 1938.

Who codifies the *C.F.R.*?
The Office of the *Federal Register* within the National Archives and Records Administration (NARA) codifies the *C.F.R.*

What is the legal status of the *C.F.R.*?
The *C.F.R.* is *prima facie* evidence of the text of the original documents (44 U.S.C. §1510).

How often is the *C.F.R.* published?
The *C.F.R.* is published annually, but on a quarterly basis. Titles 1-16 are published in January; Titles 17-27 are published in April; Titles 28-41 are published in July; and Titles 42-50 are published in October.

How is the information organized in *C.F.R.*?
The materials are arranged by title, chapter, part, and section.

How does one usually cite to a *C.F.R.* citation?
Citation is usually given to the title and section number, e.g., 29 C.F.R. 1910.

Is there a difference between a proposed and final regulation?
The proposed regulation may have an introductory statement that does not occur in the final regulation. The proposed regulation can be changed, modified, or repealed; the final regulation has approval of the agency after all changes have been completed.

Where does one find the statutory authority for the regulation?
At the beginning of the section of the regulation, an authority note identifies the statutory reference to the *U. S. Code*.

Where does one find the source for the regulation?
At the beginning of the section of the regulation, following the authority note, is the source note reference to the *Federal Register* where it was originally published.

If a subsection has been updated, there will be an additional source reference to the more recent *Federal Register*.

Can I find the cross-references to the *Code of Federal Regulations* in statutory books?
The *U.S.C.A.* and *U.S.C.S.* contain cross references under each section of the annotated codes.

Where do I find a table of authorities and rules for *United States Code* citations to the *C.F.R.* sections?
In the *C.F.R.* Index, Table 1 after the General Index provides parallel citations between the *U.S.C.* and *C.F.R.*

Where do I find a table of authorities and rules for *C.F.R.* citations to the *U.S. Code* citations?
In the *C.F.R.* Index, Table 2 after the General Index provides parallel citations between the *C.F.R.* and *U.S.C.*

Where can I find a listing of all the titles and their subdivisions in *C.F.R.*?
There is a listing of the entire contents of the *Code* in the Index and Finding Aides volume.

Why do the *C.F.R.* books have a different color each year?
It is a method by which you can identify each year's publication. It is useful because the volumes take more than a year to be printed. As a new title is published, the older title is removed from the shelf.

Title 3 includes presidential documents and has only a white color on the spine each year. Libraries keep Title 3 because the proclamations and executive orders are consecutively numbered from year to year.

Are there any annotated editions of the *C.F.R.*?
West has begun publishing annotated versions of individual titles of the *C.F.R.* containing annotations to court cases.

What are the research methods to locate information in *C.F.R.*?
There is a one-volume index published and *C.F.R. Index and Finding Aids*.

How often is the *C.F.R.* Index updated?
C.F.R. Index is updated annually.

Are there any other indexes besides the official index?
U.S.C.S. reprints the official index as a single volume.

Beginning in 2006, West Group began publishing its multi-volume paperback title: West's *Code of Federal Regulations General Index*.

Which is the most comprehensive index to use?
West's *C.F.R. General Index* contains more than 700,000 section-level references.

Can one Shepardize the *C.F.R.*?
Shepard's Code of Federal Regulations Citations is a citator for the C.F.R. titles and sections by year which provides access chiefly to court cases.

How can one find case law dealing with *C.F.R.* sections?
There are several ways to locate cases on a *C.F.R.* title and section:

First, use the citation in Shepard's *Code of Federal Regulations Citations* which will provide the case citation under each title and section.

Second, use the citation in the electronic Shepard's in Lexis or KeyCite in West-law.

Third, search the citation in the full-text case law databases of Lexis and West-law.

Fourth, use West's version of the annotated *Code of Federal Regulations*.

Fifth, use Westlaw's RegulationPlus feature that provides annotated case law to the *C.F.R.*

What is the *List of C.F.R. Sections Affected* (LSA)?
The *List of C.F.R. Sections Affected* (KF70 A34) provides cross references for updating between the *C.F.R.* and the *Federal Register*. The issue provides the *C.F.R.* title on the left hand column with a reference to a *Federal Register* page on the right hand column.

Because there is an overlap of years, the pages from the previous year's issues are in bold print to distinguish last year's volume from the current year.

How often are the *LSA* books published?
The LSA books are published monthly. There are annual issues that cumulate all of the changes for each quarterly part as listed in the previous question.

Where do you find the page numbers of the *Federal Register* published in LSA?
You can find the volume number and corresponding page number of the *Federal Register* in the last pages within the LSA book.

How do I update the information found in the *C.F.R.*? Updating the *Code of Federal Regulations*
First, one has to know the date of the volume that is listed on the front cover of the *C.F.R.* volume to begin the search, for example, Revised as of January 2007 for titles 1-16.

Second, go to the *List of C.F.R. Sections Affected* (LSA) covering the period from the date of the book forward. Check to see if there is an annual issue that updates the information for a complete year (e.g. the December issue covers Titles 1-16, March issue covers Title 17-27, June issue covers Titles 28-41, September issue covers Titles 42-50).

Third, check any later LSA pamphlets to bring the citation as up to date as possible (usually the indexes are six weeks behind the current date).

Fourth, check the back pages of the most current issue of the *Federal Register* under Reader Aids for a table of the List of C.F.R. Parts Affected During [name of month] which will provide a cumulative listing of all changes from the beginning of the month to the previous day.

Fifth, check the "C.F.R. Parts Affected In This Issue" of the current daily *Federal Register* for the most recent changes for that day.

If the paper issue is not current, one can check the daily *Federal Register* online for the current month's and/or daily changes.

Does the *C.F.R.* contain the relevant case law to the administrative rules?
The *C.F.R.* does not contain case law. One can use *Shepard's C.F.R. Citations* or the electronic databases of Shepard's or KeyCite to locate cases on a *C.F.R.* cite.

What are some of the administrative agencies?
The Interstate Commerce Commission (or ICC) was the first regulatory body in the United States created by the Interstate Commerce Act of 1887, which was signed into law by President Grover Cleveland. The agency was abolished in 1995, and the agency's remaining functions were transferred to the Surface Transportation Board.

Following the ICC, other agencies followed including the Federal Trade Commission, Federal Communications Commission, National Labor Relations Board, Federal Aviation Agency, etc. Commissions and boards include the Equal Employment Opportunity Commission, National Mediation Board, Merit Systems Protection Board, etc.

Where do I get pertinent case law for administrative rules?
Besides citators, administrative cases are referenced in looseleaf services on specific topics (published by BNA, CCH, and RIA), and in treatises and periodicals.

What are administrative law opinions?
Each administrative agency has administrative law judges who hear cases dealing with the regulations of the agency, e.g., *Decisions of the National Labor Relations Board, Reports of the U. S. Tax Court.*

What format are these administrative law opinions published?
They are published like regular court cases in slip opinions, advance sheets, and bound volumes. Some agencies publish slip opinions and bound volumes only. Some agencies post their decisions on the Internet.

Are there any commercial vendors publishing administrative law opinions?
Most administrative law decisions are published in full-text or abstract in looseleaf services published by BNA, CCH, and RIA.

Can administrative agency decisions be appealed to the regular court system?
After exhausting all appeals within the administrative agency system, cases can be appealed to the trial courts in the regular court system.

How are federal administrative regulations (*C.F.R.*, *Federal Register*) and administrative agency cases distributed throughout the United States?
Under Title 44 of the *U. S. Code*, there is a library depository program that provides free distribution of these materials to several hundred libraries of all types (university, public, state libraries) throughout the United States.

What types of materials are included in Presidential documents?
Presidential documents include proclamations, executive orders, and reorganization plans.

What is a Presidential proclamation?
Proclamations are general statements of policy that deal chiefly with ceremonial occasions like Black History Month, Greek Independence Day, etc.

Where can I find Presidential documents?
Presidential documents, like proclamations and executive orders, can be found in the *Federal Register*, Title 3 of the *Code of Federal Regulations*, *U.S. Statutes at Large*, and *U.S. Code Congressional & Legislative News*. They may also be found in the *Weekly Compilation of Presidential Documents* and the *Public Papers of the Presidents* series.

When do Presidential documents go into effect?
Documents go into effect upon publication in the *Federal Register*.

What are executive orders?
The President can issue Executive Orders to governmental officials to carry out certain policies separate from statutory law, such as the National and Community Service Program (Executive Order 13331) and American Indian and Alaska Native Education (Executive Order 13336).

Do executive orders have to be passed by Congress?
No, they are part of the President's executive authority and Congress has no control over them except to pass a law to overturn it.

Do executive orders have any legal value?
Yes, they are part of the presidential authority that gives the President the power to carry out policy through executive departments or agencies.

How are the executive orders published?
They are published chronologically and sequentially in order. Executive orders are published first in the *Federal Register* and then Title 3 of the *Code of Federal Regulations*, and the *U.S. Code Congressional & Administrative News* (West).

What are reorganization plans?
The President can reorganize departments and agencies below the cabinet level departments, e.g., add additional members to the Civil Rights Commission. Cabinet level departments can be revised with the consent of the Senate, e.g., Department of Health, Education and Welfare divided into two separate Departments of Education and Health & Human Resources.

Where are reorganization plans published?
They are published chronologically and sequentially in order. Executive orders are published first in the *Federal Register* and then Title 3 of the *Code of Federal Regulations*, and *U.S. Code Congressional & Administrative News*.

What are administrative orders?
Agencies issue orders of disposition and resolution of agency matters.

What are advisory opinions in administrative law?
Individuals request an advisory opinion to answer a hypothetical situation to see how the agency would handle a specific problem. The opinions are reliable and persuasive for determining the agency's behavior, but they are not binding on the agency.

What are no-action letters?

Individuals request no-action letters from agencies, mostly the Securities and Exchange Commission, as to their action upon a specific problem with the promise that they will not take any action against the party requesting the no-action letter. The no-action letters may be used by later parties, but the letters are not binding on the agency or the courts.

What are the dates of coverage for Presidential proclamations and executive orders in Title 3 of the *C.F.R.*?

Title 3 contains presidential proclamations beginning with Presidential Proclamation 2161 of March 19, 1936 and Executive Order 7316 of March 13, 1936. There is a two-volume set containing proclamations and executive orders of President Herbert Hoover's from March 4, 1929 to March 4, 1933.

What other information is provided in Title 3 of the *C.F.R.*?

There are tables in each volume that provide a listing of proclamations (table 1), executive orders (table 2), other presidential documents (table 3), presidential documents affected during the year of publication (table 4), and statutes cited as authority for presidential documents (table 5).

C.F.R. Finding Aids provide a Table of C.F.R. Titles and Chapters and an Alphabetical List of Agencies Appearing in the *C.F.R.*

LOOSELEAF SERVICES

What are looseleaf services?

These are single or multivolume publications that are updated on a weekly, biweekly, or monthly basis. The sets provide statutory law, case law, and administrative regulations and cases. Depending on the set, it may consist of federal and/or state materials.

All titles are updated with anywhere from a couple of pages to hundreds of pages in what is called a "release" that have to be filed by staff in each set. Each page has a release number and date on the page for the reader to identify how old the page in the volume might be. The filer also files the instruction pages for each release usually at the end of the volume. The filer has to check to see that a current release continues the numbering from the previous release before filing the new materials.

Administrative regulations and cases can be found in the looseleaf publications of the Bureau of National Affairs (BNA) and Commerce Clearing House (CCH).

Who publishes looseleaf services?

The major publishers are Pike and Fischer, Bureau of National Affairs, Commerce Clearing House, and Research Institute of America.

What are some of the major looseleaf titles from each publisher?

Bureau of National Affairs (BNA)

Antitrust Reporter
Bankruptcy Reporter
Criminal Law Reporter
Environmental Reporter
Family Law Reporter
Labor Law Manual
Federal Taxes
Tax Management Portfolios
U. S. Law Week

Commerce Clearing House (CCH)

Congressional Index
Employment Practice Guide
Federal Estate and Gift Tax Reporter
Federal Securities Law Reporter
IRS Manual
Labor Law Reporter
Medicare and Medicaid Guide
Standard Federal Tax Reporter
State Tax Reporters (each state)
Tax Court Reporter
Worker's Compensation Law Reporter

Pike & Fischer

Administrative Law. This is a three-part set. The Decisions volume contains cases from courts and agencies. The Digest volume organizes the cases by subject such as evidence, investigations, etc. A Desk Book provides the text of statutes, legislative history of important administrative law acts, implementation memoranda, agency rules, a topical index, and tables containing parallel citations and cumulative table of cases.

Research Institute of America (RIA)

Employment Coordinator
Employment Discrimination Coordinator

Federal Tax Coordinator
Pension Plan Coordinator
Real Estate Coordinator
State and Local Tax Coordinator
State Tax Reports (each state)

II. INTERNET

Is there any website that tracks federal regulations?

Justia (www.justia.com) offers regulation tracking information at http://regulations.justia.com . You can select, All, Rules, Adm. Orders, Notices, Proposed Rules, Executive Orders, Proclamation by agency and date.

Federal Register

What are the sources for *Federal Register* research?

In addition to the comprehensive legal web sites, the Government Printing Office site (www.gpoaccess.gov); the Government Regulations site (www.regulations.gov), and National Archives & Records Administration (NARA) (www.archives.gov/federal-register); and the HeinOnline site (www.heinonline.org) all provide access to the *Federal Register*.

How far back is the *Federal Register* available online?

The *Federal Register* is available from 1994 (volume 59) to the present from the GPO web site. You may browse the documents or you can perform a search.

Findlaw provides *Federal Register* entries from 1995 to the present.

HeinOnline provides the *Federal Register* (Federal Register Library) from 1936 (volume 1 to present).

What are the other information materials available from HeinOnline?

In addition to the *Federal Register*, you will also have access to *Federal Register Indexes* from volume 1 to present. Also available are:

a) Text of Administrative Procedure Act (Legislative History) 1944-1946
b) Text of Code of Emergency Federal Regulations, Volume 1 (1965)
c) *United States Government Manuals* from 1935 through 2005
d) *Weekly Compilations of Presidential Documents*, Volume 1 through Volume 42 (1965 – January, 2006)

Is there any web site that provides a daily *Federal Register*?

You can see the online version of the daily *Federal Register* from National Archives and Records Administration (www.archives.gov/federal-register) web site. It also provides a preview of what will be printed in the next day's *Federal Register*.

Can I research different sections in the *Federal Register*?

Findlaw provides a table of sections such as 'Contents and Preliminary Pages' ,'Proposed Rules', 'Presidential Documents', 'Final Rules and Regulations', 'Notices', 'Sunshine Act Meetings', 'Notices', 'Reader Aids', and 'Corrections'. You can mark one or many of those sections and run the search.

What are the different research methods (access) available?

In addition to keyword, you can also run your search by Agency, for example, "department of commerce" AND encryption; by C.F.R. cite e.g. "7C.F.R. part 33"; by Page Number e.g. "page 7426", by Federal Register citation e.g. "64 FR 618" and by Table of Contents which is available from 1998 – present from the Government Printing Office web site. You can browse or search the information.

List of C.F.R. Sections Affected (LSA)

Is the *List of C.F.R. Sections Affected* (LSA) available Online?

The LSA is available from 1949 through 2000 from the HeinOnline site covering different groups of C.F.R. titles in a particular time period.

Click on 'View All' link under 'Executive Resources' from the GPO home page (www.gpoaccess.gov) to access LSA information. The U.S. Government Printing Office (GPO) published four compilations of the LSA. These compilations span the years of: 1949-63, 1964-72 (2 vols.), 1973-85 (4 vols.), and 1986-2000 (4 vols.). Each volume is organized by C.F.R. title, then by year and includes actions taken only on finalized rules with the corresponding *Federal Register* page number. The volume number appearing at the beginning of each column indicates the year (for example, 51 FR corresponds to 1986, 52 FR corresponds to 1987).

Code of Federal Regulations (C.F.R.)

Is the *Code of Federal Regulations* (C.F.R.) available on the Internet?

The *Code of Federal Regulations* volumes are available from the 1996 edition to the current edition from the GPO web site. Click on the "Browse and or Search" link on the home page for a table covering all 50 titles from 1996 through 2006. You can select a year and title by checking the appropriate boxes and running the search.

Comprehensive legal web sites such as Findlaw and Cornell provide links to C.F.R. information available from the GPO web site.

Is it possible to locate current C.F.R. information since the publication of the bound volumes without using the *List of C.F.R. Sections Affected* (LSA) to update the Federal Register?
Yes, one can use the e-CFR.

What is e-CFR?
e-CFR is a regularly updated, unofficial, non-legal edition of the *C.F.R.*, created in partnership with the Office of the Federal Register. The *Electronic Code of Federal Regulations* (e-CFR) is a prototype of a currently updated version of the *Code of Federal Regulations (C.F.R.)*. The e-CFR prototype is a demonstration project. It is not an official legal edition of the *C.F.R.*

The e-CFR prototype is authorized and maintained by the National Archives and Records Administration's (NARA) Office of the Federal Register (OFR) and the Government Printing Office (GPO). The link for the e-CFR is available at www.gpoaccess.gov under the "view all" link of the Executive Resources or on the *C.F.R.* main page, it can be found under Related Resources.

What is the daily *C.F.R.*?
The daily *C.F.R.* is also known as e-CFR.

How does the e-CFR function?
The e-CFR. consists of two linked databases: the "Current Code" and amendment files. The Office of the Federal Register (OFR) updates the Current Code database according to the effective dates of amendments published in the *Federal Register*.

As amendments become effective, the OFR integrates the changes into the Current Code database to display the full text of the currently updated *C.F.R.*

For future-effective amendments, the OFR inserts hypertext links into the affected sections or parts of the Current *Code* to take users to the pertinent amendment files. The amendment files contain amendatory instructions, the text of amendments (if any) and their effective dates. (www.gpoaccess.gov)

Can one search the e-CFR?
Currently, one can only browse title by title.

What is incorporation by reference?
Incorporation by reference is a legal process established under the Freedom of Information Act that permits federal agencies to grant legally enforceable status to certain national consensus standards and other published materials. If agencies receive the approval of the OFR, the referenced material has the same legal status

that it would have if it were published in full text in the *Federal Register* and the *C.F.R.* (www.gpoaccess.gov)

Are there any Internet sites other than the government sites where the *C.F.R.* is available in full text?

Code of Federal Regulations (*C.F.R.*) in full text is available from most of the popular online legal research systems such as LexisNexis, Westlaw, Loislaw, Versuslaw, Firstcase (www.firstcase.com) and Casemaker (www.lawriter.net). In LexisNexis the archival C.F.R. editions are available from 1981 and in Westlaw from 1984. HeinOnline (www.heinonline.org) is the only service that provides the C.F.R. from its inception in 1938 to present.

What are the research methods to access *C.F.R.* information from HeinOnline?

You can research the *C.F.R.* content by the search method as well as the browse method. The search method offers simple and advanced search methods. You can retrieve documents by using keyword, phrase search, year and also Boolean connectors.

Are there any websites that track federal regulations?

Justia (www.justia.com) offers regulation tracking information at http://regulations.justia.com . You can select, All, Rules, Adm. Orders, Notices, Proposed Rules, Executive Orders, Proclamation by agency and date.

Presidential Documents

What type of Presidential documents are available on the Internet?

The *Budget of the United States Government*, *Economic Report of the President*, Executive Orders, Proclamations, *Public Papers of the President of the United States*, State of the Union Addresses and Weekly *Compilation of Presidential Documents* are available from the GPO web site.

Where do I get presidential proclamations?

A complete list of President George Bush's proclamations from 2001 to present is available from White House web site (www.whitehouse.gov).

Where can I get *Public Papers of the Presidents of the United States*?

Public Papers of the Presidents of the United States are available from 1991 onward covering George H. W. Bush, Bill Clinton and George W. Bush from the GPO web site (www.gpoaccess.gov/pubpapers). You can search and also browse this web site.

What are the other Presidential documents available from the White House web site?
The President's weekly radio addresses, nominations, including judicial nominations, are some of the documents available from White House web site (www.whitehouse.gov).

Presidential Executive Orders

Where can I find executive orders?
The best source to find executive orders is from the National Archives and Records Administration's web site (www.archives.gov/federal-register). From the home page click on the "Executive Orders" link which will provide you three different links: Executive Orders Disposition Table; Title 3 – The President, Code of Federal Regulations and Codification of Presidential Proclamations and Executive Orders.

Executive orders of President George Bush from 2001 to present are available from White House web site (www.whitehouse.gov). Other sites, such as The American Presidency Project (www.presidency.ucsb.edu/ws/index.php contains all executive orders from 1826 to present.

What are the research methods available to retrieve executive orders?
The "Disposition Table" link provides: executive order number; date of signing by the President; *Federal Register* volume, page number, and issue date; title; amendments (if any); and current status (where applicable). Also available is an alphabetical list of the titles of Executive Orders along with corresponding EO numbers.

How far back are the executive orders available?
The executive orders are available from the NARA web site (www.archives.gov) from January 8, 1937 through the present. Other sites, such as The American Presidency Project (www.presidency.ucsb.edu/ws/index.php contain all executive orders from 1826 to present.

Where can I find local government, city codes and ordinances?
The State and Local Government on the Net (www.statelocalgov.net) site is a gateway to thousands of city and local government web site information. Another web site is www.generalcode.com.

How do I know which state law is effecting city and municipal codes?
Municode (www.municode.com) offers prepared documents concerning how the state laws affect local codes. Currently state law summaries are available for a few states.

Are there any private sites which will provide legislative and administrative updates?

State Net (www.statenet.com) delivers vital data, legislative intelligence and in-depth reporting about the actions of government. State Net monitors bills in every state, the District of Columbia and the Congress and every state agency regulation. The Center for Regulatory Effectiveness (CRE) (www.thecre.com) is a nationally recognized clearinghouse for methods to improve the federal regulatory process. CRE ensures that the public has access to data and information used to develop federal regulations, and also ensures that information which federal agencies dis-seminate to the public is of the highest quality. CRE also conducts analyses of the activities of the OMB Office of Information and Regulatory Affairs and serves as a regulatory watchdog over Executive Branch agencies.

Where do I get the information published in the *United States Government Manual*?

The electronic version of the *Government Manual* is available from National Archives and Records Administration web site (www.archives.gov)

What web sites provide federal government administrative decisions?

Administrative decisions are available from the respective agency official web sites. For example, the Federal Labor Relations Board decisions are available from its web site, (www.flrb.gov) and Federal Labor Relations Authority decisions from 1995 to present are available from the (www.flra.gov) web site. The Federal Commerce Com-mission provides decisions from 1928 through 2002 (alphabetical list) and archival information from 1996 to present through its web site, (www.fcc.gov).

Another good site for administrative decisions and actions is the University of Virginia Library web site (http://www.lib.virginia.edu/govdocs/fed_decisions_agency.html). The information is available by agency name as well as by subject.

What is the source to obtain contract cases decided by federal contract appeals boards?

Federal Contracting web site (www.wifcon.com/courtgao.htm) provides links to:
Agricultural Board of Contract Appeals
Armed Services Board of Contract Appeals
Comptroller General
Federal Aviation Administration
General Services Board of Contract Appeals
Government Printing Office Board of Contract Appeals
Small Business Administration
United States Postal Service
Veterans Affairs Board of Contract Appeals.

What administrative agency materials are available in HeinOnline?
The U.S. Federal Agency Library is a database now available. This library contains the official case law of some of the United States' most important government institutions. The initial release included titles such as *Administrative Decisions under Immigration and National Laws, Reports of the Tax Courts of the U.S., SEC Decisions*, and many more. For a list of all titles contained in the first release or for pricing information, please email them at marketing@wshein.com.

III. LEXISNEXIS

Where is the *Code of Federal Regulations* found in Lexis?
Look under Federal Legal —U.S. directory on the main page.

How far back does the *C.F.R.* appear in the historical database?
C.F.R. goes back to 1981. Under the current document, there is a link "Go to *C.F.R.* Archive Directory."

Where does one find the historical collections?
Under Federal Legal, go under View More, Archived Code of Federal Regulations.

Can I retrieve a *C.F.R.* by citation?
Under the Get a Document tab, use Get by Citation a C.F.R. citation, e.g., 29 C.F.R. 1910.15.

Are there other methods of retrieving documents from *C.F.R.*?
Under Federal Legal-U.S., there is the *Code of Federal Regulations* (C.F.R.) Titles 1 through 50 file. The *C.F.R.* can be either searched in full text of all 50 titles at one time or just the table of contents only. Or one can select an individual title and search the whole title or select individual sections within the title to search.

In addition, each title can be broken down into its individual sections for retrieval.

Does the retrieved document appear the same as in the paper version?
Lexis provides separate headings for History, Authority, and Notes with links to the related documents under each heading. It also contains the word count for the text.

How do I move onto the next section from the retrieved document?
Select 'Book Browser' function from the menu bar and then select the 'next section' button next to the citation.

Where is the *Federal Register* found in Lexis?
Look under Federal Legal —U.S. directory on the main page.

How far back does the *Federal Register* appear in the historical database?
Federal Register goes back to July 1, 1980.

Can I retrieve a *Federal Register* by citation?
Under the Get a Document tab, use Get by Citation a F.R. citation, e.g., 48 FR 9199 or 48 Fed. Reg. 9199.

Does the retrieved document appear the same as in the paper version?
Lexis provides separate headings for History, Authority, and Notes with links to the related documents under each heading. It also contains the word count for the text.

Can I research both the *C.F.R.* and *Federal Register* at the same time?
There is a *Federal Register* and *C.F.R.*, Combined file under Federal Legal —U.S.>Administrative Agency Materials.

Where can one find Executive Branch materials?
Click on View More Sources under Federal —Legal. Executive Branch Materials library appears in the right hand column.

What files can be found under Executive Branch Materials?
There are three files: Department of State Dispatch (DSTATE) from January 3, 1984 to 1999; Executive Orders (EXECOR) from July 1, 1980 to present; and Public Papers of the Presidents (PRESDC) from March 24, 1979 to present.
    The Public Papers file contains the full text of the *Weekly Compilation of Presidential Documents* and *Public Papers of the President*.

Where can one find federal administrative decisions?
There is a Federal Agency Decisions, Combined library on the front main page under Federal —Legal.

Where can one find U. S. Attorney General Opinions?
Click on View More Sources under Federal —Legal. Then click Administrative Agency Materials on lower right column to bring up a listing of various sources including a link to the U.S. Attorney General Opinions in the left column.

How far back are U. S. Attorney General opinions available?
The opinions date from 1791 to present. Opinions of the Legal Counsel from 1977 to present.

Where can one find U.S. Comptroller General Decisions?
Click on View More Sources under Federal —Legal. Then click Administrative Agency Materials on lower right column to bring up a listing of various sources including a link to the U.S. Comptroller General Decisions in the left column.

How far back are the U. S. Comptroller General decisions available?
The published decisions date from July 1921 to present; unpublished decisions date from 1951 to present.

Where can one find the individual agency decisions?
Click on View More Sources under Federal —Legal. Then click Administrative Agency Materials on lower right column to bring up a listing of various sources including a link to Individual Agency Materials. Click on this database to obtain the individual agencies. For example, files include *Agricultural Decisions*, Motor *Carrier Cases, NLRB Decisions, SEC Docket*, etc.

Can I shepardize a federal regulation (*C.F.R.* citation)?
There is a link at the top of the document next to the cite to shepardize.

Can I find the case law for a federal regulation (*C.F.R.* citation)?
There is no display of cases under each *C.F.R.* section; however, Shepard's provides case law citations.

Where can I find state administrative codes?
Under each state's files, there is a category of Statutes, Regulations, Administrative Materials, & Court Rules. The administrative code is listed by the [State Abbreviation] Administrative Code with the file name [state abbreviation ADMN], e.g., PA-Pennsylvania Administrative Code, PAADMN.

There may also be the monthly or weekly services that update the administrative code, usually called registers but may have some other name, e.g., Texas Bulletin, Pennsylvania Bulletin. In this case the file name is the state with RGST, e.g., TX BLTN, PARGST.

It is important to check to see when the Registers begin, since they will have different starting dates. The coverage may or may not be as complete as what may be available online at the official state web site.

How can I track regulations?
Lexis has files for tracking regulations as they proceed through the administrative process, e.g., [State] State Regulation Tracking file (RGALRT).

RegAlert (RGALRT) contains the text of proposed and final regulations from most of the states from November 1997 to date. The file also includes proposals, notices, adopted regulations, rules, and other information from Departments, Boards, and Commissions. Under each state, RegAlert—State from November 1997 to date.

Where can I find state attorneys-general opinions?

Each state has a file for attorneys-general opinions with different dates of coverage, Texas from 1958, Pennsylvania from 1977, etc. The file names are [state abbreviation]AG, e.g., ILAG, PAAG.

Where can I find state administrative decisions?

Under each state's files, there is a category of Statutes, Regulations, Administrative Materials, & Court Rules. If you click on "View More Sources" for the entire category, you will find all of the department/agency decisions available in Lexis in group files or individual files.

IV. WESTLAW

Where is the *Code of Federal Regulations* found in Westlaw?

Look under U.S. Federal Materials directory on the main page and then select Administrative Rules and Regulations on the subdirectory to reach the database of Code of Federal Regulations —Current Version (C.F.R.).

How far back does the *C.F.R.* go in the historical database?

C.F.R. goes back to 1984 version.

Where does one find the historical collections?

Under Federal Legal, go under Code of Federal Regulations —Historical.

Can the *Code of Federal Regulations* be accessible by subject?

Under Administrative Rules and Regulations, the *C.F.R.* can also be accessible by Organized by Area of Practice under 29 major topics, e.g. Bankruptcy (FBKR-C.F.R.), Environmental Law (FENV-C.F.R.), Taxation (FTX-C.F.R.).

Can I retrieve a *C.F.R.* citation by using the Find command?

The Find command at the top of the page or in the left margin will retrieve documents by citation, e.g., 29 C.F.R. 1910.15.

If you have a pinpoint citation to a specific part of the chapter, appendix, etc., there is a page for standard citation formats, e.g., title, part, appendix, title, part sched., etc.

What are the fields available for research?
There are seven fields available for limiting a research query:

Citation —CI()
Prelim —PR()
Caption —CA()
Text —TE()
Note —NO()
Credit —CR()
Image —IM()

Can I retrieve the table of contents for a *C.F.R.* title?
Upon selection of *C.F.R.* for research, above the search box there are links at the top of the page for the Find by Citation, Table of Contents, and RegulationsPlus Index.

Once a document is retrieved, one can obtain the Table of Contents for the Title under Full-Text Document on the left side of the screen.

How can I move from one section to another in the *C.F.R.* database?
For all retrieved documents, there are links to the previous and next sections next to the citation at the top of the page.

What is the RegulationsPlus Index?
This is a comprehensive topical index to the *C.F.R.* located under RegulationsPlus similar to the indexes prepared for annotated statutes. Besides being located at the top of the page above the search box, it will also be found in the retrieved document on the left-side under Full-Text Document.

What is ResultsPlus in searching administrative materials?
ResultsPlus provides secondary materials which cite the search terms you entered in your query.

What is RegulationsPlus for C.F.R.?
RegulationsPlus appears on the left side of the retrieved document along with KeyCite references.

It provides links to the prior versions of the document, notes of case decisions (over 600,000 citations), references to other administrative references in the *Federal Register*, statutory authority and secondary materials that provide analysis on the retrieved document.

Can I obtain case law to *C.F.R.* citations?
Under each section Westlaw provides Notes of Decisions from the courts as well as the administrative agencies.

Where is the *Federal Register* found in Westlaw?
Look under U.S. Federal Materials directory on the main page and then select Administrative Rules and Regulations on the subdirectory to reach the database Federal Register 1981-Current (FR).

How far back does the *Federal Register* appear in the historical database?
The database dates back to 1936 when the *Federal Register* began.

In searching historical documents, there are two databases available. One Federal Register Archive (FR-OLD) covers from 1936 to 1980 only. Federal Register 1936-Current (FR-ALL) covers from 1936 to the present.

Where does one find the historical collections?
Under Federal Legal, go under Code of Federal Regulations —Historical. The Federal Register is available in two databases: Federal Register 1936-Current (FR-ALL) or Federal Register Archive (1936-1980) (FR-OLD).

Is it possible to view the *Federal Register* by Table of Contents?
The daily *Federal Register* table of contents began with volume 58 (January 1993).

Is it possible to track proposed federal rules and regulations?
The Regulation Tracking —Federal (US-REGTRK) database can be found under U.S. Federal Materials —Administrative Rules & Regulations. It contains summary and status information concerning proposed and final regulations.

In addition, there is a Regulation Tracking —All States & Federal (REGTRK) database found under U.S. Federal Materials —Administrative Rules & Regulations that combines all states and federal administrative rules and regulations for tracking purposes.

Can I research the *Federal Register* on a specific subject only?
There is a link to the Federal Register Organized by Area of Practice under U.S. Federal Materials —Administrative Rules & Regulations similar to the C.F.R. database. There are currently 28 major topics, e.g. Bankruptcy (FBKR-FR), Environmental Law (FENV-FR), Taxation (FTX-FR).

Where can I find Presidential documents?
Under U.S. Federal Materials —Other Administrative & Executive Materials, there is a link to Presidential Documents (Including Executive Orders (PRES) database.

This database contains Presidential executive orders from 1936 and proclamations and reorganization plans along with other documents since 1984.

Where can I find Presidential Proclamations?
Proclamations can be found in the PRES database and the Presidential Proclamations (USCCAN —PROC) database found under U.S. Federal Materials —U.S. Code Congressional & Administrative News directory (from 1980 onwards)

Where can I find Presidential Executive Orders?
Executive orders can be found in the PRES database and the Executive Orders (USCCAN —EO) database found under U.S. Federal Materials —U.S. Code Congressional & Administrative News directory (from 1936 onwards).

Where can I find Presidential messages or signing statements?
Presidential Messages and Singing Statements database (USCCAN-MSG) is found under U.S. Federal Materials —U.S. Code Congressional & Administrative News directory (from 1986).

What other database is available for other Presidential materials?
The *Weekly Compilation of Presidential Documents* (WCPD) database contains statements, messages, and other Presidential materials issued during the previous week.

Where can one find federal administrative decisions?
Under U.S. Federal Materials directory, there is a link for Federal Administrative Decisions which has a combined database, Federal Administrative Materials All (FADMIN-ALL) database.

This database contains documents including orders, opinions, decisions, policy statements, announcements, adjudications, releases, administrative actions, letter rulings, and no action letters prepared by the agency.

Where can one find the individual agency decisions?
Under U.S. Federal Materials directory, there is a link to Federal Administrative Decisions which leads to the individual agencies' decisions that are available.

Does each agency have its own starting date for its decisions?
Each library has its own starting date of decisions which may or may not be comprehensive back to the first volume.

Are attorneys-general opinions available?
Under Federal Administrative Decisions, there is a link to a database Attorney General Opinions at the end of the list that contains the U. S. Attorneys-General opinions (USAG)and all fifty states, e.g., AL-AG, CA-AG, NY-AG.

What types of documents are included in the Other Administrative & Executive Materials link found under U.S. Federal Materials?

There are several databases containing decisions of agencies or general information, e. g. Comptroller General Decisions (CG), Freedom of Information Guide (FOIA-Guide), Supreme Court Nominee Confirmation Hearings (SCT-CONFIRM), *U.S. Attorneys Manual* (USAM), etc.

Where can I find state administrative codes?

Under each state's databases, there is a category for Administrative & Executive Materials. The state's administrative code is a database, [state]-ADC, e.g., Pennsylvania Administrative Code (PA-ADC). In some states there may be current versions and older editions also available, e.g., California, Ohio.

There may also be the monthly or weekly services that update the administrative code, usually called registers but may have some other name, e.g., Texas Administrative Register, Pennsylvania Bulletin. In this case the file name is the state with ADR, e.g., TX-ADR, PA-ADR.

How can I track regulations?

Westlaw has two databases for tracking regulations, one for current regulations from Net Scan and one from State Net for previous years regulations, e.g., Ohio Regulation Tracking (OH-REGTRK) and Ohio State Tracking —Full Text —State Net (OH-STN-REGTXT). In some states, the tracking and full-text regulation databases are combined, e.g., New Jersey Regulation and Text Combined (NJ-REG-NET) contain the NJ-REGTRK, NJ-REGTXT together.

Where can I find state attorneys-general opinions?

Under each state's databases, there is a category for Administrative & Executive Materials. There is a database for the Attorneys-General Opinions, e.g., CA-AG, PA-AG. Coverage begins in 1977 to the present.

Where can I find state administrative decisions?

Under each state's databases, there is a category of Administrative & Executive Materials where one will find all of the department/agency decisions available in group files or individual files. Some files are grouped into folders that have more individual files for the subject under consideration, New Jersey has folders for Regulatory Insurance, Labor and Employment, and Securities Law.

CHAPTER 10

COURT RULES

Introduction: Courts issue two types of rules: one deals with conducting business in the courts, sometimes referred to as internal operating procedures, e.g., hours of operations, how to file court documents, etc. The second type deals with procedure according to the type of case being filed in court, such as civil, criminal, appellate, and evidence rules. Federal, state, and local courts contain their own rules, most of which today are published on the internet and commercial web sites. This chapter reviews the various types of federal and state rules and their sources.

I. MANUAL

What are court rules?
Court rules provide for the regulation of proceedings in court. Rules can deal with the business of the courts and procedural rules.

How are court rules created?
Legislatures create rules through statutory law or courts create rules through the issuance of rules.

How are rules created on the federal level?
Courts create rules under the Rules Enabling Act, 28 U.S.C. §2072 provided that they do not "abridge, enlarge, or modify any substantive right."

What are the different types of federal rules of procedure?
The rules are appellate, bankruptcy, civil, criminal, and evidence.

When were the rules first created?
The first rules created were the Federal Rules of Civil Procedure in 1938, followed by Criminal Procedure in 1946, Appellate Procedure in 1968, Bankruptcy in 1964, and Evidence in 1975.

Where are federal rules published?
They are published in the *United States Code* and its annotated versions in *United States Code Annotated* and *United States Code Service*.

What court rules can be found in the *U.S.C.A.* and *U.S.C.S.*?
United States Supreme Court
United States Courts of Appeal
U.S. Court of Federal Claims
Court of International Trade

Where can one find U. S. Supreme Court rules?
The rules are available in both *U.S.C.A.* and *U.S.C.S.*, individual pamphlets or from the court's web site, at http://www.supremecourtus.gov.

Where can one find U. S. Courts of Appeals rules?
The rules are available in both *U.S.C.A.* and *U.S.C.S.*, individual pamphlets, federal rules of court published with the state rules (in one volume or separate volumes), or each court's web site.

Where can one find U. S. District Court rules?
The rules are available in *Federal Local Court Rules* (West) (KF8816 A2), individual pamphlets, federal rules of court published with the state rules (in one volume or separate volumes), or each court's web site.

What titles does West publish for federal court rules for individual states?
[state name] *Rules of Court: Federal*. In some states the state rules and federal rules may be found in one volume.

What are the other materials you find in the Federal Court Rules books?
You will find the local rules of the United States District Courts, including civil rules, criminal rules, general and calendar rules, admiralty rules, magistrate judge rules, and other supplemental rules and procedures. Also found are the rules of the United States Courts of Appeals and the internal operating procedures of the United States Courts of Appeals.

Are there legislative histories for the court rules?
Rules committees post commentaries on the rules as notes after each rule.

Where can one find court cases on the Federal Rules?

Federal Rules Decisions (FRD) (KF8830 W47) from West publishes court cases on Federal rules of appellate, civil and criminal procedure. Cases are published chronologically in order.

Federal Rules Service (West) (KF8830.1 F43) publishes court cases on civil procedure by rules number. There is a digest that cumulates the cases by Rule number.

U.S.C.A. and *U.S.C.S.* provide annotated editions of the U.S. Supreme Court, U.S. Circuit Courts of Appeal, Claims Court, Court of International Trade, Federal Rules of Appellate, Bankruptcy, Civil, Criminal, and Evidence.

Where can one find court cases on Federal Rules of Evidence?

Federal Rules of Evidence Service (West) (KF8935 F4) publishes evidence cases chronologically in order. There is a digest that cumulates the cases by Rule number.

What digests are available for court rules?

West's digest system includes procedural rules from pre-trial to post-trial procedure under each topic.

Federal Rules Service contains digest of cases.

Federal Rules of Evidence Service contains digest of cases.

Are there citators for court rules?

There are two Shepard's titles: *Shepard's Federal Rules Citations* and *Shepard's Evidence Citations*.

Both Shepards and KeyCite contain court rules.

What are the standard treatises on federal rules?

The two major multivolume treaties are *Wright and Miller's on Federal Practice and Procedure* (West) (KF8840 W68) and *Moore's Federal Practice* (Bender) (KF8820 A313M6323) both covering appellate, civil, criminal, and evidence rules. Single topic treatises include *Weinstein on Evidence* (Bender) (KF8935 W4), Louisell, *Federal Evidence* (West) (KF8935 L6), and *Orfield's Federal Rules of Criminal Procedure* (West) (KF9619 07).

What is the standard work on appellate procedure before the United States Supreme Court?

Eugene Gressman et al. *Supreme Court Practice: for Practice in the Supreme Court of the United States* (9th ed. BNA, 2007) (KF9057 S8)

Are federal and state court rules the same?

No. The state rules are of the same topics —appellate, civil, criminal, and evidence —which may or may not be the same as the federal rules. In many jurisdictions, they may follow the same order but be different in context. Many states have adopted the Federal Rules of Evidence, for instance, but may have some variations within specific rules.

Who publishes state court rules?

Both West and Lexis publish Rules of Court containing both state and federal rules for each jurisdiction that they publish annotated codes.

What court rules are generally found in the state court rules books?

State appellate court rules, internal operating procedures for each court, rules of procedure, judicial administration, model rules of professional conduct, continuing legal education, bar admissions rules, and local rules.

Where can one find court cases on the state rules?

Cases on the state rules can be found in the rules volumes of the state annotated code.

Who publishes treatise material on state court rules?

West Group publishes State Practice Series that may incorporate volumes on procedure. They can also be found in state encyclopedias.

Continuing Legal Education providers have seminars on all types of procedure.

Can you find state and local rules in the citators?

State rules can be found in the Shepard's state citators. Local rules will depend on the citator.

How do I find cases on court rules if not in the citators?

Do a full-text search in Lexis or Westlaw Rules databases.

II. INTERNET

Where can I find court rules online?

Generally the rules of a court are posted on the court's official web site. However, a majority of the comprehensive legal web sites also provide links to court rules. For example, LLRX (www.llrx.com) provides user friendly links to court rules (general and local) as well as procedural rules.

What websites provide links to the court rules?

Administrative Office of the Courts (www.uscourts.gov/rules), Findlaw (www.findlaw.com), Legal Information Institute (www.law.cornell.edu), and Law Library Resources Xchange, www.llrx.com provide links to court rules.

III. LEXISNEXIS

Where can I find a comprehensive federal database for Federal Rules?

Under Federal Legal —U.S., there is a combined file of United States Code Service, U.S.C.S. —Federal Rules Annotated (RULES). The file contains U.S. Supreme Court, Circuit Courts, District Courts, specialty courts (e.g., court of international trade), etc.

Where can I find United States Supreme Court rules?

United States Supreme Court Rules (SUPRUL) can be found as part of the U.S.C.S. files under Federal Legal —U.S., Court Rules, Individual Circuit Rules.

Where can I find United States Circuit Courts of Appeals rules?

The rules of the 13 circuits can be found in the U.S.C.S. —Court of Appeals —All Circuits (CIRRUL) file under Federal Legal —U.S., Court Rules.

The individual circuits can be found in single files under Federal Legal —U.S., Court Rules, Individual Circuit Rules, e.g., First Circuit (1CRUL), Second Circuit (2CRUL), etc.

Where can I find United States District Court Rules?

Federal Local Trial Court Rules, Combined (LFDBRC) under Federal Legal —U.S., Court Rules is a combined file for all federal district courts.

Individual Federal Trial Court Rules file under Federal Legal —U.S., Court Rules, contains the individual rules listed by state, e.g., AKFRUL, CAFRUL, etc.

Where can I find United States Bankruptcy Court Rules?

The bankruptcy court rules are in the same files as the local district courts: Individual Federal Trial Court Rules file under Federal Legal —U.S., Court Rules, contains the individual rules listed by state, e.g., AKFRUL, CAFRUL, etc.

Where can I find Federal Rules of Civil Procedure?

U.S.C.S. Federal Rules of Civil Procedure (FRCP) can be found under Federal Legal —U.S., Court Rules, Individual Circuit Rules.

Where can I find Federal Rules of Criminal Procedure?

U.S.C.S. Federal Rules of Criminal Procedure (FRCRP) can be found under Federal Legal —U.S., Court Rules, Individual Circuit Rules.

Where can I find Federal Rules of Appellate Procedure?

U.S.C.S. Federal Rules of Appellate Procedure (FRAP) can be found under Federal Legal —U.S., Court Rules, Individual Circuit Rules.

Where can I find Federal Rules of Evidence?

U.S.C.S. Federal Rules of Evidence (FRE) can be found under Federal Legal —U.S., Court Rules, Individual Circuit Rules.

Where can I find Federal Rules of Bankruptcy?

U.S.C.S. Bankruptcy Rules and Official Bankruptcy Forms (BKRULE) contains the combined federal bankruptcy rules for all districts and the official set of forms.

It is also possible to use the LEXSTAT command to retrieve a specific document, e.g., U.S. bankr r 1002.

Where can I find state court rules?

Each state has a file for all state and federal rules together in one file, e.g., under Pennsylvania, Find Statutes, Regulations, Administrative Materials & Court Rules, PA —State & Federal Court Rules (PARULE).

Where can I find state trial court rules?

Each state has a file for state trial court rules for its jurisdictions (districts, circuits, counties, etc.), e.g., under Pennsylvania, Find Statutes, Regulations, Administrative Materials & Court Rules, PA —Pennsylvania Local Rules of Court (PALRUL).

Each county is listed individually for all of its local rules. The file(s) can be searched in the query box or just within the table of contents. It is also possible to use the table of contents and break each part into its individual rule numbers.

The *Pennsylvania Bulletin* (PARGST) contains proposed and final rules from October 1, 1994 to present.

IV. WESTLAW

Where can I retrieve specific court rules by citation?

Using the Find command, type "frcp rule," "frcrp rule," "frap rule," or "fre rule," followed by the number of the rule.

Where can I find a comprehensive federal database for Federal Rules?
Under All Databases, U.S. Federal Materials, Court Rules and Orders , there is a combined file of United States Code Annotated —Federal Rules (USRULES). The file contains U.S. Supreme Court, Circuit Courts, District Courts, specialty courts (e.g., court of international trade), etc.

The Federal Rules Update Orders (US-RULESUPDATES) contains court orders that updates the Federal court rules that can be found in US-RULES.

Where can I find United States Supreme Court rules?
United Supreme Court Rules can be found as part of the Federal Rules database (US-RULES).

Where can I find United States Circuit Courts of Appeals rules?
The rules of the 13 circuits can be found in the US-RULES database.

They are also available under each state's Rules database, e.g., NY-RULES, PA-RULES.

Where can I find United States District Court Rules?
State Court Rules (RULES-ALL) under U. S. Federal Materials, Court Rules is a combined file for all district and bankruptcy courts.

They are also available under the individual state rules databases, e.g., CA-RULES, PA-RULES, etc.

Individual Federal Court Rules are in a folder called Local Federal Court Rules by State folder under Court Rules & Orders, e.g., CA-TRIAL RULES, NY-TRIAL RULES, etc.

Where can I find United States Bankruptcy Court Rules?
The bankruptcy court rules are in the same files as the local district courts: State Court Rules (RULES-ALL) under U. S. Federal Materials, Court Rules & Orders is a combined file for all district and bankruptcy courts.

Individual Federal Trial Court Rules is in a folder Local Federal Court Rules by State under U.S. Federal Materials, Court Rules & Orders, e.g., AL-RULES, CA-RULES, etc.

Where can I find a database for updated state district court rules?
The Federal Rules Update Orders (US-RULESUPDATES) database contains court orders that updates the Federal court rules can be found in US-RULES database.

Local Federal Court Orders by State folder under U.S. Federal Materials, Court Rules & Orders, contains the individual state rules update orders, e.g., AL-RULE-SUPDATES, NY-RULESUPDATES, etc.

Where can I find Federal Rules of Civil Procedure?
Federal Rules of Civil Procedure can be found under the US-RULES database under U.S. Federal Materials, Court Rules & Orders.

Where can I find Federal Rules of Criminal Procedure?
Federal Rules of Criminal Procedure can be found under the US-RULES database under U.S. Federal Materials, Court Rules & Orders.

Federal Rules of Criminal Procedure is part of the Federal Criminal Justice-Rules (FCJ-RULES) database found under U.S. Federal Materials, Court Rules. The database also contains Rules for the Trials of Misdemeanors before U.S. Magistrates and habeas corpus proceedings under 28 U.S.C. §§ 2254 and 2255.

Where can I find Federal Rules of Appellate Procedure?
Federal Rules of Appellate Procedure can be found under the US-RULES database under U.S. Federal Materials, Court Rules & Orders.

Where can I find Federal Rules of Evidence?
Federal Rules of Evidence can be found under the US-RULES database under U.S. Federal Materials, Court Rules & Orders.

Where can I find Federal Rules of Bankruptcy?
U.S.C.A. Bankruptcy Rules (FBKR-RULES) contains the combined federal bankruptcy rules and official forms for all districts.

What can I find in the *Federal Rules Decisions*?
There is a combined database for cases and articles published in the Federal Rules Decisions, e.g., Federal Rules Decisions Multibase (FRD).

There is a database for articles published in the Federal Rules Decisions, Federal Rules Decisions —Articles (FRD-ART).

There is a database for cases published in the Federal Rules Decisions, Federal Rules Decisions Cases (FRD-CS).

There is a database for rules published in Federal Rules Decisions, Federal Rules Decisions Rules (FRD-RULES). It contains the five types of rules: appellate, bankruptcy, civil, criminal and evidence.

Are there other databases for specialty courts?
U. S. Court of International Trade under Federal International Law Rules (FINT-RULES), Federal Military Rules (FMIL-RULES), U. S. Securities & Exchange Commission Rules (FSEC-RULES), and U. S. Tax Court (FTX-RULES).

Is there coverage of the advisory committees to the Judicial Conference of the United States?
The Federal Rules of Practice & Procedure Advisory Committee Minutes database (US-RULESCOMM) contains all five rules committees' minutes reported to the Judicial Conference of the United States.

Is there a treatise available on the Federal Rules?
Under Court Rules & Orders, *Wright and Miller on Federal Practice and Procedure* (FPP) is a multivolume treatise that covers all procedural rules.

Where can I find state court rules?
There is a combined database for all state court rules (Rules —ALL).

Each state has a file for all state and federal local rules in one file that can be found under Court Rules & Orders, Court Rules —Individual State and U. S. Jurisdictions, e.g., California Rules (CA-RULES) Pennsylvania Rules (PA-RULES).

State Rules of Criminal Procedure can be found under Courts & Orders, Court Rules —Topical folder. Each state is listed, e.g., Criminal Justice —Alabama Court Rules (ALCJ-RULES), Criminal Justice-Arizona Court Rules (ARCJ-RULES), etc.

Where can I find state trial court rules?
Ten states have state trial court rules that can be found under Court Rules & Orders, Court Rules —Individual State and U. S. Jurisdictions, e.g., Florida State Trial Court Rules (FL-TRIAL RULES), Pennsylvania State Trial Court Rules (PA-TRIALRULES).

Where can I find state rules updates for court orders?
There is a combined database called State Rules Updates Orders (RULESUPDATES-ALL) for all state courts under Court Rules & Orders,

There is also a folder called Court Orders —Individual States under Court Rules & Orders that contains the individual state databases, e.g., Alabama Rules Update Orders (AL-RULESUPDATES).

CHAPTER 11

SECONDARY MATERIALS

Introduction: Secondary sources provide the researcher with a variety of resources to find and interpret primary sources. This chapter reviews a wide range of secondary sources including dictionaries, encyclopedias, looseleaf services, ALR annotations, legal periodicals, newsletters, and newspapers, Restatements of the Law, and treatises (nutshells, hornbooks, multivolume works, and CLE materials).

I. MANUAL

What are secondary materials?

Secondary materials help find and interpret primary sources.

What are the functions of secondary materials?

Secondary sources help to explain the law, criticize the law, propose new ideas of law, develop legal history and theory, and lead to primary sources which are available in the text and footnote references of the secondary materials.

What are the types of the secondary materials?

There are a large number of secondary sources including encyclopedias, legal periodicals, legal newspapers, legal newsletters, dictionaries, ALR annotations, *Restatements of the Law*, looseleaf services, and treatises. Digests and citators are sometimes considered tertiary sources because they help locate both primary and secondary sources.

Can I cite to secondary materials in my briefs?

Yes, secondary sources can be cited.

DICTIONARIES

What are legal dictionaries?

A legal dictionary contains the definitions of legal words and phrases. *Black's Law Dictionary* (9th ed. 2009) (KF156 B532) is the most popular law dictionary. There are various other law dictionaries available.

Do I have to have a legal dictionary?

Yes. Unlike the general English language dictionaries the law dictionaries provide citations to primary authority such as cases at the end of the definitions

What are the popular legal dictionaries?

Black's Law Dictionary, Ballantine's Law Dictionary (KF156 B3).

Are there any multi-volume legal dictionaries?

West publishes a multivolume set called *Words and Phrases* (KF156 W6712).

Where can one find definition of words or phrases in secondary legal sources?

West Digest System contains multivolumes of Words and Phrases in the *West's Federal Digest* series and in each state digest.

How many words are in the *Black's Law Dictionary*?

There are more than 30,000 words.

Who is the publisher for *Black's Law Dictionary*?

Started by Henry Campbell Black in 1891 the present 9th edition of *Black's Law Dictionary* is published by West Group of Thomson.

Are there any other legal publications cited along with the definitions in *Black's Law Dictionary*?

The 8th edition cites more than 10,000 citations to key numbers and to the *C.J.S.* legal encyclopedia.

Where can I find legal maxims?

Legal Maxims are available in the *Black's Law Dictionary* in the appendix.

Does *Black's Law Dictionary* have a thumb index?

The Deluxe Edition of *Black's Law Dictionary* has a thumb index.

What are the other important information materials available in the *Black's Law Dictionary*?

Yow will find the full texts of the United States Constitution; Universal Declaration of Human Rights; Time chart of the United States Supreme Court; Federal Circuit Court map and a table of British Regnal years.

Is there any specialty legal dictionaries?

Sloane-Dorland Annotated Medical Dictionary (RA1017 S56) contains medical definitions along with references to court cases on the definition.

When did legal dictionaries begin?

Law dictionaries date back to the sixteenth century with the publication of Rastell's *Laws of Terms*. Other important legal dictionaries include *Cowell's Interpreter* (1607), *Jacob's Law Dictionary* (1759), and more recently, *Bouvier's Law Dictionary* (3d ed. 1914).

Are legal quotations available in legal dictionaries?

Legal quotations can be found in some dictionaries.

Is there any thesaurus dealing with legal terms?

Burton's Legal Thesaurus (KF156 B856) is the single thesaurus available for synonyms.

Is there a source to define legal abbreviations?

Bieber's Dictionary of Legal Citations provides citations to more than 21,000 abbreviations.

What is *Prince's Dictionary of Legal Citations*?

Prince's Dictionary of Legal Citations is the name of the current edition of the work originally compiled by Doris Bieber. This work is published by W. S. Hein & Co.

ENCYCLOPEDIAS

What are legal encyclopedias?

A legal encyclopedia provides a useful introduction to the law of a jurisdiction, usually federal or state level.

What are the popular legal encyclopedias?

Currently, Thomson/West publishes two general law encyclopedias,
   American Jurisprudence 2d (KF154) and *Corpus Juris Secundum* (KF154).

When were *Corpus Juris* (*C.J.*) and *Corpus Juris Secondum* (*C.J.S.*) published?
Corpus Juris was published between 1914 to 1937; *Corpus Juris Secundum* dates from 1936 to the present.

When were *American Jurisprudence* (*Am. Jur.*) and *American Jurisprudence Second* (*Am. Jur. 2d*) published?
Am Jur was published between 1936 to 1948; *Am Jur 2d* dates from 1962 to the present.

How often is the information updated?
There are annual pocket parts for each volume. The volumes on the topic of taxation are revised each year.

How many topics are covered in *C.J.S.* and *Am. Jur 2d*?
There are a little more than 400 subject matter areas. *C.J.S.* calls these subject matter discussions "Titles" and *Am. Jur. 2d* calls them "Topics".

How is the information organized in *C.J.S.* and *Am. Jur. 2d.*?
Both encyclopedias contain hundreds of topics arranged alphabetically. Each topic is subdivided into subtopics, identified by section/paragraph numbers.

What information do you get by using the index to *C.J.S.* and *Am. Jur. 2d.*?
All subjects contained in the text can be found in the index by subject and section number.

Are there any other comprehensive legal encyclopedias other than *C.J.S.* and *Am. Jur. 2d*?
There are some other encyclopedias that are not as detailed in legal terminology and more for general public. They include such titles as *Gale Encyclopedia of Everyday Law*, *The Guide to American Law* (12 v.) and *Encyclopedia of the American Judicial System* (3 v.) to name a few.

Are there any state law encyclopedias?
Not every state has an encyclopedia. Lexis covers California, Florida, Pennsylvania, Texas, Virginia, and West Virginia. West covers Illinois, Maryland, and Massachusetts.

Who are the publishers for *C.J.S.* and *Am. Jur. 2d*?
Currently, West Group publishes both encyclopedias.

How do I find the information in both encyclopedias?

Both encyclopedias have multivolume paperback indexes revised each year.

Which one is the better between *C.J.S.* and *Am. Jur. 2d*?

C.J.S. provides more case law, while *Am. Jur.2d* provides more statutory references and ALR annotations. Recent volumes of *C.J.S.* provides lesser number of case law references substituted instead to the headnotes of the West Digest System.

Are there any legal subject specific encyclopedias other than these general encyclopedias?

There are some large treatises that are considered similar to encyclopedias, e.g., *Appleman on Insurance* (KF1164 A76), *Federal Procedure, L.Ed.* (KF8716.4 F4).

LOOSELEAF SERVICES

What are looseleaf services?

Looseleaf services contain primary sources on specific legal topics from federal and/or state materials including statutory law, case law, and administrative regulations. These materials are updated weekly, biweekly, monthly, quarterly basis. There are a limited number of titles that are updated daily.

How are the services updated?

Certain services are updated on a weekly, biweekly, monthly, and quarterly basis.

Who are the major looseleaf publishers?

Bureau of National Affairs (BNA), Commerce Clearing House (CCH), and Research Institute of America (RIA).

Who uses looseleaf services?

Lawyers who specialize in a particular field will use a looseleaf service to keep themselves up to date on developments in a particular field of law.

What are some of the most popular looseleaf services?

ABA/BNA Professional Responsibility (ABA) (KF305 A8A23)
Antitrust and Trade Regulation Report (BNA) (KF1632 B58)
Bankruptcy Law Reporter (BNA) (KF1507 B63)
The Criminal Law Reporter (BNA) (KF9615 C7)
Employment Coordinator (RIA) (KF3315 E472)

Environmental Reporter (BNA) (KF3775 A6E49)
Family Law Reporter (BNA) (KF501 A3F3)
Federal Tax Coordinator (RIA) (KF6272)
Labor Relations Reporter (BNA) (KF3315)
Labor Law Reporter (CCH) (KF3315 L3)
Standard Federal Tax Reporter (CCH) (KF6285 C67)
Tax Management Portfolios (BNA) (KF6289 A1T35)
U. S. Tax Reporter (RIA) (KF6285 R47U58)

TREATISES

What are legal treatises?

A treatise is a single or multivolume work on a specific subject. Treatises may be monographs with no updating or may have pocket parts or looseleaf format for updating.

How do I find them in the library?

The treatise collection is usually cataloged under the Library of Congress Classification System K system.

How are legal books arranged in the library?

American legal books are classified under KF according to the Library of Congress Classification system that arranges subjects from KF1 to KF9999.

For example legal research is KF240s, torts is KF1250s, bankruptcy is KF1515-1530, constitutional law is KF4500-4900s, and tax is KF6400 to KF6775, etc.

What are the general types of legal books?

Nutshells, hornbooks, single and multivolume treatises, Continuing Legal Education materials.

What are Nutshells?

West's Nutshell Series is more than 135 individual titles written by academic law professors. There is now a competing series called Turning Points from Foundation Press.

Several of the Nutshell titles include the topics of admiralty, Appellate Advocacy, Bankruptcy and Related Law, Constitutional Law, Contracts, Criminal Law, Criminal Procedure-Constitutional Limitations, Elder Law, Environmental Law, Family Law, Federal Income Taxation of Individuals, Immigration Law and Procedure,

Landlord and Tenant Law, Legal Ethics, Mass Communications, Oil and Gas, Products Liability, Securities Regulation, Torts, Uniform Commercial Code, Workers'. Compensation and Employee Protection Laws in a Nutshell.

What are Hornbooks?

West's Hornbook Series contains individual titles (up to 4 volumes long) on specific topics. The authors may also be the authors of the nutshell series. Some of the more published titles are on admiralty and maritime law, constitutional law, corporate income tax, evidence, legal research (how to find the law), securities regulations, torts, trusts, uniform commercial code, and UCC secured transactions,

Hornbooks began as introductory works for the students, but many individual titles are now published in a Practitioner's Edition. In addition, West has begun to publish the Concise Hornbook Series consisting of single volumes that are even shorter than the regular hornbooks.

What is the Understanding Series?

Matthew Bender publishes more than forty titles in its Understanding Series for an introduction to various topics: administrative law, bankruptcy, civil procedure, conflict of laws, criminal law, criminal procedure, juvenile law, labor law, secured transactions, securities law, and trusts and estates.

What are Casebooks?

A casebook is the textbook written by law school professors used in law school courses containing cases that students will study to learn about a specific topic. West, Foundation, Lexis, Aspen and other publishers have casebooks.

What are CLE publications?

CLE stands for Continuing Legal Education. In most states, there is an obligation upon lawyers to attend a certain amount of continuing education courses and report their attendance to a court-related office. CLE publications are the single/multivolume publication of the seminars.

Who are the major publishers for CLE materials?

The American Bar Association-American Law Institute (ALI-ABA), National Institute for Trial Advocacy (NITA), and Practising Law Institute (PLI).

What are the Practising Law Institute's series?

The Practising Law Institute publishes approximately 150 titles each year organized under the following series: Bankruptcy, Corporations, Intellectual Property, Litigation, Real Property, Tax and Estates.

Are there state publications for CLE?

On the state level, many of the states have their own CLE publishers, e.g., California Continuing Education Board, Pennsylvania Bar Institute, etc. National Business Institute, Lorman Publishers, and Professional Education Systems Inc. offer state-specific seminars for all fifty states.

RESTATEMENTS OF THE LAW

What are *Restatements of the Law*?

This is a series of books created by the members of the American Law Institute (ALI).

What is the American Law Institute?

ALI began in 1923 in Philadelphia as a professional organization of law professors, judges, and lawyers who attempt to compile various titles on specific topics to describe the common law at the time the volumes are written. There are approximately 2,500 members of the Institute.

Are *Restatements* available for every legal topic?

No. The current list is: Agency 2d, Conflicts of Laws 2d, Contracts 2d, Foreign Relations Law of the United States 3d, Judgments 2d, Law Governing Lawyers 3d, Property 1st, Property 2d Landlord and Tenant, Property 2d Donative Transfers, Property 3d Wills and Other Donative Transfers, Property 3d Mortgages, Property 3d Mortgages, Property 3d Servitude, Restitution 1st , Suretyship and Guaranty 2d, Torts 2d, Torts 3d Apportionment of Liability, and Torts 3d Products Liability, Trusts 2d, Trusts 3d Prudent Investor Rule, Unfair Competition 3d. (KF395 or each title under its individual call number)

How many series are there?

The first series began in the 1940s; the second series covers from 1960s to present; third series covers from 1990s to present. As new titles are added, they are published in the 3d series.

How much time does it take to publish titles in the Restatements?

The number of years for each title will vary from topic to topic, e.g., Restatement of Torts 2d took fourteen years.

How is a title produced?

Specialists in each area have a committee headed by a reporter. The committee creates tentative drafts, proposed official drafts, final drafts, and then when completed, final bound volumes. Each draft has to be approved by the members of the Institute.

How are the *Restatement* volumes organized?
Each topic is broken down into points of law listed in bold print. It is followed by reporter's notes, illustrations, and case digests.

How are the volumes updated?
The volumes are updated annually with pocket parts or supplementary pamphlets.

Where can I find the case law to the *Restatements*?
Case law references can be found in the appendices of the Second Series. In the Third Series titles, case law digests are found under each section.

How do I know what states follow the *Restatements*?
Information on states following the Restatements can be found in the indexes to the volumes where citations to state statutory law can be found. One can also search a particular Restatement citation in the caselaw databases of Lexis and Westlaw to find any cases citing to the Restatements.

Are there any indexes to the *Restatements*?
There is a single volume general index to the first series of *Restatements*. The second and third series have indexes at the end of each title.

LEGAL PERIODICALS

What are the types of legal periodicals?
Law school publications, bar association publications, specialty organization periodicals, and private publisher journals.

What are the law reviews?
All law schools publish at least one law review of general subjects as well as specialty subjects, e.g., international law, taxation, gender, criminal law, etc. Harvard Law School, for instance, has thirteen law reviews.

Are there any subject oriented legal periodicals?
There are hundreds of subject periodicals covering such topics as international law, women and gender, criminal law, taxation, property law, etc.

What are student-run law reviews?
The students are organized in their second and third years. There is an editor-in-chief, articles, comments, case notes, book review editors; business manager, production editors, student cite checkers. There are usually one or two faculty who serve as advisors, but the work is done by the students.

What are faculty-run law reviews?
Faculty actually do all of the work in selection, editing, and publishing of the reviews, e.g., *Supreme Court Review* of the University of Chicago Law School.

What are bar association publications?
National organizations, like the American Bar Association, state, regional, and local bar associations publish journals monthly, bimonthly, quarterly, semiannual or annually. The articles are shorter, little or no footnotes compared to law reviews, and are on current topics including changes in the law, law office practice, regular columns on writing, ethics, and other topics.

What is the leading national bar association called?
American Bar Association

What is the periodical called that it publishes?
American Bar Association Journal or *ABA Journal*.

How is the American Bar Association organized?
It is organized by divisions, sections, committees, special committees, task forces, etc.

What are the divisions of the ABA?
Division for Bar Services
Division for Judicial Services
Division for Public Education
Division for Public Services
Division of Media Relations and Communication Services
General Practice, Solo and Small Firm Division
Law School Division
Senior Lawyers Division
Young Lawyers Division

What are the sections of the ABA?
Section of Administrative Law and Regulatory Practice
Section of Antitrust Law

Section of Corporation, Banking and Business Law
Section of Criminal Justice
Section of Dispute Resolution
Section of Economics of Law Practice
Section of Environment, Energy, and Resources
Section of Family Law
Section of General Practice
Section of Individual Rights And Responsibilities
Section of Insurance, Negligence and Compensation Law
Section of Intellectual Property
Section of International Law
Section of Labor and Employment Law
Section of Law Practice Management
Section of Legal Education and Admissions to the Bar
Section of Litigation
Section of Mineral and Natural Resources Law
Section of Public Contract Law
Section of Public Utility Law
Section of Real Property, Probate and Trust Law
Section of Science and Technology
Section of State and Local Government
Section of Taxation
Section of Tort Trial and Insurance Practice

Does each state have a bar association?
Yes, all states have state bar associations as well as many counties and even cities.

Are there any other national bar associations?
Yes, National Bar Association for African-American lawyers and The Federal Bar Association for lawyers who practice in the federal courts.

What are the specialty-organization periodicals?
Various legal organizations sponsor law periodicals similar to the law reviews. The reviews may be associated with an academic law school for student assisting. American Society for Legal History publishes *Law and History Review*, American Society of International Law publishes *American Journal of International Law*, and American Society for Law and Medicine publishes *American Journal of Law and Medicine*.

What are commercial vendor periodicals?

Publishers like Matthew Bender, Warren Gorham & Lamont, Aspen, etc. publish periodicals that are oriented towards the practicing bar, e.g., *Journal of Taxation*, *Journal of Corporations*. These periodicals are published several times a year to keep the reader up on new developments in their field.

Who contributes the articles to law reviews?

Judges, law professors, attorneys, other academic professionals, and law students write articles.

What types of articles are generally published in law reviews?

Any topic can be written on for a law review from strictly legal topics to interdisciplinary articles dealing with sciences, social sciences, mathematics, languages, etc.

Do students also contribute to law reviews?

Second and third year students write comments on a topic that is broader than just one case; first year students write case notes or recent decisions upon one specific case from either a federal or state court. Law Reviews can publish articles written by students as well, but they probably are from schools other than which the law review is published.

How do I recognize an article written by students in the law reviews?

Generally the student written articles are published under the headings such as: Notes; Comments; Case Comments; Recent Developments; Surveys. The student name will appear at the end of the article.

What is a symposium issue in a periodical?

Many periodicals offer symposium issues in which there are at least two to ten articles published on a specific subject, e.g., symposium on the European Union or last year's U.S. Supreme Court cases.

How do book reviews differ from book reviews in other academic periodicals?

Law review book reviews are generally much longer (can be more than 20 pages long) compared to half page-full page reviews in academic reviews. Generally, there are fewer book reviews published in law reviews. *Michigan Law Review* dedicates one issue a year to just law reviews.

How do I track the articles published in law reviews?

Periodical indexes and citators provide references to periodicals.

What published paper indexes are available?
Index to Legal Periodicals and Books (*ILPB*) (K33 I534) and *Current Law Index* (*CLI*) (K33 C37).

Do both *ILPB* and *CLI* cover the same time period?
ILPB dates back to 1908, while *CLI* began in 1980.

How many periodical titles are indexed in *ILPB* and *CLI*?
There are more than 600 in *ILPB* and more than 1,000 in *CLI*.

How are the *ILPB* and *CLI* arranged?
Both have author/subject indexes, statutes, cases, and book reviews by author. *CLI* also has a title index that *ILPB* does not have. The *ILPB* also contains references to new books along with the periodical titles.

How are the two indexes kept up to date?
Both have monthly paperback advance sheets that cumulate quarterly and an annual bound volume. Before 1980, the *Index to Legal Periodicals* has three-year cumulative volumes, e.g., September 1976-August 1979.

Are there any other periodical indexes available?
Current Index to Legal Periodicals (*CILP*) is published weekly by the University of Washington Gallagher Law Library. Each issue has between twenty and forty titles indexed by subject and by table of contents of each issue.

Index to Periodical Articles Related to Law (1958-) publishes law-related articles from non-legal periodicals and magazines.

What is the *Jones-Chipman Index to Legal Periodical Literature*?
Leonard Jones and Frank Chipman, An *Index to Legal Periodical Literature* (published between 1888-1937) is a five-volume periodical index of legal periodicals covering from the early nineteenth century to 1930.

What is *Legal Resources Index (LRI)*?
This is the online version of the *Current Law Index*. It is a cumulative index from 1980 to present. It also contains legal newspapers in its coverage with more than 1.5 million articles. This database is available in Lexis and Westlaw.

Early citations are bibliographical only; more recent citations may contain an abstract (a paragraph summary of the article) or full-text.

The index can be searched basic or advanced. Basic provides subject searching. Advanced includes author, title, subject, keyword, periodical, and date searching.

What is *LegalTrac*?

LegalTrac is the same database as *Legal Resources Index* but its name is associated with Gale Publisher's InfoTrac databases that covers business, academic, reference, legal, and other databases.

What is the coverage on the Lexis and Westlaw databases?

Full text of legal periodicals dates back to the mid-1980s, but full coverage will vary from journal to journal, many not starting until the 1990s.

What is HeinOnline?

Hein Online is a commercial database of full-text academic periodicals retrievable in pdf format from their beginning date, thereby providing extensive coverage not found in the Lexis and Westlaw databases.

HeinOnline also now includes a complete set of *United States Reports* for the U.S. Supreme Court, complete backfile of *Federal Register*, U.S. Attorneys-General Opinions, and a Legal Classics Library of more than one thousand important legal treatises.

All documents can be printed or downloaded for patron use.

What is *Government Periodicals Index*?

Government Periodicals Index is a publication of the Congressional Information Service (CIS) that indexes more than 700 periodicals published by the departments and agencies of the Federal Government. It is available through LexisNexis.

How do citators provide periodical information?

Law review coverage depends on the Shepard's title. In the federal citations, there are references to the top twenty law reviews (Harvard, Yale, Columbia, University of Pennsylvania, etc). These may also be found in the Shepards Citations for each state in addition to the general law reviews published in each state, e.g., Montana has the *Montana Law Review*; Pennsylvania has Duquesne, Penn State, Temple, University of Pittsburgh, Villanova, and Widener law reviews/journals. Shepards for regional reporters have no law reviews.

Electronically, both Shepards and Keycite provide references to hundreds of law reviews found in Lexis and Westlaw respectively.

What types of information are available in *Shepard's Citations to Law Reviews*?

Shepard's Citations to Law Reviews provides both caselaw and periodical citations to more than 300 law reviews.

LEGAL NEWSPAPERS & NEWSLETTERS

What is the purpose of legal newspapers?
A legal newspaper provides articles as well as schedules for trials within the jurisdiction covered by the legal newspaper.

How many legal newspapers are there?

There are approximately 12 to 15 major legal newspapers:
New Jersey: *New Jersey Law Journal* (weekly)
Pennsylvania: *Pennsylvania Law Weekly* (weekly)
Chicago: *Chicago Daily Bulletin* (Daily)
Los Angeles: *Los Angeles Daily Journal* (Daily)
New York City: *New York Law Journal* (Daily)
Philadelphia: *Legal Intelligencer* (Daily)
Pittsburgh: *Lawyers Journal* (biweekly); *Pittsburgh Legal Journal* (daily)
Washington, D.C.: *Legal Times of Washington* (weekly)

Are there any legal newspapers devoted to legal technology?
Law Technology News published by American Lawyer Media Inc.; *Legal Management* published by the Association of Legal Administrators; *Information Today* published by Information Today Inc. are the popular ones.

What are legal newsletters?
Legal newsletters are generally published monthly on a specific subject by law firms or commercial vendors like Andrews or Mealys. Bar Association newsletters published by sections and/or committees of the bar may be published weekly, biweekly, monthly, bimonthly, four, six times a year.

Where can I find a listing of legal newsletters?
Arlene Eis publishes *Legal Newsletters in Print* (InfoSources) (KF1 L44).

AMERICAN LAW REPORTS (A.L.R.) ANNOTATIONS

What does *A.L.R.* stand for?
A.L.R. stands for *American Law Reports* (KF132 A5) that began in the early 20th century.

What are *A.L.R.* annotations?
Annotations are a secondary source containing articles that vary in length from a few pages to hundreds of pages on one topic derived from a reported federal or state court case.

A.L.R. began as competition to the West's regional reporter system. Each volume contains eight to 15 annotations, containing a case and an annotation that derives from a specific point of law in the case. Current series contain the annotations with the cases at the end of the set; previous series contain the case first and then the annotation.

Who writes annotations?

Company attorneys and outsides attorneys write annotations on a per-annotation-pay basis.

When was the first *A.L.R.* started?

The first series began in 1918, but there was an earlier set Lawyers Reports Annotated that covered from the 1880s to 1917.

Is *A.L.R.* a case reporter?

A.L.R. began as a specialized reporter competing against West's reporter system. Although cases are published, today the set is used primarily for the annotations.

Who publishes *A.L.R.*?

A.L.R. was originally published by Lawyers Cooperative Publishing Co, which now is part of the Thomson Corporation. *A.L.R.* initially began as a competitor to the West Regional Reporter series, but its annotations became more important than the reporting of the actual cases.

What is the series coverage?

A.L.R. 1st
A.L.R. 2nd
A.L.R. 3rd
A.L.R. 4th
A.L.R. 5th
A.L.R. 6th
A.L.R. Federal
A.L.R. Federal 2nd

What is the current series?

The current series is A.L.R. 6th series and A.L.R. Federal 2d series.

What is the difference between the numbered series and A.L.R. Federal series?

A.L.R. 1st to 3rd cover both federal and state cases. Since 1969, *A.L.R.* 3rd, 4th, 5th, and 6th series cover state topics; *A.L.R. Fed* 1st and 2nd series cover only federal topics.

How are the series updated?

*A.L.R. 1*st has the Blue Book Decennial volumes to look for updated references.

A.L.R.2d has *A.L.R.2d Later Case Service*, a multivolume series updating the 100 volumes of the 2nd series.

*A.L.R. 3d-6*th series and *A.L.R. Federal* 1st & 2nd series have annual pocket parts.

Do they cover both federal and state issues?

A.L.R. is broken down into *A.L.R.* 1-6 series and *A.L.R. Federal* 1st and 2nd series. Beginning in 1969, in the middle of the A.L.R.3d series, the company started *A.L.R. Federal* covering just federal annotations and *A.L.R.3d* onwards covers just state annotations.

What are the leading cases?

This is the case that provides the basic point of law upon which an annotation is written upon.

Are cases available in full text format?

The leading cases for the annotations are available in all of the *A.L.R.* series. *A.L.R. 5*th and 6th series and *A.L.R. Federal 2*nd have cases published at the end of the volume; earlier series contain the case first and then the annotation.

No other cases are reprinted in full-text.

What are the parts of an *A.L.R.* annotation?

Every annotation will have the following parts: Title; Author; Table of Contents; Article Outline; Research References (Total Client-Service Library References); Research Sources; Index and Jurisdictional Table of Cited Statutes and Cases, and the annotation itself.

What *A.L.R.* information is available in Shepards Citations?

Shepards provides references to volume and page reference of *A.L.R.* annotations for the numbered series and *A.L.R. Federal*.

How can one find citations to cases listed in the *A.L.R.* series?

There are two multivolume sets of table of cases for *A.L.R. 5*th and 6th series and another set for *A.L.R. Federal* 1st and 2nd series. These are published as paperback volumes and updated annually.

What is the Jurisdictional Table?

The jurisdictional table in the front of each annotation provides the references to both federal and state statutory law and case law with references to specific sections within the annotation.

How do I find annotations on my research topic?

There is a multivolume index at the end of the set that covers all series.

There is also a *Quick Index for A.L.R. for 3*rd, 4th, 5th, and 6th, and a *Quick Index for A.L.R. Federal 1*st and 2nd.

Cases are also arranged by a multivolume digest.

Is there any other research method in addition to Indexes?

A.L.R. annotations are also cited in Shepards Citations.

What is Annotation History Table?

The History Table contains a listing of all annotations that have been supplemented or superseded since the First Series.

Where is the Annotation History Table published?

The Annotation History Table is published in each volume of the *A.L.R.* Index. It is also updated in the pocket parts.

What is a Superseding Annotation?

If the laws have changed such that the original annotation should be rewritten.

What is a Supplementing Annotation?

If the new, more recent cases were merely adding to the cases cited in the original annotation. Sometimes only one section of an annotation may be updated in a later annotation.

What is *West's A.L.R. Digest*?

This multivolume set, recently published in 2004, has court decisions and annotations with research references (formbooks, legal encyclopedias) arranged by the West Key Number Digest System.

For every key number they have the annotation followed by headnote references.

FORM BOOKS

What are form books?

Form books provide forms for topics (commercial law, real property, etc.) jurisdictions (federal or state jurisdictions) and procedural forms for a specific court (West's Federal Forms have volumes for U.S. Supreme Court, U.S. Courts of Appeals, U.S. District Courts, U.S. Bankruptcy Courts) or procedural forms (appellate, bankruptcy, civil, criminal and evidence).

What are the general forms sets available. Form books, Bibliography

Am Jur Legal Forms (Thomson) (KF170 A542)
West's Legal Forms (Thomson) (KF170 W47)
Nichols Cyclopedia of Forms Annotated (Thomson) (KF170 N5)
Rabkin and Johnson Current Legal Forms with Tax Analysis (Matthew Bender) (KF170 R3)

What title covers forms for the federal courts?

West's Federal Forms, (KF8836 W4) is a multivolume set containing forms arranged by three federal courts: U.S. Supreme Court, U.S. Circuit Courts, U.S. District Courts, and U.S. Bankruptcy courts.

What titles cover trial practice?

Am Jur Pleading and Practice Forms Annotated (West) (KF8836 A45) is a multivolume set containing from pre-trial to post-trial procedural forms.

How does one access the forms?

There are usually index volumes to access the information.

Where can one find federal forms?

Federal Procedural Forms, L.Ed. (KF8836 F4) is a multivolume set containing forms by subject and by department/agency of federal government.

II. INTERNET

Dictionaries

Are legal dictionaries available on the web?

Web sites such as Nolo, Findlaw, Cornell, HeirosGamos, Mega Law and Law Guru have links to online legal dictionaries.

Nolo: <www.nolo.com/glossary.cfm> Law.Com: <dictionary.law.com>, and Cornell: <www.law.cornell.edu/wex>; are some of the major sources for legal dictionaries.

Dean's Law Dictionary (www.deanslawdictionary) which is a commercial product includes 185,773 legal rules and definitions in 21,309 digital pages (as of Sep. 2006). Since it is in digital format, new legal rules and definitions are added continuously to the existing one (from the web site).

Encyclopedias

Are there any legal encyclopedias found on the Internet?

Currently, there are no web sites where you can get legal encyclopedia information. However, some sites are in the developmental stage: Jurispedia, <www.jurispedia.org>, Cornell, <www.law.cornell.edu/wex>, and Wiki Law, <www.wiki-law.org>.

Legal Periodical Literature

Are there any sites that provide legal periodical articles?

The majority of the comprehensive legal sites such as Findlaw, HeirosGamos, Virtual Chase provide links to legal periodical titles. You may go directly to a specific law review site or select a law review from the list provided by the comprehensive sites.

Law Reviews Org (www.lawreviews.org) provides links to an alphabetical list of law reviews and other national and international legal periodicals.

HeinOnline (www.heinonline.org) is the only site that provides articles published in law school law reviews as well as other legal periodicals in full text from the inception of the periodical. You have to be a subscriber to access HeinOnline.

Are there any Internet services that provide legal periodical abstracts?

Legal Scholarship Network (LSN) provides a wide selection of abstracts from journals, working papers, and articles accepted for publication as well as selected full-text papers and articles to the subscribers. It is searchable by using author, keyword, journal or topic.

What are the research methods (access points) to retrieve articles from HeinOnline?

You can retrieve articles by author, title, subject, keyword, and also by citation.

Is there any source that publishes the table of contents (TOC) for legal journals?

Table of contents (TOC) of law journals are available from the Washington & Lee Law School (law.wlu.edu/library/CLJC) . Currently, the contents pages are available for a little over 1,500 law journals. You can search this online service by keywords and by author.

What is LegalTrac?

LegalTrac (www.legaltrac.galegroup.com) is a subscription based service which offers indexing for almost 900 major law reviews, legal newspapers, specialty law publications, bar association journals and more than 1,000 business and general interest titles containing more than 1.5 million articles.

Legal Forms

How can one find free legal forms online?

You may find links for free legal forms from comprehensive legal web sites. Some sites provide free legal forms and for a fee. LexisOne (www.lexisone.com) provides free forms and for fee automated forms which are powered by Hot Docs ® document-assembly software.

Are there any sites for court related forms?

LLRX (www.llrx.com) provides links to court related forms.

Do Federal and State governments provide forms for free?

Federal and state governments do provide free forms through their official web sites. For example, federal government forms are available from the www.forms. gov site. You may also obtain free forms by visiting individual government agency web sites.

Are there any web sites for legal forms for a fee?

Westlaw and Lexis has several databases for various types of legal forms. Find Legal Forms (www.findlegalforms.com) and U.S. Legal Forms (www.uslegalforms. com) are a few of the several comprehensive sources available to obtain legal forms for a fee. Other good sites for free legal forms are www.Allaboutlaw.com and www.yourfreelegalforms.com.

III. LEXISNEXIS

Are legal dictionaries available on Lexis?

In Lexis there is a dictionary of Modern Legal Usage, as well as many other specialized dictionaries. Click on the "Reference" button on the right side of the home page/directory page. Select "Law" link on the right column. At the top of the left side you will see the *Dictionary of Modern Legal Usage* (DMLU), *Ballentine's Law Dictionary* 3rd edition (BTINES) and several other legal dictionaries.

Are legal encyclopedias available on Lexis?

Select "Jurisprudence & ALR" under the heading "Secondary Legal". You will find links to *American Jurisprudence 2d* (AMJUR) and several state law encyclopedias such as *Florida Jurisprudence 2d, Illinois Jurisprudence, Pennsylvania Law Encyclopedia*, etc.

The encyclopedias can be searched using full-text searching or by using the Table of Contents. Searching can be done using either Terms and Connectors or Natural Language.

State encyclopedias are available under each state's materials, e.g., *Pennsylvania Law Encyclopedia* (PLE).

Where can I find a listing of the law reviews available on Lexis?

Select "Secondary Legal" on the home page and then select "Law Reviews and Journals." You will see several combined files as well as links to 'Law Reviews by Jurisdiction'; 'Law Reviews by Area of Law'; 'Individual Law Reviews & Journals' and 'ABA Journals' categories.

The category of U.S. Law Reviews and Journals, Combined" includes academic law reviews and selected bar association journals.

What are the dates of coverage for legal periodicals?

In general, coverage goes back to only the 1980s. Each periodical will have a different starting date and coverage, e.g., *Harvard Law Review* dates from 1982; *Indiana Law Review* from 1998.

Can I research legal periodical information by jurisdiction?

Under "Law Reviews and Journals," select "Law Reviews by Jurisdiction" for a state-by-state listing, e.g., New York Law Reviews, Combined, for all law reviews published by schools within New York State.

Can I research legal periodical information by topic or area of law?

Under "Law Reviews and Journals," select Law Reviews by Area of Law" for a listing of more than twenty topics, e.g., Banking Law Review Articles, Criminal Law Review Articles, Tax Law Review Articles.

Can I research legal periodical information on individual law reviews?

Under "Law Reviews and Journals," select "Individual Law Reviews & Journals" for an alphabetical listing of periodicals.

Can I research an individual periodical published by the American Bar Association (ABA)?

Under "Law Reviews and Journals," select "ABA Journals" for an alphabetical listing of periodicals published by the ABA.

Is there an index to the legal periodical literature?

The Legal Resource Index (LGLIND) file indexes both legal periodicals and newspapers back to 1977 is available in Lexis under "Law Reviews and Journals."

What is LexisNexis Academic Universe?

Lexis Academic service provides full text documents of close to 6000 news, business, legal, medical and reference publications. Newspapers such as *New York Times, Wall Street Journal* and several law school law reviews etc. are included. Many academic libraries and law libraries subscribe to Academic Universe and make it available free to students and other registered borrowers. It has limited access to LexisNexis legal databases and does not have all of the "bells and whistles," e.g., the database does not provide links to all primary sources cited in cases or limits Shepard's Citations to only U.S. Supreme Court cases.

Can I research legal newsletters?

Under Secondary Legal, Mealey Reports & Conferences contains a variety of legal newsletters by jurisdiction (state-by-state), practice area (construction, toxic torts), reports and files from various states (by topic and by state).

What types of treatises are available on Lexis?

Lexis offers a wide variety of treatises on many different areas of the law. Select "Secondary Legal" and find on the right side "Area of Law Treatises" link. Lexis will then list for you an extensive list of general and state-related treatises available, e.g., *Appleman on Insurance Law, Corbin on Contracts, Wigmore on Evidence, Colorado Landlord-Tenant Law, Massachusetts Domestic Relations*, etc.

Can I research treatises by publisher?

There are several major legal publishers available such as ABA, Aspen, BNA, Matthew Bender, Practising Law Institute, and John Wiley.

Are continuing legal education publications available?

Under Secondary Legal, there are links to Individual ALI-ABA Materials, NITA, Practising Law Institute's course handbook series, and a few states' CLE publications.

A more restrictive listing can be found under a link for "CLE Materials" on the right side that provides links only to ALI-ABA, NITA, and a few states' CLE publications.

Is a complete set of *A.L.R.* available for research?

Under "Secondary Legal," *American Law Reports* (ALR) is available as a single file (LEDALR) or combined with Restatements, Jurisprudences and Law Reviews (SS-MEGA), or Law Reviews and ALR (LRALR).

As a single file, *A.L.R.* begins with *A.L.R.* 2d to the present and includes *Lawyers Ed.* 2d as well.

There is a separate file for *U. S. Supreme Court Lawyers' Edition* annotations (LED2D) only.

Can I research *Restatements of the Law* in Lexis?

Under "Secondary Legal" click on "Restatement of the Law" that provides links to two combined files: Restatement Rules Combined (RULES) and Restatement Annotated Case Citations Combined (CITES) and also links to individual restatement titles such as property, torts, etc.

IV. WESTLAW

Are legal dictionaries available on Westlaw?

On the home page under Directories, Reference, there is a folder for dictionaries. Cllick on the link to retrieve *Black's Law Dictionary*, 8th ed. (BLACKS) and other dictionaries, *Dictionary of Occupational Titles* (DICOT) and *Stedman's Medical Dictionary* (STEDMANS).

If you are a law school student using lawschool.westlaw.com you will see a number of options on the left side of the screen. You will see a link to the *Black's Law Dictionary*. Upon selection enter any desired word to retrieve definitions from the *Black's Law Dictionary* 8th edition.

Are legal encyclopedias available on Westlaw?

On the home page under the Treatises, CLEs, Practice Guides, there are links for *American Jurisprudence 2d* (AMJUR) and *Corpus Juris Secundum* (CJS).

State encyclopedias are available under each state's materials, e.g., *Maryland Law Encyclopedia* (MD-ENC).

Where can I find a listing of the law reviews available on Westlaw?

On the home page under Legal Periodicals & Current Awareness, click on Law Reviews to obtain the Law Reviews, Bar Journals & Legal Periodicals databases. There are a number of individual and combined databases.

Texts and Periodicals Combined (TP-ALL). The TP-ALL database contains documents from law reviews, texts, *American Law Reports* (ALR), legal encyclopedias (*American Jurisprudence 2d* and *Corpus Juris Secundum*), CLE course materials, bar journals and legal practice- oriented periodicals. A document is an article, a note, a symposium contribution, a product review, or other material published in one of the available periodicals; an ALR annotation; or a section from one of the available texts or encyclopedias

Journals & Law Reviews Combined (JLR) contains a link for all academic law reviews, various CLE course materials, and bar journals.

Where can I find a listing of the law reviews available on Westlaw?

Under "Law Reviews, Bar Journals & Legal Periodicals," select "Law Reviews & Bar Journals in JLR & TP-ALL. "There is an alphabetical listing by title.

What are the dates of coverage for legal periodicals?

In general, coverage varies from periodical to periodical including differences of selected versus full coverage, e.g., *Harvard Law Review* dates from 1949; *Indiana Law Review* from 1983 in selected coverage and full coverage from 1993.

Can I research legal periodical information by jurisdiction?

Under each state's directory, there is a file "Law Reviews, Bar Journals & Legal Periodicals" that provides the database for the individual titles, e.g., *Temple Law Review* (TMPLR) as well as the combined databases (PA-JLR).

Also, under the main directory, Law Reviews, Bar Journals in JLR &TP-ALL has a link to "State Journal & Law Review Databases" that provides the individual state periodical databases, e.g., California Journals & Law Reviews (CA-JLR).

Can I research legal periodical information by topic or area of law?

Under the Directory, select "Topical Materials by Area of Practice" and then under each topic, there is a Law Reviews Texts & Journals database, e.g., Bankruptcy topic (BKR-TP) as well as individual titles, e.g., *California Bankruptcy Journal* (CABKRJ)

Can I research legal periodical information on individual law reviews?

Under the main directory, click on "Law Reviews, Bar Journals & Legal Periodicals, to link to "Law Reviews, Bar Journals in JLR &TP-ALL" that provides an alphabetical list of all of the titles, e.g., *Harvard Law Review* (HVLR), *Stanford Law Review* (STNLR).

Is there an index to the legal periodical literature?

There are two periodical indexes available under Periodical Indexes under "Law Reviews, Bar Journals & Legal Periodicals. *Current Index to Legal Periodicals* (CILP) is a weekly publication of the University of Washington Gallagher Law Library that indexes approximately 570 periodicals by subject and title of the periodical.

The Legal Resource Index (LRI) database indexes both legal periodicals and newspapers back to 1980.

Can I research legal newsletters?

Under Law Reviews, Bar Journals and Legal Periodicals, there is a Legal Newsletter Multibase (LEGALNEWSL). There are two smaller databases, Legal Newsletters Listed by Publisher and Legal Newsletters Listed by Title. The publishers' list includes Andrews, ABA, American Lawyer Media, RIA, A. S. Pratt, etc.

Legal Newsletters Listed by Title database has more than one hundred different newsletter databases. Andrews Litigation Reporters (ANDREWS) database and its individual newsletters are available. There are various topics covered including newsletters dealing with state-by-state coverage of employment and environmental law databases.

Can I research legal newspapers?

Legal Newspapers Database contains a comprehensive databases (LEGALNP) and individual titles, e.g., *American Lawyer* (AMLAW), *Legal Times* (LEGALTIMES), *New York Law Journal* (NYLJ), etc. The coverage of each newspaper varies from title to title.

Can I research a specific legal periodical?

'Legal periodicals and current awareness' link under directory will provide an alphabetical list of the periodicals available in the Westlaw service.

What are the search options available to conduct research in the periodical database?

Several search options are available to retrieve the desired documents. Fields such as CI (if you know the citation); TI (Title of the article); SO (Publisher's name); AU (Author of the article); TE (searching in the text of the document) are available. If you know the proper citation to the article you can also retrieve the article by using the FIND function.

Are there other sources for current legal news information?

Under Legal Newsletters, Highlights, and Notable Trials, Highlights contains current information sources like Westlaw's Topical Bulletins, e.g., Antitrust (WTH-ATR), Bankruptcy (WTH-BKR), Family Law (WTH-FL), etc., providing a various number of court cases based on a date restriction.

Other Current Awareness provides links to a number of general databases on current affairs, e.g., American Political Network, Death Penalty, Iraq Gulf War Documents.

What types of treatises are available on Westlaw?

Under the Directory, select "Forms, Treatises, CLEs and Other Practice Material." This will give you an extensive listing of the specific titles (databases) of single and multivolume treatises covering specific topics and also state-specific topics.

If you have a specific area of law that you are attempting to research you can enter a keyword, for example "Contracts", and this will bring up the directories that apply to that key word. In order to search within a directory you can simply click the link for that directory, and it will bring up a query box allowing you to do a keyword search within that specific directory. Or if you wish to search within multiple directories you can click the selection box to the left of each category, and then scroll down to the bottom of the screen and click "Ok". This will bring up a query box that will allow you to do a key word search within each of these directories. You will see the selected directories above the query box.

Are treatises available by publisher?
Under Forms, Treatises, CLEs and Other Practice Materials, Warren Gorham & Lamont has a separate folder consisting of a listing for its treatises and periodicals and Practitioners Publishing Company has a folder of its tax publications as well.

Are continuing legal education publications available?
Under Forms, Treatises, CLEs and Other Practice Materials, there is a folder for Practice Guides and CLE Materials that contains databases alphabetically by state publications as well as National Business Institute publications and Practising Law Institute course handbook series.

Is the complete set of A.L.R.s available for research on Westlaw?
Under Treatises, CLEs and Practice Guides, heading from the directory listing can be found the *American Law Reports* database (ALR) covering *A.L.R. 1st* to *A.L.R. 6th* series and *A.L.R. Fed.* And *A.L.R. Fed. 2d*. The database is updated weekly for all series except for the first series that is updated annually.

Is an index to *A.L.R.* available on Westlaw?
To retrieve the *A.L.R.* Index, use the citation field search CI (index). Jump markers in the index can be used to retrieve additional index documents and the full text of the annotations indexed from *A.L.R.* 3d, *A.L.R.* 4th, *A.L.R.* 5th, *A.L.R.* 6th, *A.L.R.* Fed, and *A.L.R.* Fed 2d. You can also use segment IN to find listings on a particular topic.

Is a topical *A.L.R.* available rather than the whole *A.L.R.* database?
Westlaw provides *A.L.R.* databases for individual topics including Business Organizations (*A.L.R.*-BUS), Family Law (*A.L.R.*-FAM), etc.

What are the search options available to retrieve relevant annotations on a specific topic?
AU (author); TI (Title of the annotation); JUR (jurisdiction of the case from the jurisdictional table); TE (Text of the annotation) are some of the useful fields.

Can I research *Restatements* in Westlaw?
Under Forms, Treatises, CLEs, and Other Practice Materials, click on Restatements. The complete *Restatements* are available in a combined database (REST) and individual databases by topic, e.g., *Restatement of the Law of Agency* (REST-AGEN), *Restatement of the Law of Torts* (REST-TORT), etc. Each database contains rules, annotations, tentative drafts, current pocket parts or interim pamphlets.

There is also an archive database in a combined database (REST-ARCHIVE) covering Agency, Law Governing Lawyers, Property, Torts, and Trusts or the individual topics, e.g., torts (REST-TORTSAR).

Can I research a specific title of *Restatement*?
Westlaw provides separate databases for each Restatements, e.g., REST-AGEN for Restatement of Agency, (REST-AGEN), Restatement of Torts (REST-TORT) etc.

Are there other American Law Institute publications available on Westlaw?
The annual Proceedings of the Institute from 2000 to present are available as ALI Proceedings (ALI-PROCEED).

CHAPTER 12

LEGAL ETHICS

Introduction: Legal ethics deals with how judges and lawyers interact with each other and with individuals as litigants in the judicial system. Legal ethics codes for lawyers and judges have developed over the decades and are adopted in most states today. The American Bar Association adopts a Model Code of Professional Conduct for lawyers and a Model Code of Judicial Conduct for judges that are updated irregularly as needed. These codes are then available for adoption by each state's highest court for the judges and lawyers of that jurisdiction.

I. MANUAL

What is legal ethics?

Legal ethics deals with the conduct of lawyers and judges in carrying out the practice of law.

Where can one find the standard rules for lawyers?

The standard rules can be found in the *Model Rules of Professional Conduct*.

Who composes the rules?

The American Bar Association through its Center for Professional Responsibility produces the rules.

When were rules first created?

George Sharswood, Chief Justice of the Pennsylvania Supreme Court and Professor at the University of Pennsylvania Law School, wrote the first treatise on legal ethics entitled *A Compend of Lectures on the Aims And Duties of the Profession of Law* in 1854. In later editions it was entitled *An Essay on Professional Ethics*.

What was the first state to adopt a code of legal ethics?

The first state to adopt a code of legal ethics was Alabama in 1887.

When did the American Bar Association first adopt conduct rules?
In 1908 the ABA adopted Rules of Professional Ethics partly based on Sharswood's book and the 1887 Alabama Code.

When did the American Bar Association create new rules?
The ABA adopted the *Model Rules of Professional Responsibility* in 1969. Each state then had to adopt the rules through their regular procedure.

How were the Model Rules broken down?
The Rules were divided into Canons, Ethics Decisions (EDs) and Disciplinary Rules (DRs)

When was the *Model Rules of Professional Conduct* created?
The American Bar Association adopted the *Model Rules of Professional Conduct* in 1983 that are published in *Annotated Model Rules of Professional Conduct* (6th ed, 2007) (KF305.A2).

How many states have adopted the Model Rules?
Forty-two states have adopted them through court rules.

What are the Model Rules?
CLIENT-LAWYER RELATIONSHIP

Rule
1.1. Competence.
1.2. Scope of Representation.
1.3. Diligence.
1.4. Communication.
1.5. Fees.
1.6. Confidentiality of Information.
1.7. Conflict of Interest: General Rule.
1.8. Conflict of Interest: Prohibited Transactions.
1.9. Conflict of Interest: Former Client.
1.10. Imputed Disqualification: General Rule.
1.11. Successive Government and Private Employment.
1.12. Former Judge or Arbitrator or Law Clerk.
1.13. Organization as Client.
1.14. Client Under a Disability.
1.15. Safekeeping Property.
1.16. Declining or Terminating Representation.

COUNSELOR
2.1. Advisor.
2.2. Intermediary.
2.3. Evaluation for Use by a Third Person.

ADVOCATE
3.1. Meritorious Claims and Contentions.
3.2. Expediting Litigation.
3.3. Candor Toward the Tribunal.
3.4. Fairness to Opposing Party and Counsel.
3.5. Impartiality and Decorum of the Tribunal.
3.6. Trial Publicity.
3.7. Lawyer as Witness.
3.8. Special Responsibilities of a Prosecutor.
3.9. Advocate in Nonadjudicative Proceedings.
3.10. Issuance of Subpoenas to Lawyers.

TRANSACTIONS WITH PERSONS OTHER THAN CLIENTS
4.1. Truthfulness in Statements to Others.
4.2. Communication with Person Represented by Counsel.
4.3. Dealing with Unrepresented Person and Communicating With One of Adverse Interest.
4.4. Respect for Rights of Third Persons.

LAW FIRMS AND ASSOCIATIONS
5.1. Responsibilities of a Partner or Supervisory Lawyer.
5.2. Responsibilities of a Subordinate Lawyer.
5.3. Responsibilities Regarding Nonlawyer Assistants.
5.4. Professional Independence of a Lawyer.
5.5. Unauthorized Practice of Law.
5.6. Restrictions on Right to Practice.
5.7. Responsibilities Regarding Nonlegal Services.

PUBLIC SERVICE
6.1. Pro Bono Publico Service.
6.2. Accepting Appointments.
6.3. Membership in Legal Services Organization.
6.4. Law Reform Activities Affecting Client Interests.

INFORMATION ABOUT LEGAL SERVICES
7.1. Communications Concerning a Lawyer Services.

7.2. Advertising.
7.3. Direct Contact with Prospective Clients.
7.4. Communications of Fields of Practice.
7.5. Firm Names and Letterheads.
7.6. Advertising a Certification.
7.7. Lawyer Referral Service.

MAINTAINING THE INTEGRITY OF THE PROFESSION
8.1. Bar Admission and Disciplinary Matters.
8.2. Statements Concerning Judges and Other Adjudicatory Officers.
8.3. Reporting Professional Misconduct.
8.4. Misconduct.
8.5. Disciplinary Authority; Choice of Law.

Where can one find these rules?
Martindale-Hubbell Law Directory contains the various ABA Codes. The ABA publishes an *Annotated Model Rules of Professional Conduct* (2007 ed.).

Annotated editions of the state rules can be found in the annotated codes for each state usually with the Rules of Civil Procedure. They also can be found in the State Rules of Court volumes published by West Group.

Where can one find cases on the *Model Code of Professional Conduct*?
The West Digest System contains cases under Attorney & Client §32, Regulation of Professional Conduct, In General:.

(1)   In general
(2)   Standards, canons or codes of conduct
(3)   Power and duty to control
(4)   Attorney's conduct and position in general
(5)   Persons subject to regulations
(6)   Limitations on duty to client, in general
(7)   Miscellaneous particular acts and omissions
(8)   Dignity, decorum, and courtesy; criticism of courts
(9)   Advertising or soliciting
(10) Duty to accept or decline representation
(11) Frivolous, vexatious, or meritless claims
      Relations, dealings, or communications with witness, juror, judge, or opponent
(12) Client's confidences, in general
(13) Candor, and disclosure to opponent or court
(14) Extrajudicial comments.

One can also search ALR annotations.

What are the leading treatises on legal ethics?
Geoffrey C. Hazard, Jr. and W. William Hodes, *Law of Lawyering* (3d ed 2001) (KF306 H33 2001);. Ronald D. Rotunda and Michael Krauss, *Legal Ethics in a Nutshell* (3d ed. 2007) (KF306.Z9R668 2007); Ronald D. and John S. Dzienkowski, Legal Ethics: *The Lawyer's Deskbook on Professional Responsibility* (Annual) (KF306.R68)

Has the American Law Institute created a *Restatement* for legal ethics?
In 2000, it adopted the *Law Governing Lawyers, Restatement of the Law, Third Series*. (KF300.R48 3rd or KF395 G613A7)

Are the Model Rules available in Shepards and Keycite?
There is a bound volume entitled *Shepard's Professional Responsibility and Judicial Conduct Citations*. Both online citators provide for cite checking the Model Rules.

What are formal and informal ethics opinions?
The ABA publishes formal and informal ethics opinions.

Where can I find ethics opinions?
The ABA publishes a looseleaf service of both types of opinions. They are also digested on the ABA Center for Professional Responsibility website, at www.abanet.org/cpr.

Where can I find state bar ethics opinions?
Full text ethics opinions can be found in *National Reporter for Professional Responsibility and Legal Ethics* and in Lexis and Westlaw databases.

Where can I find cases on the Ethics Opinions?
The ethics opinions can be found in *Shepard's Professional Responsibility and Judicial Conduct Citations* and Keycite.

What is the looseleaf service on the Model Rules of Professional Conduct?
The Bureau of National Affairs publishes *ABA/BNA Lawyers Manual on Professional Conduct*.

It is divided into a biweekly current events periodical. The Reference Manual is published monthly with detailed information on model standards, the chapters of the Model Code, and ethics opinions.

What are the Model Rules for Lawyer Disciplinary Enforcement?
The ABA passed these rules in 1993 providing for types of discipline and the procedure for implementing disciplinary hearings.

How are lawyers disciplined on the state level?

States have disciplinary boards to handle the investigation of cases. The boards usually are under the state court administration.

What are the Model Rules for Federal Lawyer Disciplinary Enforcement?

These rules, created in 1978, apply to those serving in the federal courts.

What is judicial ethics?

Judges, like lawyers, have an ethical code of conduct in serving as a judge. The ABA approved the Canons of Judicial Ethics in 1924 followed by the Model Code of Judicial Conduct in 1990 and has been updated four times since that time. The most recent version is from 2007.

Who publishes the *Model Code of Judicial Conduct*?

The ABA publishes an *Annotated Code of Judicial Conduct*.(2008 edition).

What are the contents of the *Model Code of Judicial Conduct*?

Preamble

Terminology

Canon 1. A judge shall uphold and promote the independence, integrity, and impartiality of the judiciary, and shall avoid impropriety and the appearance of impropriety

Canon 2. A judge shall perform the duties of judicial office impartially, competently, and diligently.

Canon 3. A judge shall conduct the judge's personal and extrajudicial activities to minimize the risk of conflict with the obligations of judicial office.

Canon. 4 A judge or candidate for judicial office shall not engage in political or campaign activity that is inconsistent with the independence, integrity, or impartiality of the judiciary

Application

Application Chart

Where can I find the Code on the state level?

The state rules of court published by West includes the Code of Judicial Conduct.

Where can one find cases on judicial ethics?

The West Digest System contains Judges §11.

   ALR annotations may also have cases.

What is the major treatise on judicial ethics?
James J. Alfini, *Judicial Conduct and Ethics* (4th ed. 2007).

II. INTERNET

Where can I find the Model Rules of Professional Conduct, Code of Judicial Conduct, etc. online?
ABA Center for Professional Responsibility has the Model Rules of Professional Responsibility, Professional Conduct, Code of Judicial Conduct, Lawyers Disciplinary Rules, etc., at www.aba.net/cpr

Where can I find state Model Rules of Professional Conduct?
The Legal Information Institute (LII) has an Ethics Library that contains annotated editions of the a limited number of states. It is located on the left side under special libraries, www.law.cornell.edu

Where can I find ABA ethics opinions?
Summaries of the opinions can be found at the ABA Center for Professional Responsibility web site, at
  http://www.abanet.org/cpr/pubs/ethicopinions.html

Where can I find ethics codes of different legal and nonlegal organizations?
Illinois Institute of Technology has a Center for the Study of Ethics in the Professions where one can find codes of ethics online for various professions, Health Profession, Law and Legal, Real Estate, etc., at
  http://ethics.iit.edu/codes/coe.html

What codes are covered under the Law and Legal category?
American Arbitration Association
Code of Ethics for Arbitrators in Commercial Disputes
Code of Professional Responsibility for Arbitrators of Labor-Management Disputes
American Bar Association (Currently, ABA's codes are only available for a fee)
American College of Forensic Examiners
American Correctional Association
American Federation of Police

Arbitration and Mediation Institute of Canada, Inc.
Court Interpreters and Translators Association, Inc.
Idaho State Bar Association Code of Professional Responsibility
International Association of Chiefs of Police
Canons of Police Ethics
Law Enforcement Code of Ethics
International Bar Association
International Code of Ethics (1988)
International Code of Ethics (1964)
Judicial Conference of the United States
NALS..the association for legal professionals
National Association for Court Management
National Association of Judiciary Interpreter and Translators
Roscoe-Pound American Trial Lawyers Foundation
American Lawyer's Code of Conduct, Public Discussion Draft
Code of Conduct
State of Arizona Supreme Court
State Bar of California (link only)
United States Courts
Judiciary Policies and Procedures

III. LEXISNEXIS

Are ethics materials available in Lexis?

Under Area of Law —By Topic, click on View All to obtain the Ethics file.

Can I research ethics cases from an individual state?

Ethics cases can be searched in Ethics Cases —All States (COURTS) or by individual state, California Ethics Cases (ETHICS). (Both files have no state designation to it.)

Is there a database that contains both state cases and ethics opinions?

There is also a combined state case law and ethics opinions database for all states (ETHCAS) or for individual states, e.g., California Case Law and Ethics Opinions (CAETH).

Are the Code of Professional Conduct and the Code of Judicial Conduct available?

There is a single file containing both Codes and the previous Model Code of Professional Responsibility (CODES) under Find Statutes and Rules.

Is there an annotated edition of the Code of Professional Conduct available?
The *ABA/BNA Lawyers' Manual on Professional Conduct* (MPCMAN) is available under Search Analysis, Law Reviews, & Journals.

Can I search the codes and ethics opinions in one database?
The file ABA Codes & Ethics Opinions Combined (ETHICS) contains the codes and formal and informal ethics opinions from 1959 to present.

Can I search all state codes at one time for ethics information?
The State Codes, Constitutions, Court Rules & ALS, Combined (ALLCDE) contains all states annotated codes with legislative pamphlets.

Is there any individual state ethics codes available?
The New York State Bar Association's Lawyer's Code of Professional Responsibility (NYCPR) is available from 1976 to present. The database contains Canons, Ethical Considerations, and Disciplinary Rules.

Are the ABA Formal and Informal Ethics Opinions available?
There are two separate databases for ethics opinions: Formal opinions (FOPIN) (from 1924 to present) and Informal opinions (INFOP) (current only to number 1530 dated 10/20/1989).

Is there a commercial publication available for state ethics opinions?
The *National Reporter on Legal Ethics and Professional Responsibility* (ETHOP), published by the University Publications of America, contains both formal and informal opinions from individual states excluding Delaware, Louisiana, Nevada, North Dakota, Oklahoma, and Puerto Rico. Dates of coverage varies.

Are judicial ethics opinions available?
The Judiciary Advisory Opinions file (JUDETH) contains opinions from individual state ethics commissions. The file contains opinions from seventeen states only. The individual state files can be found under Search Legal Ethics Opinions, By State —View more sources to obtain additional state files.

Are other secondary sources available for research?
Under Search Analysis, Law Reviews & Journals, there are several treatises dealing with ethics, e.g., Sarbanes-Oxley Deskbook (PLISOD). Under View More Sources, the Restatement 3d, Law Governing Lawyers by section (LAWGV2) or case citations (LAWGV3) are available.

What law reviews are available under the ethics topic?
Legal Ethics Law Review Articles Combined (ETHLR) contains articles from a wide range of legal periodicals including *Georgetown Journal of Legal Ethics*, etc.

What news services are available for current information?
Under Search News, New York Times Ethics Law Stories (NYTETH) from June 1980 to present, Martindale-Hubbell Legal Articles —Ethics Law (ARTETH) from 2004. The *ABA Journal* (ABAJNL) is available under Legal News, while *New York Times*, Dow Jones, Reuters, and Barron's files are available under General News.

IV. WESTLAW

Are ethics materials available in Westlaw?
Under Topical Materials by Area of Practice, click on View All to obtain the Legal Ethics & Professional Responsibility database.

Can I research ethics cases?
Ethics cases can be searched under federal or state databases which are folders under Legal Ethics & Professional Responsibility. The federal cases can be searched in one comprehensive database Federal Cases —All Courts (FETH-CS) from 1789 to present or the individual Supreme Court, Courts of Appeals, or District Courts databases.

Under the State Cases folder, there are the Multistate Database (METH-CS) or individual state databases, e.g., California (CAETH-CS).

Can I search ethics opinions by topics under the West Digest System?
Under both Federal Cases and State Cases, there is a folder for Key Number Service Topics which lists Attorney and Client, Attorney General, Contempt, District and Prosecuting Attorneys, Judges, and Justices of the Peace.

Are federal government ethics materials available?
Under Federal Administrative Materials folder, the *C.F.R.*, *Federal Register*, and the United States Office of Government Ethics Opinions (FETH-OGE) are available.

Are the Rules of Professional Conduct and the Code of Judicial Conduct available?
There are three files containing the unannotated Model Rules of Professional Conduct (ABA-MRPC), annotated Model Rules of Professional Conduct (ABA-AMRPC), and the Code of Judicial Conduct (ABA-CJC).

Is there a commercial annotated edition of the Rules of Professional Conduct available?
The *ABA/BNA Lawyers' Manual on Professional Conduct* (ABA-BAN) is available under the ABA Materials folder. It may also be further broken down into the Reference Section (ABA-BNA-MOPC) and Current Reports (ABA-BNA-MOPCNL) .

Can I search all state codes at one time for ethics information?
The State Rules of Professional Conduct permits searching of all states or individual state databases, e.g., New Jersey Court Rules (NJ-RULES).

Are the ABA Formal and Informal Ethics Opinions available?
The American Bar Association Ethics Opinions contains both Formal opinions (ABA-ETHOP) (from 1924 to present) and Informal opinions (from July 1961 to present).

Is there a commercial publication available for state ethics opinions?
The National Reporter on Legal Ethics and Professional Responsibility (ETHOP), published by the University Publications of America, contains both formal and informal opinions from individual states excluding Delaware, Louisiana, Nevada, North Dakota, Oklahoma, and Puerto Rico. Dates of coverage vary.

Are disciplinary opinions available?
Under the Disciplinary Opinions folder, there are databases for Colorado, Connecticut, Illinois, Kansas, Massachusetts, New York, Virginia, and Washington, that may cover lawyer and/or judicial discipline, e.g., New York Commission on Judicial Conduct —Judicial Opinions (NYETH-DIS).

Are judicial ethics opinions available?
The Judiciary Advisory Opinions file (JUDETH) contains opinions from individual state ethics commissions. The file contains opinions from seventeen states only. The individual state files can be found under Search Legal Ethics Opinions, By State —View More Sources to obtain additional state files.

Are there other judicial sources available?
Under Other Legal Materials folder, the *Judicial Conduct Reporter* (JCR) contains articles, summaries, reviews and indexes published in the *Judicial Conduct Reporter*. The *Judicial Discipline and Disability Digest* (1963-1993) (JDDD) contains published and unpublished abstracts prepared by the American Judicature Society.

Are other secondary sources available for research?
Under Law Reviews, Legal Texts & Periodicals, there are several treatises dealing with ethics, e.g., Prosecutorial Misconduct (PROMIS). The Restatement of the Law-- Law Governing Lawyers (REST-LGOVL) is a single database, while an archive collection contains the earlier tentative drafts (REST-LGOVLAR).

Also under Forms, Treatises, CLEs and Other Practice Material, there are several other individual treatises, e.g., *Criminal Defense Ethics: Law and Liability* (DEFETH-ICS), *Sarbanes-Oxley Deskbook* (PLIREF-SAROX).

What law reviews are available under the ethics topic?
Under Law Reviews, Legal Texts & Periodicals, there are specifically-related legal periodicals, e.g., *Georgetown Journal of Legal Ethics*, *Journal of the Legal Profession*, etc.

The individual periodicals are available as single databases.

Are forms available under legal ethics?
Under Forms, Treatises, CLEs and Other Practice Material, a Forms-All (FORMS-ALL) database provides forms from more than fifty different form sets and treatises.

CHAPTER 13

INTERNET

This chapter is not on Internet research, but the Internet itself. It deals with terminology of the Internet and its various components.

What is the Internet?

In simple terms the Internet is the network of computers and networks. There are three major components that are important to legal researchers.

1) Email, 2) Usenet (news groups/listservs), and 3) the World Wide Web. Others are Intranet, Extranet and add-ons such as free email and messenger services, auctions, stocks, travel maps, etc.

What are the main components of the Internet?

As far as legal research is concerned, the following are the main components of Internet: Email, Listserv, Intranet, Extranet and World Wide Web.

What is the operating system?

The operating system is the most important software you will ever use on your computer. It is the program that controls your computer and all its peripherals. The operating system most commonly in use is Microsoft's Windows XP and Windows Vista.

What is TCP/IP?

TCP/IP stands for Transmission Control Protocol/Internet Protocol. TCP is the protocol that allows your computer to make a direct connection with another computer along with handling other parts of the transmission, while IP is the address used to locate where the data is going to as it moves between the two connected computers.

What is an IP address?

Each machine on the Internet is assigned a unique address called an IP address. Every machine on the Internet has a unique IP address. IP stands for

Internet Protocol, and these addresses are 32-bit numbers normally expressed as four "octets" in a "dotted decimal number" A typical IP address looks like this: 216.27.61.137 *(www.howstuffworks.com)*

What does DNS means?

A set of servers called Domain Name Servers (DNS) map the human-readable web address names to the IP addresses. These servers are simple databases that map names to IP addresses. The servers are distributed all over the Internet. Most individual companies, ISPs, and universities maintain small name servers to map host names to IP addresses. *(www.howstuffworks.com)*

What are servers and clients?

The Internet is made up of millions of machines, each with a unique IP address. Many of these machines are server machines, meaning that they provide services to other machines on the Internet. You may have heard of many of these servers: email servers, web servers, FTP servers, Gopher servers, printer servers and telnet servers, to name a few. *(www.howstuffworks.com)* Your personal computer is known as the client (receives services); a server does not provide services.

What is email?

Email, or electronic mail, allows you to exchange information electronically via the Internet. Through email you may send legal documents such as cases, statutes, articles, etc. to other people in real time. It is more efficient than using the U.S. Postal Service because messages and files can be sent (and therefore received) in a fraction of the time it would take for a letter to travel from one person to another. Email is also the foundation for listservs and news groups. You can email from home or workplace. Many ISP's (Internet Service Providers) and web browsers provide email accounts free of charge. Hotmail (operated by the Microsoft Network), Yahoo mail, and G-Mail (Google mail) are examples of the more popular free email services, while Eudora and Microsoft Outlook are examples of popular commercial email programs.

How does email work?

Email messages are stored on email servers. Email servers use SMTP (simple mail transfer protocol), POP3 (post office protocol) or IMAP (instant messaging access protocol) to send and receive messages. Most email systems that send mail over the Internet use SMTP to send messages from one mail server to another.

What are email clients?

Email clients are the software or programs used to retrieve email messages from an email server. Common email clients include: Microsoft Outlook, Eudora, etc. using either POP3 or IMAP protocols.

What is web-mail?

Web-mail or web-based email is similar to email except that you can access web-mail from any computer that has an Internet connection and a web browser. Web-mail may be more convenient because you do not need to configure your machine for any additional protocols such as telnet, etc. Web-mail providers such as Yahoo mail, G-mail and Hotmail require a browser and user registration to enable personal email accounts. By using these accounts, it is possible to send email along with attachments to other email addresses.

What is G-mail?

Google offers G-mail, a free email service that gives users more than one gigabyte (100 megabytes) of email storage space. That's the equivalent of 500,000 email pages – more than 100 times what most other free web-mail services offer.

What is L-mail?

L-mail is a service offered by www.L-mail.com . You write an email using an online Web form and the Website prints the letter, stuffs it in an envelope, stamps it and mails it for you for a reasonable fee. You can request your letters to be converted as Braille letters and as audio format (they make as CD).

What does VOIP mean?

Voice Over Internet Protocol (VOIP) is the routing of voice conversations over the Internet.

What is a byte?

The byte is the basic unit of measurement for compute storage. The fundamental data unit of personal computers, a byte is eight contiguous bits.

What are the names of the current measurements for storage?

Kilobyte - One thousand bytes
Megabyte - One thousand kilobytes
Gigabyte - One thousand megabytes
Terabyte - One thousand gigabytes
Petabyte - One thousand terabytes
Exabyte - One thousand petabytes
Zettabyte - One thousand exabytes
Yottabyte - One thousand zettabytes

What are news groups?

News groups may sometimes be called electronic bulletin boards. News groups are collections of articles called postings, and Usenet is a collection of news groups. Each news group focuses on one topic. The topic covered by each news group is evidenced by the name of the group. You can read postings and post information to a news group without subscribing, but it is easier to find the news groups in which you are interested if you subscribe to them. If you find that you are no longer interested in a certain group, you can always cancel your subscription.

What is Usenet?

Usenet consists of news groups and listservs. News groups are similar to electronic bulletin boards and the terms may be used synonymously. There are news groups on thousands of topics. Members of each news group will post information for others to read and comment. It is a forum intended to encourage discussion by those interested in the similar topics. To find the names of relevant news groups, you can visit: http://www.tile.net/.

Electronic newsletters are called listservs. They are forums to share ideas and problems. Listservs are subscription services. Unlike email that is a one-to-one means of exchanging messages or Usenet where anyone may look at the postings and jump in with their own post, the listserv requires users to subscribe to the service. Most popular listservs are moderated by an organization or individual.

For a list of listservs and forums visit: http://www.deja.com, which has now merged with Google groups at: http://www.groups.google.com.

What is a listserv?

A listserv is an electronic mailing list. Listservs allow you to contact a large group of people who also belong to the same listserv. For example, if you have information that you want to send to a large group of people, such as other lawyers who practice in your field, you can post that information to a listserv rather than sending or emailing it to each recipient individually. All of the members of that listserv will then have access to that information.

What is threading?

Message threading is an organization method found on mailing lists and Usenet newsgroups. Threads consist of replies to the original post. Threads will often contain the same subject name as the original email, allowing the user to view the history of the conversation.

What is a posting?

A "posting" is a message that is posted to a listserv or a newsgroup. The original posting will often start a discussion. The subsequent postings made in response to the original will constitute the thread for that subject. Oftentimes, when you are looking for information, you will ask other members of the listserv or newsgroup a question. Asking a question is otherwise known as posting. The response postings will make up that subject thread.

Where can I find law-related listservs?

Each listserv deals with a particular topic. Because listservs are focused on a specific subject, they are a good place to share ideas, problems, and to get assistance with research questions. Generally, you must subscribe to each listserv from which you want to view information. Listservs may provide a large amount of information (emails), so it is best to subscribe to only one or two that meet your needs and interests. "Law Lists" maintained by Lyonette Louis-Jacques of University of Chicago Law School is the best web site for locating law- related listservs. Another good site to find various groups and listservs is http://www.washlaw.edu/listservs/.

How can I subscribe to a listserv?

First you select the listserv you want to join. Since some listservs may distribute hundreds of email messages a week, if not a day, depending on how active the list is, you may not wish to subscribe to more than one or two listservs. Any valid email account may be used to subscribe. However if possible, it is best to create a new email address to receive and view these emails. Separate email accounts allow you to quickly scan new listserv emails and prevent personal or other business related emails from becoming mixed in with the large number of listserv messages. Use the email program you wish to receive the listserv emails on to subscribe to a listserv.

To join, compose a new email message and insert the appropriate listserv email address in the "To" line of the email program. In the message area, type the word 'subscribe' followed by the list address and your first and last name on one line. For example, if you want to subscribe to liibulletin to receive United States Supreme Court case summaries (do not use the quotation marks):

Message to:listsev@listserv.law.cornell.edu

Message area: subscribe liibulletin "first name and last name"

To subscribe to the Bankruptcy Law discussion listserv type in:

Message to:bankrlaw@polecat.law.indiana.edu

Message area: subscribe bankrlaw "your name"

What is Internet Relay Chat?

Internet Relay Chat (IRC) allows people all over the world to converse with one another in real time over the Internet.

What is Instant Messaging?

Instant Messaging (IM) allows users to converse in real time with other users who are using the same instant messaging program. Essentially, the software, several versions of which can be downloaded for free, allows users to conduct online conversations in real time without all that annoying and time-consuming spam. It also allows users and their contacts to say whether they are logged off, busy or available, something email typically does not do unless a user creates an automatic reply. There are several popular IM programs: MSN Messenger, AOL Instant Messenger, Yahoo Messenger, and ICQ.

What is telnet?

Another method of accessing information on the Internet is telnet. Telnet is an Internet tool that makes one computer a terminal for other computers on the Internet. Telnet permits the local user to use a program located on the remote computer.

What is FTP?

FTP (File Transfer Protocol) is software that enables you to transfer a file from a remote computer to your local machine.

What is open source?

Open source software includes programs that are not controlled by a single company. The software can be developed by anyone, with few restrictions. The best known such software is the Linux operating system, which can be downloaded free from the Internet.

What is an intranet?

An intranet is an in-house version of the Internet found within companies and organizations. Typically, only those within the company or organization have access to the company's intranet. Most of the computers used in a firm are connected to the firm's intranet. Law firms commonly use intranets to post all information related to a particular practice area. More than one practice area may be included on a firm intranet.

A company's intranet is often connected to the Internet giving the company's computers access to the web. The company is able to regulate this web access in order to prevent any security breaches to its own computers. However, users of the Internet must be careful when downloading suspect programs or opening suspect emails on their computers. Viruses and damaging programs can bypass the intranet's security mechanisms when users request a download or open unknown emails. Because all of the company's computers are connected via the intranet if one user's computer gets infected it can quickly infect all the computers connected to the intranet, causing major problems.

What is an extranet?

A network designed to provide, disseminate, and share confidential information externally with clients using the look and feel of the World Wide Web.

Extranets serve as repositories of information relevant to clients' cases. The extranets also offer new technical Web applications. For instance, software can allow clients to:

- Use templates to generate legal documents, such as nondisclosure agreements, based on specific business rules;
- Track agreements so clients can monitor the cases handled by the law firm
- Track legal trends within clients' industries and produce reports (Richard A. Weiss, *Legal Times*, Oct 23, 2006).

What is a firewall?

A firewall allows users from inside an organization to access the Internet but keeps outside users from accessing the computers or networks.

Firewalls are hardware and software combinations that are built using routers, servers, and a variety of software. They "sit" at the most vulnerable point between a corporate network and the Internet, and they can be as simple or complex as a system administrator wants to build them. There are many types of firewalls. Firewalls allow anyone on the corporate network to access the Internet, but they stop crackers, hackers, or others on the Internet from gaining access to the corporate network and causing damage. (Gralla, Preston, *How the Internet Works*)

What is RSS?

RSS are "feeds" which allows you to see when sites from all over the Internet have added new content. You can get the latest headlines and articles (or even audio files, photographs or video) in one place, as soon as they are published, without having to remember to visit each site every day.

RSS (known as Rich Site Summary or Really Simple Syndication) have started to make waves in content management and delivery of information, and they are a guiding force for professionals interested in keeping abreast of what is going on in their profession. RSS feeds are written in XML (Extended Markup Language) code.

Where can I find a list of available RSS feeds?

No single source provides a list of all available RSS feeds. The best way to find feeds is to watch for them as you find web sites with content that interests you. Most blogs and news sites have feeds. (Robert J. Ambrogi, 2007 USA 68)

How do I read RSS feeds?

A news aggregator (sometime called newsreader) is your tool for gathering, organizing, and reading RSS headlines. A news aggregator is simply a kind of software that periodically polls a specified set of web sites or blogs and then pulls the latest headlines and displays them on a single page.

What are the popular newsreaders for RSS feeds?
There are number of tools available for reading RSS feeds, including desktop and web-based styles. Some of the popular news aggregators are:

Bloglines (www.bloglines.com)

Feedster (www.feedster.com)

Newsgator (www.newsgator.com)

Awasu (www.awasu.com)

FeedDemon (www.feeddemon.com)

Do courts make their cases available as RSS feeds?
Some courts now make their cases available as RSS feeds which can be located on Findlaw.com.

What is Atom?
Atom is a simple way to read and write information on the web, allowing you to easily keep track of more sites in less time, and to seamlessly share your words and ideas by publishing to the web.

Atom is a format quite similar to RSS. It was created by people who felt that RSS could be improved upon, and others that disagreed with some of the politics regarding RSS. The basic difference is that while Atom is somewhat more complex (for *producers* of Atom feeds), it is also able to carry more complex information, and it is consistent across the syndication, storage, and editing of information. You can learn more about Atom at the official web site, www.AtomEnabled.org.

What is XML?
XML (extended markup language) is used to write RSS feeds etc.

What is a blog?
Blogs, short for "Web logs," are web sites belonging to an individual consisting of diaries, journals, opinions, reviews, clippings, musings and other personal tidbits posted, typically daily for others to read. What makes blogs differ from other personal noodling or dairy writings is blogs may take advantage of hyperlinks. Additionally, they may provide quick answers to hot topics before they are available in the standard literature.

What is a blawg?
Law related blogs (legal blogs) are knows as blawgs. Denise Howell coined the terms "blawg" and "blawgosphere" for the community of legal bloggers.

What are the popular legal blawgs?
The following are few of the many popular blawgs:

Law Professors (www.lawprofblogs.com)
How Appealing (appellateblog.blogspot.com)
Be Spacific (www.bespacific.com)
Inter Alia (www.inter-alia.net)
Bag and Baggage (http://www.bgbg.blogspot.com)

What are the index tools for blogs / weblogs?
Index tools assist a user in finding particular weblogs as well as providing a search engine for particular topics located among the various weblogs.

Daypop (www.daypop.com)
Technorati (www.technorati.com)
Blogdex (blogdex.media.mit.edu)

Is there any index exclusively for legal blawgs?
BlawgSearch (http://blawgsearch.justia.com) indexes law related blawgs. Content of this index is organized into: Most Popular; Categories; Recent Search Terms; Blawg Post Tags; Recent Posts; and Featured Blawger.

Are blawgs cited in the court opinions?
Recently courts have started citing legal blogs (blawgs) in their opinions, e.g., *U.S. v. Booker*, 543 U.S. 220, 277 n4 (2005) (Stevens dissent), *U.S. v. Scott*, 450 F.3d 863, 894 n5 (9th Cir. 2006). Law X.0 blawg has an ongoing article on "Cases Citing Legal Blawgs."

What are micro-blogs?
Mobile Internet devices and online communities are merging with a new kind of web diary "microblogging", where people fire off terse missives about what they are doing or thinking at any given moment. The postings are bare-bones, on-the-go versions of online journals in which people share their lives and dreams – hence the name micro-blogging. Example are Twitter, www.twitter.com, Jaiku, www.jaiku.com, Utterz, www.utterz.com etc.

What is mobblogging?
Mobblogging refers to the ability to add materials such as text, photos etc. to one's blog when away from a computer.

What is a vlog?
A vlog or video blog is a blog (short for weblog) which uses video as the primary content. The video is linked to a videoblog post and is usually

accompanied by supporting text, images, and additional metadata to provide content (Wikipedia).

How can I create my own blog?

There are several companies that allow you to create blogs. One of the more popular companies is Blogger (www.blogger.com). Using this web site you can produce your own blog in less than five to ten minutes by following the directions listed on the web site. You are not required to know any markup language to create a blog.

What is podcasting?

Podcasting is a way to receive audio files over the Internet. Many content providers offer podcast feeds at no cost. These feeds deliver audio broadcasts to your desktop. You can listen to these files on your computer or load them on to your MP3 player and listen to them at your leisure.

Several law firms are using podcasts as recruiting tools. Law firms are creating "pod centers" where the prospective student employees can hear testimonials of the previous hires and learn about various job related issues.

How do I listen to podcasts?

All you need to get started is podcasting software. Once you have download and installed the software, simply add the podcast feeds. The podcasting software will automatically check for updates and download the files to your computer so you can load them onto your MP3 player.

Here are some popular podcast programs:

Bloglines (www.bloglines.com)

iTunes (Windows/OS X) (www.apple.com/itunes/download/) **Juice** (Windows/OS X/Linux) (juicereceiver.sourceforge.net/index.php)

jPodder (Windows) (www.jpodder.com/)

iPodderX (OS X) (ipodderx.com/)

Depending on the software used, to listen to a specific podcasting segment, it is usually just a matter of selecting the "play audio" option. The MP3 file will play directly on your computer.

Where can I find legal podcasts?

http://blawgfm.justia.com offers several legal podcasts.

What are the popular legal podcasts?

The following are some of the podcasts available for and by lawyers:

Legal Talk Network (www.legaltalknetwork.com)
May It Please the Court (www.mayitpleasethecourt.net)
Legal Underground (www.legalunderground.com/podcasts)
Family Law News and Views (familylawnewsandviews.blogspot.com)
Internet Cases (www.Internetcases.com)
Criminal Law (www.criminallaw.blogspot.com)

What is a widget?
A widget is a small application that runs on your desktop. The widget pulls data – news, pictures, videos, games, etc. from one source/place and displays that information on your own sites. Google, http://desktop.google.com/plugins, Yahoo, http://widgets.yahoo.com provide several useful widgets.

What is a lawcast?
Lawcast is a podcast about a legal topic. Denis Howell coined the term "plawdosphere" for the community of legal professionals with podcasts.

What is VODcast?
VOD (Video On Demand) is a syndicated video content. Many web sites will offer video broadcasts of prerecorded information that can be either downloaded or streamed directly from the web site.

What is a Wiki?
A wiki is a collaborative web site comprised of the collective work of many authors. Similar to a blog in structure and logic, a wiki allows anyone to edit, delete, or modify content that has been placed on the web site using a browser interface, including the work of previous authors. A wiki may be continuously edited and updated. The first wiki (wiki means "quick" in Hawaiian language) was created by Ward Cunningham in 1995.

What is pbwiki?
Pbwiki (www.pbwiki.com) allows a person to create their own wiki free of charge. Another free hosting site is www.wikihost.org.

What is Wikipedia?
Wikipedia is an encyclopedia written collaboratively by many of its readers. It uses a special type of web site, called a wiki that makes collaboration easy. Lots of people are constantly improving Wikipedia, making thousands of changes an hour, all of which are recorded on article histories and recent changes. Inappropriate changes are usually removed quickly (Wikipedia).

What is JurisPedia?

JurisPedia (www.jurispedia.org) is an encyclopedic project of academic initiative devoted to worldwide law, legal, and political sciences.

What is Miki?

Miki is a wiki program for mobile applications, in a move aimed at extending wikis to cell phones and other mobile devices.

What is 3Book?

3Book is a digital book that has the appearance of a real book on the computer screen. A reader can turn its pages by touching the corner of each page or touching the edge of the display to flip through pages quickly.

Flipviewer (www.flipviewer.com) and NextbookMedia are other digital book programs which publish magazines using digital technology to flip through the pages of the magazines.

What are viruses?

Computer viruses are typically spread through email attachments. Do not open attachments with ".exe", ".bat" or ".com" file extensions. The Klez virus can infect your computer without opening the attachment. Computer viruses can now affect your machine just from visiting a web page. It is advisable to have an anti-virus program installed on your computer.

What is spam?

Spam is unsolicited and unwanted junk email. Spam is named after a famous Monty Python skit on the canned meat product. Email marketing is cheaper than telemarketing and direct mailings, but is generally less effective. As a result spammers send massive amounts of messages often indiscriminately. To avoid spam, use blocking features, unique email addresses, and email filters.

What is spyware?

Spyware is software installed on your computer without your knowledge or explicit permission and serves some nefarious purpose. In general, spyware gathers confidential information from your computer and automatically transmits back to the individual or organization that planted it on your computer.

An example of spyware is a "keystroke logger", which is a program that runs in the background on your computer and records every keystroke you make.

What is adware?

Adware is software that gathers information about your web-surfing habits in order to target you with pop-up advertisements for products and services that might be of interest to you. Unlike spyware, adware is generally installed with the user's knowledge and permission, usually in exchange for software that is free but supported by advertisers.

What is sneakware?
Sneakware uses deceptive means to sneak onto your computers. Users grant permission for the software to be installed, but the user is often unaware he is granting permission. Unlike adware, which tracks browsing activities and delivers pop-up ads, sneakware often makes changes to your system.

What is malware?
Malware, or malicious software, enters a PC (through infected emails or downloads) and converts it into a bot or zombie. By creating a network of 1,000s of bots that work as one entity controlled by the originator, these networks can be used for launching targeted mass attacks on other PC's, including sending spam, spreading viruses, or even stealing data.

What are cookies?
Cookies are text files web servers save on your PC. Many cookies are beneficial. Some sites remember your user ID or password to make logging-in easier. Others provide customized news or weather updates. Shopping sites might keep track of items you want to buy. The site reads small bits of identifying information it left on your hard drive the previous time you visited, links it up with additional data, and sends customized pages to your desktop. Cookies let web sites know who you are. Some sites, however use cookies for more sneaky purposes. For instance, ads embedded in web sites might plant third-party cookies of their own.

What is phishing?
Phishing scams – named for the way victims are baited and reeled in – are mass emails and web sites mimicking authentic communications and sites of financial institutions. Warnings of identity theft or pending account cancellations prompt victims to "confirm" financial information in an email response or on a fake web site. The information is actually relayed to the scammer, who uses it to clean out bank accounts or fraudulently open lines of credit.

What is site spoofing?
Spoofing means parody. On the web, people create a site similar to the original or official site but then provide bogus information. Other sites aim to criticize the original site or simply provide humor. Some examples are:

www.MyPyramid.gov vs. www.MyPyramid.org

www.whitehouse.gov vs. www.whitehouse.org

www.WTO.org vs. www.GATT.org

What is a desktop search?

Desktop search programs search your computer's hard drive packed with documents, spreadsheets, pictures, email, music and video files along with Internet sites. The big web search sites, including Google (www.desktop.google.com), Microsoft's MSN (www.toolbar.msn.com), and Yahoo (www.desktop.yahoo.com) offer desktop search programs. Free for the download, they take just minutes to install. Afterwards, you can search your computer's hard drive just as if you were using a search site. Type a keyword or phrase and documents, email or files that contain it appear as search results.

What is a federated search?

Federated searching aggregates multiple channels of information into a single searchable point. This blends e-journals, subscription databases, electronic print collections, other digital repositories, and the Internet. The vendors of these search engines offer their products as a way to search multiple subscription resources at one time through an easy to use front-end. The user does not need to know which database offers a particular journal title or learn a search syntax for each service. The federated search product searches the services subscribed to by the researcher's library and returns a combined search results list.

Are there any federated search engines for legal information?

Lexis and Westlaw introduced "Total Search" and "KM" products respectively for law firm usage. For example, the Lexis Total Search allows an attorney to search both Lexis databases and the law firm's own documents simultaneously. The researcher will obtain two sets of results, one from Lexis and one listing in-house documents. Thus, "Total Search" ensures that an attorney using Lexis for a legal question will be made aware if there are in house briefs or memoranda addressing the issue.

What is Search Engine Optimization (SEO)?

Search Engine Optimization (SEO) is the science of search as it relates to marketing on the web. It is mostly technical in nature, combining programming with business, persuasion, sales, and a love for competitive puzzle solving into a written form capable of maintaining desired revenue goals while achieving high rankings in the organic sections of search engine results pages. (www.bruceclay.com/wb_rank.htm)

What are user-created content sites?

User-created content sites, like Amazon and You Tube —give individuals the ability to create customer reviews, post messages, videos, etc.

What is social networking?
Sharing views, photos, etc. among people through free web sites offered by online services.

What are the popular social networking web sites?
The popular social networking sites are: Facebook (www.facebook.com), MySpace (www.myspace.com), Friendster (www.friendster.com),

Xanga (www.xanga.com), and WeIshare (www.weishare.com).

Wink, http://wink.com, Spock, http://spock.com, Zoominfo, http://zoominfo.com are few of the many popular people search Internet sites.

Lawyers can make contacts with several companies and corporations through the following web sites: Accenture, www.accenture.com, WebCrossing Inc., www.webcrossing.com, Jigsaw Data Corp., www.jigsaw.com.

When you are looking for a job and share your resume Linkedin (www.linkedin.com) is a good source. If you are looking for a job and would rather get in touch with your real geographic community including government officials, I-Neighbors (www.i-neighbors.org) is a good source.

Are there any social networking web sites for attorneys?
There are social networking sites exclusively for the legal community, e.g., Martindale-Hubbell, www.martindale.com/connected, American Bar Association site, legallyminded.com, lawlink, www.lawlink.com. In addition, social networking sites such as Linkedin (www.linkedin.com) has more than 90,000 lawyer members.

What is social bookmarking?
Social bookmarking is an increasingly popular way to locate, classify, rank and share Internet resources through the use of shared lists of user-created Internet bookmarks, the practice of tagging, and inferences drawn from grouping and use of such tags (Wikipedia). To create a collection of social bookmarks, you have to register with a social bookmarking cite.

What are the popular social bookmarking tools?
There are several social bookmarking tools in the market. The following are some of the popular social bookmarking tools.

De.Icio.Us http://del.icio.us
CiteULike: http://www.citeulike.org
BlinkList: http://blinklist.com
Furl: http://www.furl.net

What are virtual worlds?

Virtual worlds are online, computer-based simulated environment, where people create their own avatars to interact with each other, e.g., Second Life.

What is the Creative Commons?

The Creative Commons (CC) is a non-profit organization devoted to expanding the range of creative work available for others to legally build upon and share.

The Creative Commons web site enables copyright holders to grant some of their rights to the public while retaining others through a variety of licensing and contract schemes including dedication to the public domain or open content licensing terms. The intention is to avoid the limitations and problems current copyright laws create for the sharing of information (Wikipedia).

What is open access?

Open access includes an author's agreement to distribute published work for free, as well as to create the technical structure responsible for distribution on the Internet. In open access, the public can access the work, but no modification can be made. On the other hand, peer review of published articles is encouraged. (Shelli Shaw, *Information Today*, p.24, Sep. 2006)

What is open content?

Open content, which allows any given published work to be modified unlike open access information which cannot be modified.

What is web monitoring?

Using web site monitoring software, web-tracking services can monitor any sites that users have specified and notify them when any changes have occurred on that particular page. Web users do not have to return to each page every day to see if any changes have occurred. The software will do it for them.

What are the popular web monitoring services?

Watch that Page (www.watchthatpage.com), Infominder (www.infominder.com), Track Engine (www.trackengine.com), web site Watcher (aignes.com), Tracelock (www.tracelock.com), and Change Detection (www.changedetection.com).

What are bookmarklets?

Bookmarklets are links, but they do not link to web pages, they link to a tiny JavaScript program. Each bookmarklet is a tiny program, a JavaScript application, contained in a bookmark. The URL is a 'javascript:' link, which can be saved and executed from Internet Explorer's "Favorites" panel.

Bookmarklets are used in the same way you would use normal bookmarks, but with more features and more control over what you see. Power Bookmarklets present you with bookmarklets for Page Data, Page Look, Power Navigation, Power tools and Power Search. Each of these bookmarklets gives you control over the way you navigate through different web sites and improves your surfing experience.

How do I get bookmarklets?

To add a bookmarklet to your link bar (Internet Explorer), click down on the link, and drag it onto the link bar. If you do not see a link bar, go to *View > Toolbars* and make sure that *Links* is checked off. To add it anywhere else, right-click on the link and select *Add to Favorites*. If you see a warning that says the link may not be safe, click 'ok.' All of these bookmarklets are safe (Faganfinder).

How do I use bookmarklets?

When you are on any page, just select the bookmarklet as you would a normal link. If you are using Internet Explorer and have the bookmarklet on your link bar, then just click on the link.

What do "parked" web sites mean?

Trademark counterfeiters often set up "parked" web sites, which exist for no purpose other than to attract and redirect Internet traffic to other sites.

What is meant by "typosquatting"?

"Parked" web sites characteristically draw in users by incorporating or imitating well-known names and trademarks in their domain names. For example, a user trying to reach Citibank's web site might accidentally type www.citibabnk.com instead, and find they are at a parked web site with multiple links to other sites.

What is Wi-Fi?

Wi-Fi, short for "Wireless fidelity", is a term for certain types of wireless local area networks (WLAN). Many airports, hotels, and fast-food facilities offer public access to Wi-Fi networks. These locations are known as hot spots. (www.whatis.com)

What is hot spot?

For users of portable computers equipped for wireless, a hot spot (or *hotspot*) is a wireless LAN (local area network) node that provides an Internet connection and virtual private network (VPN) access from a given location. For example, a business traveler with a laptop equipped for Wi-Fi can look up a local hot spot, contact it, and get connected through its network to reach the Internet and their own company remotely with a secure connection. Increasingly, public places, such as airports, hotels, and coffee shops are providing free wireless access for customers.

The Wi-Fi Alliance provides a list of hot spots through its Wi-Fi Zone program. A number of companies such as Sprint and Cometa plan to provide a nationwide network of hot spots. (www.whatis.com)

CHAPTER 14

WORLD WIDE WEB

Students are introduced to the terminology of the web including types of browsers, domain names, saving and bookmarking of urls.

What is the World Wide Web?

The 'Web', short for the World Wide Web (WWW), is part of the Internet. Web pages are written in HyperText Markup Language (HTML). To make web pages interactive several software packages and languages have been developed. Some of them are Javascript, Java, Perl, and C. Currently there are more than one billion web pages. Web pages include hypertext links, graphics, audio and video files. Some of the documents are available in portable document format (PDF). Web pages include several hyperlinks connecting them to other web pages. For easy identification the hyperlinks are in a different color and generally underscored.

What is Web 2.0?

The term Web 2.0 was given by Tim O'Reilly, founder of O'Reilly Media. Web 2.0 mainly included works of collaboration and social networking. Also the RSS feeds, Wiki's, and Podcasts are part of Web 2.0

Who invented the Web?

Tim Berners-Lee invented the Web.

What is a web site?

A web site is where information is located. It is similar to a database in Westlaw or a library and file in Lexis. Each web site is made up of many web pages.

What is a web page?

A web page is found within a web site. When you use the Internet, you view web pages one at a time. Many web pages contain hypertext links to other related web pages. They allow the user to click on a link in order to move directly to the linked page.

How are web pages written?

The main language used to write a web page is HTML (HyperText Markup Language). However, to create dynamic web pages authors use DHTML, XML, script languages such as Javascript, C+++, Perl, CGI-script, Flash, etc.

How much information is available on the Internet?

The amount of information on the web varies depending on who compiles the statistics. Some say it is in billions of pages if you include the invisible web. However, Google, which is the most popular search engine, has indexed more than ten million web pages and continues to expand its indexes. According to Netcraft's Rich Miller there are now 100 million websites with domain names and content on them.

How can I access the information on the World Wide Web?

You can access the World Wide Web through a web browser.

What are the popular browsers now?

Internet Explorer and Firefox.

What are popular alternate browsers?

Mozilla (www.mozilla.org); Opera (www.opera.com); and google chrome, www.google.com/chrome.

Do I need to have an alternative browser also?

It is good to have an alternative browser such as Firefox, Opera or Amaya in addition to your regular browser for various reasons: for speed, security, pop-up blocker, voice controlled features etc.

What is tabbed browsing?

Tabbed browsing means that instead of needing to open multiple windows for each web site you visit, you can see multiple sites simultaneously within one window. This allows you to open one Internet browser window and view a number of web sites at the same time. Firefox, Opera, Amaya all offer tabbed browsing.

What is a voice feature in a web browser?

The Opera browser has a voice feature that allows you to control the interface by talking, provided you have a microphone and are using a PC running Windows XP. When you give it the command to speak, Opera can read the site content and email messages.

What are browsing companions?

Browsing companions are simple desktop utilities that facilitate searching, gathering, and managing items of interest from the Internet. They make the entire process of surfing the web much simpler. Some popular examples are various tool bars provided by search engines such as Yahoo toolbar, Google toolbar, etc.

What is browser-based search?

A majority of the browsers such as Internet Explorer, Firefox, etc. have a built-in search feature. Most utilize Google, Yahoo, or other search engine to perform the search.

Can I view a web page in a foreign language other than English?

All of the major general purpose search engines such as Google, Yahoo, Ask, MSN do provide an option of converting web sites from English to other foreign languages (use advanced search feature). You can even translate the text of a document from language to language. For example, Altavista (www.altavista.com) provides a translation service called "Babel Fish Translation".

What is the "find" feature?

When faced with a long web page and a need to quickly locate a particular word, you can use Internet Explorer's "Find" (on the page) tool (click on the 'edit' button from the menu bar) to search the web page you are currently viewing. You may also use the keys 'Control' and press 'F' to get a "Find" dialog box. The dialog box will contain options which allow you to locate a specific word found on that web page.

What is TLD?

TLD stands for Top Level Domain name. The first batch of approved TLD's are: .com, .edu, .gov, .org, .net, .mil, and .co. (for countries followed by the two letter country code). For example .co.uk for United Kingdom.

Who provides the TLDs?

TLDs are approved by ICANN.

What is ICANN?

The Internet Corporation for Assigned Names and Numbers is an internationally organized, non-profit corporation that has responsibility for Internet Protocol (IP) address space allocation, protocol identifier assignment, generic (gTLD) and country code (ccTLD) Top-Level Domain name system management and root server system management functions.

What are ICANN-approved TLDs?
The World Wide Web was initially subdivided into generic and country code top-level domains (gTLDs and ccTLDs.) The original set of seven gTLDs were .com, .edu, .gov, .org, .mil, .net, .int, In 2000, an additional seven gTLDs were added: .aero, .biz, .coop, .info, .museum, .name, and .pro. In 2004 ICANN announced a plan for the introduction of more gTLDs. In 2005, the employment, e-commerce, and tourism gTLDs - .jobs, .mobi, and .travel were approved.

What are unsponsored TLDs?
Generally several organizations or people request for TLDs for variety of reasons. There are seven unsponsored domain names: .biz, .com, .info, .name, .net, .org. and .pro.

What are sponsored TLDs?
There are seven sponsored TLDs: .aero, .museum, .coop, .travel, .jobs, .mobi, and .cat. These are sponsored by various organizations.

What are the good domain names for lawyers and law firms?
The TLDs .pro, .info, and .biz are useful for the legal community. The TLD .pro is exclusively available only to lawyers along with accountants and doctors. .info and .biz are useful for law firms to advertise their information.

What is meant by domain name tasting?
Where speculators register a large number of domain names and try them out under the Internet Corporation of Assigned Names and Numbers (ICANN) 5-day money back guarantee. (Correy E. Stephenson, 2007LUSA 223)

Where can I register a domain name?
You may buy most of the domain names from many sources such as Yahoo (www.yahoo.com), Godaddy (www.godaddy.com), Networksolutions (www.networksolutions.com), Register (www.register.com) etc. for a very nominal fee. However, .pro and other new domain names are available only from a few web sites. You may register a web site using the .pro TLD from Register (www.register.com).

What is the title bar?
The title bar will have the name of the web site or title of the page you are viewing. It is found on the top, left-hand corner of your screen. This horizontal blue bar runs across the entire width of your screen. On the right side of the bar you will see the "minimize," "restore," and "close" buttons.

What is the menu bar?
The menu bar is the horizontal band that contains commands and options that can be chosen. In Internet Explorer, these selections are File, Edit, View, Favorites, Tools, and Help.

What is the address bar?
The address bar or address box or locator box provides you the location or address of the current page you are viewing. Each web page has a unique address called a Uniform Resource Locator or URL.

What is a homepage?
A homepage is the page that appears first when you enter an URL (web address) in the browser. You will automatically see the default page set for your browser, unless you choose to select a different page for your home page.

How do I change my default homepage?
The way you change your home page depends on the type of browser you use. If you use Netscape, select 'Preferences' from the 'Edit' menu and enter the desired URL and the click 'O.K.'. If you use the Internet Explorer, choose 'Internet options' under the 'Tools' menu and enter the desired URL and click 'O.K.'

What is a URL?
URL stands for Universal Resource Locator. It is the address or location of a web site. The URL or web address is typically composed of four parts: A protocol name (a protocol is a set of rules and standards that enable computers to exchange information); the location of the site; the name of the organization that maintains the site; and a suffix that identifies the kind of organization it is. For example, this URL http://www.duq.edu shows *http://* to denote this is a web server that uses Hypertext Transfer Protocol (HTTP), the most common protocol on the Internet. The *www* indicates that this site is on the World Wide Web. The *duq* indicates that the web server is at Duquesne University; and the *edu* indicates the URL is from an educational institution.

What is HTML?
HTML stands for Hyper Text Markup Language. This is the basic language used to create a web page.

How do I find the HTML code for every web page?
Click on the 'View' option from the browser menu and click on 'Source' to reveal the html code used to create that page.

What are the main HTML tags used to create web pages?
The main tags used to create a web page are: <html>, <title>, <head>, and <body> tags. Once the desired text is filled for every field, those tags have to be closed by adding a backward slash, </html>, </title>, </head>, and </body>

However, there are several tags to create links, forms and other options necessary to create more elaborate web pages.

Are there any other languages or scripts needed to create web pages?
In addition to HTML, web authors may use XTML, DHTML, Java, Javascript, Pearl, CGI script, C++, Flash, and other languages to make more dynamic web pages.

What is .shtml in a url?
A web file with the suffix of ".shtml" (rather than the usual ".htm") indicates a file that includes some information that will be added "on the fly" by the server before it is sent to you. A typical use is to include a "Last modified" date at the bottom of the page. (www.searchSOA.com)

If I have to create a web page do I have to know all these languages and scripts?
Web editors such as Microsoft's Frontpage, Macromedia's DreamWeaver, and other programs will help you to create web pages without knowing HTML and other scripting languages. Many word processors allow you to save a document as HTML.

Can I read the web pages when I am not connected to the Internet?
You can save web pages as you normally would by selecting 'Save As' from the "File" option on the toolbar. However, some hyperlinks may not work if you do not have all the pages of the site saved. Netscape and Internet Explorer both will allow you to save web sites as off-line and read them even when you are not connected to the Internet.

How can I access a specific web site?
Once you know the web site address, also known as the URL (Universal or Uniform Resources Locator), replace the existing one by typing it in the location box. For example if you are in Findlaw, you will see its address as: http://www.findlaw. com in the location box when you use Netscape or in the address box when you use Internet Explorer. Replace the address by typing: http://www.law.cornell.edu to access the Cornell Site.

Do I need to remember the web address every time I use it?
Once you know that you use a particular web site, bookmark it for future use. In Netscape it is called a bookmark and it is known as a favorite in Internet Explorer.

How do I bookmark?
When you are viewing a particular web site, click on the "Bookmarks" option from the Netscape main menu and then select "Add bookmark". Similarly you may do the same thing by selecting "favorites" within Internet Explorer. When you have added several bookmarks/favorites to your list, you should organize them into separate files. For example, you can group all federal legal sites under the file heading, 'Federal' and all Pennsylvania sites under the file heading, 'Pennsylvania.'

How can I save web pages?
You can save your web pages by printing through your printer by selecting the print option from the File menu, or you can save to your disk by selecting 'Save As' from the File menu or you may also email the entire web page or selected text to your own email address.

What is WebCD?
"WebCD" is a concept of creating your own virtual CD on the Web. By selecting different songs and adding them to your WebCD, you can create dozens of collections of your favorite music available to you anytime and anywhere. You can use your WebCD anywhere you have Internet access. (www.smashits.com)

What are the bookmark managers?
Bookmark managers are software programs designed to help users keep track of their favorite web sites, as well as their favorite blogs and subscription feeds. Link Commander (www.linkcommander.com), Bookmark Buddy (www.bookmarkbuddy. com), iFaves (ifaves.com), SiteBar (www.sitebar.com) are some of the popular bookmark managers.

Sometimes I cannot connect to a web site. What is the reason?
Generally web addresses are case sensitive. If you receive any error messages such as 404 File Not Found or Moved to New Address, it is because the server is unable to find the DNS (Dominion Name Server) entry, or the site is moved to a new host, or the current server is under maintenance. However, when there are a lot of users trying to access information you will see a message on your browser's bottom function bar 'trying to connect'. In those circumstances click on 'stop' and retry by clicking on "Enter" to allow the browser to use a different router.

How can I conduct research on a specific issue?

As you know, there are more than a billion web pages. Search engines visit those pages and index them and store them as a database. You have several general search engines such as Yahoo, Looksmart, Lycos, Altavista, Google, Alltheweb to name a few. There are several specific subject oriented search engines that only index web pages related to the specific subject. For example, when you are doing legal research you should use Findlaw or Law.com rather than Yahoo.

CHAPTER 15

SEARCH ENGINES

Students are introduced to the different types of general-purpose search engines. The questions explain how general search engines gather information and how they display the information to the user.

What are search engines?

A search engine is a tool (web site) that searches the information available on the Internet, then classifies, categorizes and indexes it for easy retrieval by users. When you enter your query in the dialog box, the search engine looks for matching web pages stored in its indexed databases to assist you with your inquiry.

When did search engines emerge?

The first group of search engines emerged in 1993. However, some of the popular search engines used today, for example, Yahoo, were created in 1994.

What are the popular search engines?

The top four search engines are: google (www.google.com); Yahoo (www.yahoo. com); MSN (www.msn.com); and Ask (www.ask.com). However, there are several other popular search engines such as Lycos (www.lycos.com); Altavista (www. altavista.com); Looksmart (www.looksmart.com); and Hotbot (www.hotbot.com), etc.

What does "Search within Results" mean?

For Google, Ask, Yahoo.

Google: After you enter your initial search into the query box a list of hits will appear on the page. At the bottom of the page, underneath the query box, is the button "search within the results". Once you select this option, a new query box will appear. When you enter the new parameters for the search, Google will only search within the results of the original search. This allows you to narrow your inquiry displaying web sites that are pertinent to your search. This option is useful when you are looking for a very specific topic but are having a hard time finding a relevant web site.

Ask: Ask does not have a traditional "search within the results" option. After you enter your initial search into the query box, and your results are displayed, you will find several options on the right side of the screen. These options allow you to narrow, expand, and choose a particular person that may be relevant to your search. However, once you select these terms it does not search within the results, it instead carries out a new search based on the selected option.

Yahoo does not allow a user to search within the results, but a user can make a search more specific by choosing the advanced search option found to the right of the query bar on the results page.

Do I have to use upper case letters when I use connectors in my query?

No. Yahoo, Google, and Ask do not require you to use upper case connectors when performing a search. In fact, searches are not case sensitive and the search engine will often ignore the common term in order to accelerate the search.

What is a cached link?

Yahoo, Google, Ask: After you enter your search into the query box, the search engine will display the results of your search. You will notice that underneath each result there will be a link called "cached". If you click on this link it will take you to a previously saved version of that web page. Each search engine will periodically search the web itself in order to index web sites so they are available when a user runs a search. The cached link is the saved version of that web site the search engine found when it last searched that web page. As a result, when you click that link you may be looking at an old version of the web page dating back to the last time that particular search engine updated its index. Caching allows the user to view a web site that may not be available when the user runs his or her search by showing the cached version of the web page.

Sometimes the search engine will not have cached a particular web page, and will not give you the option to view the cached results.

What are similar pages in the search results?

Yahoo and Ask do not offer the similar pages option.

Google: When you come to the results page, after entering a query, you will notice that there is a "similar pages" link located near the bottom of each result. When you select this link, Google will conduct a new search of the web for other web sites related to this link. This can be useful when you need to narrow your search and you find a specific web page that is pertinent.

What are indented results?

Indented results are not offered by Yahoo or Ask.

Google: When you enter your search into the query box Google will display the results. Sometimes these results will be indented, and you will notice that the indented results originate from the same web page as the previously listed result. The indented result occurs when Google finds multiple results from the same web site, the most relevant result is listed first, with other relevant pages from that site indented below it. This assists the user by allowing him or her to go directly to the relevant information without having to navigate through several web pages.

How do I differentiate actual results from sponsored results?

Google: Sponsored links are found on the right hand side of the page, and will be marked as "Sponsored Links". Web sites pay for the privilege of having their web sites listed prominently on the results page.

Yahoo: Yahoo will list their sponsored links either at the top of the page or on the right hand side of the page depending on how many sponsored links correspond with your search. Yahoo will mark these links as "Sponsored Results."

Ask: Ask will post their sponsored links at the top of the page above the regular search results. They will be found in a lightly shaded box and will also be marked "Sponsored Results."

Generally the sponsored results are not numbered.

What does the summary bar contain?

Google and Yahoo: After you run a query and come to the results page, you will find the summary bar located within a small shaded area above the listed results. The summary bar will display the total number of results found by the search engine, as well as the specific number of results listed on that page. This bar will also display the time taken to complete the search and the specific words used to initiate the search. When a word can be defined, such as when it is not a proper name, Yahoo and Google will link the search terms located in the summary bar with a dictionary allowing you to easily look up the meaning of the words used.

Ask: The summary bar on Ask can also be found above the results within a red shaded area. However, Ask will only display the total number of results found and the number that can be found on that immediate page. Directly underneath the summary bar, Ask provides dictionary, encyclopedia, and thesaurus links for the search terms used when this information is available.

What is an advanced search?

Yahoo: After you run a search, you will notice a link called "Advanced Search" found to the right of the query box on the results page. When you click that link, Yahoo directs you to a new page that allows you to narrow your search. Yahoo offers a wide assortment of options that allow you to tailor your search for specific information. This can be useful when a regular search is bringing up a large number of results that are impossible to fully examine. By making the search more specific you can hone in on the information that you are looking for.

Google: Google gives you the option to run an advanced search directly from the homepage. If you look to the right of the query box you will see the option advanced search. Once you click that link, Google will take you to a new web page that displays all of the options you can use to narrow your search. Google contains many of the same options used by other search engines.

Ask: Ask has a list of search tools found in a box on the right side of the homepage. You may have to scroll through the options, but the advanced search option is located here. Once you click this link Ask will take you to a new web page that displays all of the options used to narrow your search. These available options are similar to the ones offered by other search engines.

What is a terms and connectors search?
In Lexis and Westlaw the users can formulate their queries by using Boolean connectors (OR; AND; BUT NOT) and proximity connectors (Within a certain number on the same page and same paragraph and phrase search). You have to use advanced search feature to use Boolean connectors on the Internet.

What is a natural language search?
A natural language search is an alternative to the terms and connectors search where users can enter the entire issue or a concept in sentence form without using terms and connectors. Both Lexis and Westlaw offer natural language search methods in addition to the terms and connectors method. In a way, the Internet allows the natural language searching by default.

What other products are available from search engines?
Google: Google offers a wide assortment of products through its web site. To access these, go to the Google homepage and click the "more" link located above the query bar. This will bring up a short list of options. If you then click "even more," Google will direct you to a web page that lists all of the products available

for use. Some of the more popular of these are Google Earth, which shows detailed satellite imagery of the Earth, as well as Google Maps, which makes maps of the world available to the user.

Yahoo: Yahoo also offers a wide variety of sources. Yahoo's homepage contains most of the options available to the user. These can be predominantly found above the tool bar, and within the shaded area along the left side of the screen. However, in order to access all of Yahoo's services click on the "More Yahoo Services" link on the left side of the page, then click "All Yahoo Services", and this will bring you to all of the services offered by Yahoo. You can also link to Yahoo Next through this web page. At Yahoo Next, Yahoo presents all of Yahoo's newest products, some of which are still in the testing phase (beta).

Ask: Ask displays additional options in the search tools box located on the right side of the homepage. Ask allows you to edit and rearrange these options at will, allowing for easier access to them. The options located here are not as numerous as those found on Yahoo or Google, but they do provide the most popular options such as maps, dictionary, etc.

What does "More from this site" mean?
Not an option on Google and Ask.

Yahoo: After you run a search, Yahoo will present you with the results. Next to the "cached" link at the bottom of each result you will find a "more from this site" link. Once this option is selected, Yahoo will search other web pages within that web site for the terms used in your original query. This allows you to navigate directly to the desired web page instead of navigating through the whole web site to find your information.

Can I customize my search engine?
http://google.com/coop seems to be the kind of service that librarians would have considerable interest in. It allows anyone to create a customized Google search engine. You supply a list of URLs and Google allows any users to limit their search to those sites. I did one with a list of U.S. Law School websites at: http://lawlib.wlu.edu/searchlawschools.htm. So you could do something like "dean search" and see only results from U.S. law schools. Lots of possibilities for creating subject domains, such as English legal history, etc. (John Doyle Washington & Lee Law School Library).

Can I save my searches for future use?
Google does not allow you to save a search for future use.

Yahoo: Once you reach the results pages, after having performed a search, you will notice a link marked "save" at the bottom of each result. This link allows you to save the results for later reference. However, Yahoo requires the user to register with Yahoo and create an account to which Yahoo will save your information. While there are more steps required to use this save option, it does allow you to save links for a long period of time, and it permits you to send links via email to other people.

Ask: Once you reach the results page, after having performed a search, you will notice a link marked "save" at the bottom of each result. One you click this link, Ask will save this result for future reference. In fact, even if you close your browser window, and then open a new one, you can still access your saved results. To do this, start a new browser and go to the Ask homepage. Once there go to "My Stuff" located within the search tools box, and click the link. This will bring you to all of your saved results. Ask also allows you to edit, delete, and email this information.

How do search engines collect information?
Search engines employ a software program (automated agents) called spiders (also known as bots or crawlers).

What are spiders / bots / crawlers?
Spiders/bots/crawlers visit and collection information from various web sites and pages and create searchable indexes that can be searched by keywords.

What are sitemaps?
Sitemaps, http://sitemaps.org, "are an easy way for webmasters to inform search engines about pages on their sites that are available for crawling. In its simplest form, a Sitemap is an XML file that lists URLs for a site along with additional metadata about each URL (when it was last updated, how often it usually changes, and how important it is, relative to other URLs in the site) so that search engines can more intelligently crawl the site." (From http://sitemaps.org)

What is the difference between browsing and searching?
The difference between browsing and searching is that in browsing you do not have a place where you can enter your query. You simply have to click on the hypertext link to read the information. Whereas, in searching method you will have an opportunity to enter a query in a dialog box to retrieve information. Some web sites will have both options.

Are there any web sites that show the results in graphical presentation?
Grokker and Kartoo show results in graphical presentation.

What is a portal?
A portal is a gateway to variety of information. It will generally have a directory, a search query box and several add-ons (additional information such as stock quotes, travel, auctions, news etc.)

What is a vortal?
A web site that offers a wide range of resources and services on a specific subject or product is termed a "vortal" or "vertical portal".

What are links?
Once you are on a web site, you will notice some references are highlighted/ underscored with a different color than the text. You may visit those sites by clicking the link and then return to your original site by clicking the "Back" button on the browser's menu.

Do I need to be very specific in my research request?
If you are not specific, you will retrieve several web sites. Generally, each search engine will have a "Help" button or link to explain the general search and advanced search techniques along with some examples. The following are some of the search techniques that may be useful:
- Select a specific web site rather than a general one (e.g. Use Findlaw for legal materials rather than Yahoo).
- Use 'and' 'or' and 'not' when available with search engines.
- Use phrases in quotation, e.g. 'Sexual harassment'
- Look for higher percentages of relevance. Most of the search engines will provide a percentage sign in front of the web sites. Google automatically provides web sites that are most relevant to your research query.
- -Use the + sign to have a specific word(s) in the retrieved list, e.g. "Rule 1008" +"federal rules of evidence". Similarly use the - sign to not have a specific word(s) in the retrieved list, e.g. Lincoln -car when you are looking for president Lincoln. Please remember you have to have a space before the + and - signs.

How do I enter my legal specific query when using general purpose search engines?
When you are using general purpose search engines such as Google, Yahoo, or Altavista, the more specific you can be, the better. For instance, "secured transactions" is better than "uniform commercial code." If you want law specific to Pennsylvania, include Pennsylvania in the search terms. Also, think in terms of key words or phrases rather than full sentences. For example, "estate probate

Pennsylvania" will yield better results than "passing property to the next genera-tion; under Pennsylvania law."

The other thing you have to remember is that the general purpose search en-gines are multi-disciplinary. As such, legal terms of art may give them problems. For example, the terms "will" and "trust" carry special meanings in a legal context. If you use words such as these in a search, you will get many results that are not related to the meaning lawyers attach to them as terms of art.

How do I cite Internet information in a legal document?

You will find proper citation formats for Internet publications under rule 18.2 in the eighteenth edition of the Blue Book. The following is an example: Dittakavi Rao, Digests (last visited Sep.17, 2009) <http://www.pennsylvanialegalresearch.com>

What is "My Module?"

In order to make them more personal, several Internet sites allow users to change the appearance of the site by selecting important links that are generally used for everyday use. For example, "Findlaw" allows users to select federal, a particular state, secondary materials, or specific topic (subject) information so the links appear on the first page. This will allow users to go directly to the links they frequently use rather than going through multiple links.

What are tabbed pages?

Westlaw and Lexis offer users the ability to create tabs on the first page of the screen. In Westlaw users can click on "My Westlaw" and then select the databases they want to see on the main page. In Lexis, click on the "Add/Edit tabs" link under "Look for a Source" and select the jurisdiction and/or area of law and then click on the "Done" button to configure the selected tabs on the main page. You can also email these tabs to your colleagues and clients.

What are the types of search engines?

There are two main types: general purpose search engines and subject specific search engines.

What does a general purpose search engine do?

By entering a keyword or phrase in the query box, you can obtain information on any topic from general purpose search engines such as Google, Altavista. Yahoo, MSN, or Ask.

What does a subject specific search engine do?

Unlike general purpose search engines, the subject specific search engines will provide information only on one topic or subject area since their databases are specifically meant for that topic. For example, Findlaw, HeirosGamos, Law Guru, etc. only provide legal information.

Are all search engines the same?

Every search engine is unique and can differ with regard to:
Data collection
Data display
How often the spiders visit
How much they index
De-duplication

What is searchandizing?

The word is a combination of *search* and merch*andizing*. It is an electronic commerce term used to describe using your own site search to promote products when users search for certain keywords or phrases, akin to merchandizing a retail store for up-selling, cross-selling or promoting specific merchandise. Also called *multi-faceted search*. (webopedia.com)

What are hybrid (directory) search engines ?

Most search engines are hybrids as they usually include a directory consisting of categories and a search engine whereby you will be provided with a query box to enter your query.

The information available on web pages is organized into several categories of a directory. The categories are then organized in hierarchical order from general to specific. Directories generally depend on the human factor where editors review the web pages. Dmoz (www.dmoz.org) is a good example of a directory based search engine. Currently Yahoo and other search engines provide an option to search via a directory or a general web search.

Can you provide examples of directory type search engines?

In recent times several search engines changed from directory to portal type. The best example of this is Dmoz (www.dmoz.org).

Are there any examples of directory type specific to legal information?

The information in Westlaw and Lexis are mechanically organized into directories. All of the approximately sixteen thousand databases in Westlaw are organized into fourteen or fifteen categories in its directory.

What are pure search engines?

The search engines described in this category will generally only have a query box. Some do provide a limited search directory option as well.

What are the popular pure search engines?
Google (www.google.com), Teoma (www.teoma.com), and Wisenut (www.wisenut. com).

What are meta search engines?
Meta search engines, also known as parallel search engines or multi-threaded engines, are web sites that search multiple general purpose search engines simultaneously for information matching your search words or terms.

What are some of the popular meta search engines?
Surfwax (www.surfwax.com); Dogpile (www.dogpile.com); Mamma (www.mamma.com); Vivisimo (www.vivisimo.com); Zapmeta (www.zapmeta.com); and Gigablast (www.gigablast.com).

What are human search engines?
Human search engines are also known as online advisors, interactive Q & A databases, people portals, and knowledge networks. A few employ their own experts and some serve as a matchmaking service between a customer and an expert.

What are the popular human search engines?
Ask (www.ask.com); Internet Public Library (www.ipl.org); Google (www.answers. google.com); and Yahoo (answers.yahoo.com).

The cha cha web site (www.chacha.com) offers real-time search assistance with a real, live expert anytime, day or night. After entering your query select "search with guide" option.

What is online syndication?
During the past couple of years there has been a growth of online syndication services due to the growing number of site owners and network managers that are looking for efficient ways to supply third party content to their end users. Generally they provide news, financial, consumer and business sites to other web sites. For example, Lexis launched a syndication service called Verocity that delivers real-time news from more than 1,200 sources to business web sites. Google (www.news.google.com); Moreover (www.moreover.com); and Isyndicate (www. isyndicate.com) are other examples.

Kayak (www.kayak.com) is a syndicated web site providing travel information from various other travel specific sites and Indeed (www.indeed.com) provides information related to jobs by collecting information from various job search web sites.

What is the invisible web?

The invisible web describes a collection of resources which are available on the web, but are not crawled or indexed by the general purpose search engines such as Google, Yahoo, etc. The invisible web is also known as the deep web / net or the hidden web or the dark web.

What are the popular invisible web search engines?

Completenet (www.completenet.com); BrightPlanet (www.brightplanet.com); Pro-Fusion (www.profusion.com); and Turbo10 (www.turbo10.com).

How do I determine if the information available is authentic and reliable?

One can usually be assured that sites belonging to reputable educational institutions and government organizations (sites with .edu and .gov as domain names) are dependable. However, legal researchers must diligently verify the accuracy of the information found on the web just as they would for print sources. For more information, read the article entitled, "Getting it Right: Verifying Sources on the Net" by Sabrina I. Pacific (www.llrx.com/features/verifying.htm).

In order to verify the authenticity and reliability of information available on the Internet, the following points should be considered: authority (of author); accuracy (of the information); objectivity (of site); currency (of the information); comprehensiveness (of the information), and if there are any reviewing sources available (about the site and its information).

Are there any tools to evaluate the search engines?

In order to keep your research current and accurate, you need to know which search engines do the best job of updating the information they use to produce search results. One way to quickly evaluate the credibility of a search engine is use: Search Engine Watch (www.searchenginewatch.com) or Search Engine Showdown (www.searchengineshowdown.com) web monitoring sites.

How do I know what information is available on a web site?

Web sites cannot display all of the information it contains on their homepage. Generally, they will have links such as 'Site Map', 'View All', 'A-Z Resource List', 'Site Index' etc. These will give you a more detailed list of the information available on that web site. Furthermore, it will allow you to link directly to that information for quick access.

Is there an Internet archive where I can find old web sites?

The Wayback Machine (www.archive.org) is an Internet archive. It is a non-profit organization that was founded to build an Internet library, with the purpose of offering permanent access for researchers, historians, and scholars to historical collections that exist in digital format. Simply type the URL in the query box and you will then see all the previous versions of the site.

www.archive-it.org was designed mainly for institutions (state archives, state libraries, and university libraries) that have a mandate to archive their web content and that lack resources (staff, budget, and technical capabilities) to do so.

Can I have a personal web where I can keep all my web sites permanently?

Furl (www.furl.net) is a free service that saves a personal copy of any page you find on the web, and lets you find it again instantly by searching your archive of pages. Once you register, which is free, each member gets a 5-gigabyte searchable personal archive.

Can I create my own personal search engine?

Rollyo (www.rollyo.com) allows you to create your own search engine in which you can include your list of selected web sites and give a name. You can search that list (your search engine) every time you conduct your research.

Yahoo! Search Builder (builder.search.yahoo.com) allows users to create a specialized search box to search several user-selected sites. Google allows you to create your own custom search engine. Google has created a wizard (google.com/coop/cse) that leads you through the process in a few simple steps. You can specify sites you want to include or exclude from your search engine. You can also prioritize sites, giving some more precedence than others.

What is mobile search?

"Mobile search is different from standard, PC-based Web search in three ways," said Matt Tengler, Product Manager at JumpTap, a Massachusetts-based firm that helps wireless operators deliver a mobile search experience for subscribers and advertising partners:

Content: "Currently, mobile content is dominated by mobile consumables, such as ring tones," he said.

Form factor: "The first page becomes the first few search results," he said.

Opportunities: "A personal device is always on," he said, "presenting more customized advertising opportunities." (Shari Thurow, www.searchenginewatch.com)

What is Direct navigation?

Direct navigation or type-in traffic practice whereby users often type what they are looking for into a browser's address bar and add".com". For example if you need wedding shoes, type in "weddingshoes.com" and you will land on what looks like a shoe-shopping portal, filled with links from dozens of retailers. (Paul Sloan, The Man Owns the Internet, CNN article, 2007)

What is iterative searching?
The most important concept in constructing searches is "iterative searching." As you search, keep refining or changing your search terms and strategies based on what you find. For example, when you are asked to find a law that governs incorporating a business in Nigeria, your first search simply 'nigerian business incorporation'. Although you do not retrieve the law, your first result is a summary of the law from the Nigerian Embassy. The summary includes and name of the law: The Companies and Allied Matters Act, 1990. By copying and pasting this name as a new search, you immediately retrieve a copy of the law. (Marcy Hoffman & Mary Rumsey: *International and Foreign Legal Research: A Coursebook*, 2008)

CHAPTER 16

LAW FIRM/ LAW PRACTICE/

COURTROOM TECHNOLOGY

Students are introduced to some of the technology and software pack-
ages used in law firm practice. Today, the sole practitioner to the largest
firm incorporates technology in conducting business whether it is word
processing or databases, case management systems, or a complicated
Knowledge Management system. As the courts become more technologi-
cally advanced, the practicing bar has a need to keep up with new devel-
opments and update their practices.

What technology is used in the law firm?
Law firm technology includes: case-filing, case management, client management,
billing and time management, case preparation, research, electronic evidence,
witness preparation, docket retrieval, docket tracking, etc.

What are the online data backup systems?
There are several online data backup systems in the market for law firms. www.
ibackup.com, www.carbonite.com, www.livevault.com, ww.mozy.com/pro are a few
of them.

Where do I get information regarding law firm and practice technology?
Most of the comprehensive legal web sites such as Findlaw, HeirosGamos; Cornell,
Law Guru; Megalaw, Virtual Chase provide links to technology used in the law firm.
There are virtually hundreds of commercial vendors including Lexis and Westlaw
that offer technology tools. Product information of the commercial vendors can
be found in any issue of *Law Technology News* (www.lawtechnologynews.com),
and other legal newspapers and magazines. *Law Technology News* is the best
source for information regarding law firm office technology. Another good source

is LitTech (www.littech.org). Brett Burney's Legal Tech Reviews column at www. llrx.com contains useful reviews.

What are the sources to find white papers written by law firm attorneys?

Findlaw (www.findlaw.com) has links to white papers related to electronic discovery and other law technology issues. Similarly American Lawyer Media (www.law. com) has links to legal white papers written by attorneys of law firms.

What is meant by managed services?

A managed service is one in which the service provider, rather than the customer, takes full responsibility for the outcome, including the management of resources for delivery of the service. (Heinan Landa, Outsourcing Technology, *Legal Times*, Apr. 23, 07)

What are the benefits of the managed services (outsourcing technology) for law firms?

There are several distinct benefits to managed services: First, because of the usage-based pricing model, firms can reduce potential budgetary surprises. Second, the proactive approach to systems management reduces overall downtime. Third, these services can grow with the law firm. Finally, the best managed service providers include high-level technology guidance with their service. (Heinan Landa, Outsourcing Technology, *Legal Times*, Apr. 23, 07)

What is PACER and who operates it?

Public Access to Court Electronic Records (PACER) is an electronic public access service that allows users to obtain case and docket information from Federal Appellate, District and Bankruptcy courts, and from the U.S. Party/Case Index via the Internet. Links to all courts are provided from this web site (pacer.psc.uscourts. gov/cgi-bin/links.pl). Electronic access is available by registering with the PACER Service Center, the judiciary's centralized registration, billing, and technical support center.

Each court maintains its own databases with case information. Because PACER database systems are maintained within each court, each jurisdiction will have a different URL. Accessing and querying information from each service is similar, however, the format and content of information provided may differ slightly. PACER is a service of the United States Judiciary. The PACER Service Center is operated by the Administrative Office of the United States Courts. (PACER Web site)

Where do I get information about witnesses?

Versuslaw (www.versuslaw.com) in association with Witnessinfo (www.witness-info.com) provides many types of records related to witnesses. The following are some of the services Witnessinfo offers:

1. Locate witnesses or persons related to a case.
2. Gather comprehensive historical data about the people involved in a legal proceeding.
3. Gather asset information, corporate affiliations and personal affiliations on witnesses.
4. Reduce the costs associated with research.

(Witnessinfo web site)

Can I Shepardize the cases from any Internet site?
You may find cases citing to your case but you will be unable to determine if these cases are still applicable law, or how these cases relate to your current case. Once you retrieve a case from the United States Supreme Court, Findlaw provides you with other cases which cite to this case. Shepards on Lexis and KeyCite in Westlaw are the only sources that validate and explain the treatment of your case. Loislaw offers Globalcite which only provides cases that cite to your case.

What are West Court Records?
West provides the largest collection of records and briefs for the U.S. Supreme Court in a space-saving DVD, micrographic fiche, or roll-film format. These records constitute the landmark cases in constitutional law and evidence of the evolution of *American Jurisprudence*. All materials for cases from 1832 are included. The following are some of the documents: briefs of appellees and appellants, petitioners' briefs and briefs in opposition, *amicus curiae* briefs, testimony, depositions, memoranda, and other evidence from lower courts and rulings from courts of original jurisdiction. (Thomson brochure)

What is Westlaw for Litigators?
Westlaw along with American Lawyer Media offers various products which are useful to the law firms for every phase of litigation. These products help attorneys in the evaluation, investigation, negotiation, case preparation and case presentation.

What is Westlaw CourtExpress?
Westlawcourtexpress.com is a single, easy-to-use location where you can perform all of your docket research and document retrieval tasks, including: Order a hardcopy document from any location or courthouse, and have it delivered to any destination; Access the world's largest collection of online dockets on Westlaw, with more documents from more state and federal courts; Create Profiler Litigation History Reports – a deep well of integrated information about attorneys or judges involved with a case; Receive an automatic email whenever there's a change or

new filing in your case; and Docket alerts notify you of newly filed cases. (Thomson/West brochure)

What are profiler litigation history reports on Westlaw?
Profiler Litigation History Reports (Westlaw) provides insightful and authoritative analysis in a flexible format that helps you evaluate the litigation experience of attorneys and judges. (Thomson/West brochure)

What is West's CiteAdvisor?
CiteAdvisor automates the formatting of citations and creates tables of authority in briefs, opinions, etc.

What is Case Evaluator on Westlaw?
Case Evaluator helps to accurately evaluate the legal merits and monetary value of a potential case. Once you describe your client's case, and Case Evaluator generates a custom report that lays out the settlement you can expect; the actual briefs, pleadings, and other documents filed in similar cases so you can see how they were argued, and the most effective experts for your situation.

What is Westlaw legal calendaring?
Westlaw legal calendaring is a new online tool to give litigation assistance in managing critical trial dates and filing logistics. It automatically calculates litigation dates from the first complaint filed through the final appeal, and it tracks every event change requiring recalculation, helping litigators and support staff stay abreast of dates and updates throughout a trial (www.litigator.westlaw.com) (Online, Vol.32, no.3, 2008)

What is NetScan?
NetScan is a fast, accurate provider of web-based legislative and regulatory information for all 50 states and the federal government. NetScan includes HPTS (Health Policy Tracking Service); LegAlert (legislative tracking service); RegAlert (proposed regulation, adopted regulations, repealed regulations, and emergency regulations) and PUCAlert (public utility information). (Thomson/West brochure)

What is LexisNexis Courtlink?
CourtLink is a product from LexisNexis which has a collection of more than 200 million dockets from federal and state courts and allows the user to view motions, orders, pleadings, and other supporting documents. CourtLink litigations tools include: strategic profiles; document retrieval, search, track and alert that can be used throughout your workflow to help you argue your cases more effectively. (Lexis brochure)

What is LexisNexis' "File & Serve?"

File & Serve is a case-file management tool that allows the user to e-file information in jurisdictions where the court has implemented e-filing. With File & Serve, firms can file, serve, and access documents online.

What is LexisNexis' "Applied Discovery?"

Applied Discovery is a product of LexisNexis that provides electronic discovery services to the law firms. The Applied Discovery product performs the critical tasks such as consulting, data gathering, media restoration, data processing, online review, document production, and reporting. (Lexis brochure)

What does LexisNexis' "HotDocs" mean?

HotDocs is a document preparation and automation tool for law firms. It gives you the option of turning your best documents, prepared in Word or WordPerfect formats, into templates that you can easily adapt for a variety of clients and circumstances. (Lexis brochure)

What is LexisNexis' Time Matters™?

The Time Matters™ program effectively manages the elements of your workday – cases, clients, contacts, deadlines, communications, research, documents, billing etc. This integrated research manager tool includes: cases/matters, outlines, contacts/clients, calendars, to do's/tasks, documents, web research, email/messages/phone/fax, mail/courier, notes, billing, and mobility. (Lexis brochure)

What is LexisNexis' "SmartLinx?"

SmartLinx is a research tool that makes logical connections between LexisNexis public records and delivers comprehensive summary reports to your desktop in just seconds. Information includes: documenting the chain of ownership for a business or property, compiling connections and conflicts of interests among people and business, uncovering business and personal assets, plus mortgage, lien and bankruptcy liabilities, find business associates, neighbors, "lost" people, potential witnesses, etc. (Lexis brochure)

What is "Total Litigator?"

LexisNexis' Total Litigator is web-based platform containing everything you need to build your best litigation strategies. It is intuitively organized by the tasks litigators typically perform over the course of a case. These tasks include: the drafting, filing and sending of documents, planning and conduct of discovery, conducting legal research, gathering intelligence and alerts as well as tracking dockets. (Lexis brochure)

What is "CaseSoft?"

CaseSoft software is a product of LexisNexis which is specifically designed to help litigators organize the major components of a case – the facts, the legal issues, the people and businesses involved. The CaseSoft line of software tools currently consists of CaseMap; TimeMap; TextMap; NoteMap; and DepPrep.

CaseMap organizes and links information about key facts, documents, parties and legal issues in every litigation matter.

TimeMap provides visual timelines that depict and analyze evidence uncovered at any time during the litigation workflow.

TextMap is a database of electronic transcript files from case depositions, examinations and other proceedings that stand alone or integrate into CaseMap resources.

NoteMap helps to process key facts from vast numbers of documents typically processed in litigation. It also helps in creating and editing outlines quickly and effectively.

DepPrep grooms witnesses for their depositions quickly and easily. (LexisNexis Information Professional Update brochure)

What is Concordance?

Concordance is a powerful database tool (LexisNexis product) that reviews images of each document on their computers and searches through thousands of records using keywords. In addition, they can create 'tags' or names for their search results, annotate documents with notes, assign issues to specific paragraphs, print out customized reports, and more (*Lawyers Guide to Concordance*, ABA)

What is Courtroom Connect?

Courtroom Connect is a company founded in 2001 which addresses communications infrastructure within courthouses. Courtroom Connect provides videoconferencing, streaming, and Internet services to law firm offices on a permanent basis as well as on a temporary basis for legal events, such as trials, jury research, war rooms, and presentations. There are several companies providing all or selective services to law firms.

What is video streaming capture and encoding for litigation?

The Video Streaming Capture and Encoding Component captures legal events on video as they occur and digitally encodes the content in real time. Industrial strength encoders take the video and audio sources, digitize and compress the signals, and then deliver them over the IP network. (www.courtroomconnect.com)

What is a blackberry?
Blackberry is a handheld device made by RIM (Research in Motion) which handles wireless e-mail and also provides several Internet services. For the legal community it offers wireless access to time and billing systems, customer relations management software and integration with third-party research and case management applications. Several law firms use Blackberries to keep their attorneys connected to clients, colleagues and information. It helps attorneys access the legal data that drives their day, including legal references, case management tools, legal documents and time entry and billing information.

What are cyber courts?
Cyber courts or virtual courts, are courts resolving disputes through electronic communication with the lawyers and parties without their physical appearance in a traditional court room, and allow the conducting of court proceedings electronically. And at the discretion of the judge, pursuant to the court rules all proceedings of the cyber court are open to the public on the Internet *(www.globalcourts.com)*

Where do I get the information about cyber courts in the United States?
National Center for State Courts (www.ncsconline.org) and the Court Room 21 Project (www.legaltechcenter.net) provides comprehensive information.

What is Courtroom 21?
Located in the College of William & Mary Law School's McGlothlin Courtroom, Courtroom 21, "the Courtroom of the 21st Century Today," is the world's most technologically advanced trial and appellate courtroom.

The Courtroom 21 project is an international demonstration and experimental effort which seeks to determine how technology can best improve all components of the legal system. Courtroom 21 is a joint project of the Law School and the National Center for State Courts.

What is Courtroom 23?
History

For the Ninth Judicial Circuit, the Courtroom of the future is here today. The Judges' vision of an integrated high-tech courtroom has become a reality. The project began in March of 1997, when a contingent from the Ninth Judicial Circuit traveled to Williamsburg to tour the preeminent hi-tech courtroom, Courtroom 21. The goal of the project was to create a hi-tech courtroom that seamlessly integrated the latest in courtroom technology and enhanced courtroom performance and presentation. On May 14, 1999, after much planning, discussion, and hard work, the Ninth Circuit formally opened one of the world's most technologically advanced and integrated courtrooms.

Design

In June of 1998, six months after moving into the new Orange County Courthouse, the Court contracted with Applied Legal Technology (ALT) to design and implement a plan to integrate cutting edge courtroom technology for the Roger A. Barker Courtroom, located on the 23rd floor (i.e., Courtroom 23). A team consisting of judiciary, court administration, and an architectural firm completed the design.

What is E-Court?

"These E-Courts represent a profound and fundamental change in the way court proceedings are conducted," said Superior Court Presiding Judge Colin F. Campbell. "Widespread use of technology during trial enhances the way evidence is presented, allowing facts, concepts and ideas to be more readily understood by jurors, litigants, spectators, lawyers and the Court."

What is courtroom technology?

Lawyers and legal researchers should be familiar with the new technologies related to their profession. New technologies include: e-filing, electronic evidence, video depositions, case management, knowledge management, etc.

Is there any virtual trial practice center available?

Robins, Kaplan, Miller & Ciresi law firm has created a half a million dollar virtual trial practice center with all the latest technology gadgets. The web site is www.rkmc.com/Trial_Practice_Center.aspx.

What is an automated courtroom?

An automated courtroom is a courtroom with sophisticated electronic equipment including evidence display systems, real-time court reporting, and other technology systems.

What is an evidence display system?

An evidence display system is a computerized system that displays evidence via monitors to the judge, jury, counsel, and the public simultaneously.

What is videoconferencing?

Videoconferencing is a private broadcast between two or more remote locations with live image transmission, display, and sound.

What is real-time court reporting?

Real-time court reporting is a computerized court reporting system where a witness's testimony is immediately converted from a court reporter's notes to a transcript in real-time.

What is an Internet deposition?

An Internet deposition is a process that allows an attorney to join, monitor, or take a live deposition from a witness from any location with a personal computer and Internet connection.

What is electronic case filing?

Electronic case filing (ECF) or e-filing allows legal documents that are generated using a word processor or scanner to be transferred to a court using the Internet or other electronic method. Currently, electronic case filing is mandatory in some courts. Most of the courts require you to send the documents in portable document (PDF) format.

By the end of the December 2005, well over half of the federal bankruptcy filings were done electronically, as were over 35 percent of all federal filings. (ABA Journal, December 2005)

What is CM/ECF system?

The federal judiciary's Case Management and Electronic Case Files (CM/ECF) system has been implemented in almost all district and bankruptcy courts. CM/ECF allows the courts to have case file documents in electronic format and to accept filing via the Internet. The CM/ECF system stores case and related information as PDF files.

How many federal courts use the CM/ECF system?

CM/ECF systems currently are in use in 89% of the federal courts: 89 district courts, 93 bankruptcy courts, the Court of International Trade, and the Court of Federal Claims. Most of those courts accept electronic filings. More than 35 million cases are on CM/ECF systems, and more than 400,000 attorneys and others have filed documents via the Internet.

How does CM/ECF system work?

Attorneys practicing in courts offering the electronic filing capability can file documents directly with court via the Internet. When documents are filed electronically, the system automatically generates and sends a verifying receipt by electronic mail. Other parties in the case automatically receive notification of the filing. Litigants receive one free PDF copy of every document electronically filed in their cases.

Does the public have access to these documents?

CM/ECF provides courts the ability to make their documents available to the public over the Internet via the Public Access to Court Electronic Records (PACER) program.

Users once registered with the PACER service center can obtain comprehensive case and docket information as PDF files from federal appellate, district, and bankruptcy courts via the Internet.

What is Portable Document Format (PDF)?

PDF lets legal professionals capture and view information – from any application, on any computer system – and share it with anyone around the world. PDF files can be viewed and printed on any computer system – Macintosh, Microsoft windows, UNIX, and many mobile platforms.

Adobe PDF files look just like original documents, regardless of the application used to create them. Paper documents scanned to PDF look just like their hard-copy counterparts and can be quickly turned into computer-searchable files.

What is a PDF file?

A PDF file is a standardized format that can contain both images and text. Many different types of documents can be converted into PDF format, allowing them to be sent over email and appear in exactly the same condition that they were created in. This standardized format allows many different users to view the same document in its original form without having to buy new software, other than download a free reader.

What types of programs utilize the PDF format?

Adobe Systems created the PDF format. Adobe also created Adobe Acrobat, and Adobe Reader which utilize the PDF format.

What is the difference between Adobe Reader and Adobe Acrobat?

Adobe Reader is the free version of the Adobe Acrobat software. Adobe Reader will allow you to view and print PDF files but you will not be able to access many of the options found in Adobe Acrobat. For example, Adobe Reader will not allow you to edit, create, or modify PDF files, these functions can only be done in Acrobat. Adobe Acrobat is the full version of the program. Adobe offers Adobe Acrobat Standard and Adobe Acrobat Professional as well. Both of these programs allow you to create, edit, and modify PDF documents. However, Adobe Acrobat Professional also allows you to create standardized forms on your computer.

What is the advantage of using the PDF format?

PDF files will display the same way on any computer that they appear. This allows you to use as many decorative fonts in a document that you would like, email that document as a PDF file, and be assured that it will appear exactly the same to the person receiving the file. For example, you can create a document on Microsoft word, "print" that document to PDF, then email that document to another person. If that person has Abode Reader (which is free) or Adobe Acrobat they can open your file and it will appear to them in exactly the same manner you created it in. Thus, if one law firm uses Microsoft Word, and another firm uses WordPerfect, both of these firms can send each other their documents in PDF format, and each firm can read them using Adobe Reader or Acrobat. These firms will also receive the documents in the exact form that they were sent, and will avoid any of the formatting differences that result when attempting to bring up a WordPerfect document in Microsoft Word or vice versa.

How can I create PDF files?

Once installed, Adobe Acrobat adds a "print to PDF" option on many of your computer programs. For example, it will add this option to Microsoft Word, Excel, and PowerPoint, as well as WordPerfect. What Acrobat actually does is create another printer on your computer. This is not an actual printer, but it is a printer driver that Acrobat uses to create the PDF document. Once you select this printer and "print" the document the Acrobat printer will create a PDF version of that file and save it onto your computer. Thus, "print to PDF" is the way Adobe creates PDF files, and allows you to use them.

You can also create PDF files using a scanner. To do this go to the Acrobat program, and choose the create PDF file from scanner option. You will be given a variety of options depending on the scanning software you use, then hit scan. Acrobat will create a PDF file of the item that you scanned.

You can also create PDF documents out of existing documents. There are two ways to accomplish this. The first is to run the Acrobat program, and then drag and drop the file you want to convert into the open Acrobat window. The second way, is to again, run the Acrobat program and then choose the create PDF button, and choose "from file". Then choose the specific file you want converted.

It is also possible to convert web pages into PDF format, this is explained below.

What is web capture?

Web capture is an option offered on Adobe Acrobat. This option allows you to convert a web site into PDF format. In order to access this option you must be in Abode Acrobat. Then choose the web capture feature under the create PDF button. Acrobat will then ask you for the web address of the site, and it will give you the option to convert the entire site, or just the "first level". Acrobat gives the option of just converting the first level (initial web page) or converting successive levels. By converting successive levels Acrobat is converting both the initial page as well as all of the links on that page. For example, if you chose to convert 2 levels of a web site, Acrobat would convert the initial web page to PDF, and then it would also follow the links on that page, and convert those web pages to PDF. This allows you to save successive web pages for access at a time when you might not have Internet access, or when you might need to send someone an exact copy of a web site. However, be careful, converting a whole web site as this can create a very large file that can take a significant amount of time to convert.

What are PDF bookmarks?

Bookmarks are specifically marked areas of a document. They often act as a table of contents for a PDF document. For example, as you work with a PDF document you can highlight specific text and delineate that text as a bookmark. The bookmarked areas then show up on the left hand side of the page, and act like links to those book marked pages. Thus, if you create a large PDF document, and you want to enable easy scanning of that document you may break up each chapter with a bookmark. The bookmark would be displayed on the left hand side of Acrobat, and would allow the user to go directly to the specific book marked areas of the text instead of having to scan the whole document manually.

Can I use PDF files as slide shows and multimedia presentations?

Adobe Acrobat allows you to create and present slideshows using one program. Furthermore, it allows you to create the slideshow in Microsoft PowerPoint, transfer the PowerPoint document into PDF, and present the slideshow on Adobe Acrobat. Using Acrobat, and creating the slideshow in PDF format allows a larger audience to view your slideshow, as the only required program for viewing is Adobe Reader, which is free of charge, and found on the Internet.

What is a binocular search?

The Acrobat Reader has a binocular tool on the toolbar to help you find words or phrases in a document. Unless you click one of the other options, the search will find any place in the document where the letters you have entered in the search box occur. You may also use the key combination "CTRL-F" to bring up the "Find" function.

Can I copy the text from the PDF document?

First select the "select text tool" from the Basic toolbar. Then drag this tool over the text you wish to copy. Once this text is selected, go to edit and choose the copy button from the menu. You can now paste this text anywhere else in that document, or move it to a new Word or WordPerfect document and paste it there. However, you may not be able to use this method on some documents which have been scanned as images.

Can I convert my Word or WordPerfect documents into PDF documents?

The "print to PDF" option on your word processor will transform that document into the PDF format. It will then save the PDF document onto your computer for your future use.

Can I convert my PDF documents into Word or WordPerfect documents?
Simply open the PDF document in Adobe Acrobat. Then click save as, and choose the option to save the document as a".word" file. Then merely open Microsoft Word and open the newly saved document. Most of the formatting should be correct, however, at times there may be small errors, so be sure to check the document.

Can I fill out legal forms that are in PDF format?
In Adobe Acrobat, using version 7 or later you can type over any PDF document. While most forms require that interactive fields be defined in order to be accessed, this new option allows you to type on top of any PDF file. In order to use this option you must have downloaded the 7.05 update. To do this, simply go to the help menu and click "check for updates now". This will automatically install any updates to your Acrobat program. Then go to Tools à Typewriter à Typewriter. This will enable the typewriter program. Now simply click the typewriter icon on the toolbar and you can type wherever you would like in the open document. Thus if you have a form in which the fields are not defined yet, you can still enter the pertinent information without creating defined fields within the document. This will save you a lot of time and can be a great asset when you are in a hurry.

What are the legal-specific features of Adobe Acrobat 8?
Acrobat 8 Professional has included for the legal professionals functions such as Bates numbering, redaction and metadata removal.

What is OpenDocument Format?
OpenDocument Format (ODF) is an ISO standard (ISO/IEC JTC 1/SC 34N0681). An open file format enables users of varying office suites to exchange documents such as text documents, spreadsheets, charts, or databases, freely with one another. Any software maker can ensure its own applications can read and write this format.

What is Bates numbering?
Bates numbering means applying sequential numbers to individual pages of documents, usually in the course of litigation. Acrobat 8 Professional offers legal professionals the ability to add Bates numbers to individual or multiple PDF files.

What is redaction?
Legal professionals must often share documents with other parties. However, in many instances, not all information in those documents should or can be shared. When the information is marked for redaction Acrobat 8 removes the marked text or selected images permanently and securely from the PDF file.

What is metadata removal?

In addition to removing visible content from documents, legal professionals also need to verify that no hidden information exists in their documents, including metadata (data about data), before those documents are distributed. Acrobat 8 new Examine Document feature scans through the documents and alerts you to hidden information that you may not be aware of, including metadata, comments, file attachments, and other elements.

Do courts require that briefs be in PDF format?

Many courts require that an electronic copy of a filing be filed with the court. Furthermore, they also require that the electronic filing be in PDF format. This helps relieve the court of paper filing, and allows all users to access the PDF documents through Adobe Reader.

Are there any web sites that explain more about PDF?

www.pdfforlawyers.com: A blog for lawyers that contains information on how to apply Adobe Acrobat to your practice.

www.adobe.com/legal: This is Adobe's own web page which gives you an overview of how Acrobat can be used in the legal profession.

blogs.adobe.com/acrolaw: This is another web site dedicated to displaying the abilities of Acrobat to the legal field.

Are there legal publications available in PDF?

Most of the court cases, legal forms and legal periodical articles are currently available in PDF.

What is a CD-ROM brief?

A CD-ROM brief is an identical copy of the paper brief. The purpose of a brief on CD-ROM is to give the court a copy of the paper brief which takes up less physical space and is in a format that is easier for judges and their clerks to use. A CD-ROM with 650 megabytes of storage capacity holds 20,000 images or 100,000 word-processed pages. The main advantage is granted by hypertext linking cases, statutes, and cites to the appendix or exhibits in the brief. The final product is an integrated filing that enables the judge or clerk to move easily through the brief and referenced materials with the click of a mouse instead of wading through a huge pile of paper.

The U.S. Court of Appeals for the First Circuit requires a disk to accompany all paper briefs filed, and permitting submission of CD-ROM briefs at the discretion of counsel. (Jurist)

What is an e-brief?

An e-brief is an electronic version of a paper brief or motion in which all of the documents that constitute a traditional submission to the court are digitally stored on CD-ROM or a hard drive and hyperlinked from the main document. Hyperlinks allow for immediate, one-click access to all imaged exhibits, case citations, transcript references, joint appendices or other sets of supplemental documents.

What is electronic evidence?

Courtroom technology is primarily a means of putting evidence before everyone in the courtroom – the judge, the jurors, the opposing lawyers, the courtroom support staff and even onlookers seated in the courtroom. Courtroom technology is a means to draw attention to particular points, to emphasize certain aspects of evidence and to make visible that which otherwise might only exist as a mental picture formed by listeners.

Are electronic signatures legit?

The Global and National Commerce Act (E-SIGN)was enacted in June 2000 confirmed the legitimacy of electronic signatures as a matter of national policy. This act promotes commerce on the Internet by declaring that electronic signatures will not be denied legal effect.

How does an electronic signature work?

A workable electronic signature has to do three things. First, it must inform the signer about what he is doing as he approves a document. Second, a workable signature must keep a good record or transcript of the signing event so it can later be determined in court who the signer was, which document he thought he was signing, and what he intended for his signature to mean. Third, a good signature will be applied to a document in such a way that the entire document – including all of the signature evidence and audit trail itself – can be given to and stored by both the signer and the receiving party (such as a lender).

What are the types of electronic signatures?

Some of the types of electronic signatures are: Sign-it EX (www.ecomaus.com); voiceprints, eye patterns, keys stored in smart cards, or even credit card numbers. (Benjamin Wright, *Uniformity in Electronic Signatures*, 2000.)

What is a digital certification?

The new domain name (.pro) provides a digital certification, which enables secure electronic communication through the web site. This certification allows attorneys to put a digital signature and encryption on their email communication. Digital signature and encryption provide the following levels of digital trust: authentication (proof of digital identity), confidentiality (maintains privacy and confidentiality of content), integrity (ensures that the content has not been changed or altered), and non-repudiation (provides proof that the communication was sent).

What does encryption mean?

Encryption runs a message through an encoder that uses an encrypting key to alter the characters in the message. Unless the person wanting to read the message has the encryption key needed to decode it, the message appears unreadable.

What is document management software?

This is the software that organizes, controls, distributes, and allows for extensive searching of electronic documents, typically in a networked environment.

What is electronic billing?

Electronic billing allows law firms to bill clients using electronic means such as the Internet.

What is a case management program?

Some of the features found in case management programs include docket control (scheduling/ appointments), to do list, contact information database (name, address, email, phone, fax, etc.), by case (parties, co-counsel, opposing counsel, judges, etc.), case notes, document assembly, and document tracking/ management.

What are the popular case management software programs?

There are several software programs currently available. The following are a few of the case management software programs:

Abacus (www.abacuslaw.com)
Compulaw (www.compulaw.com)
Prolaw (www.prolaw.com)

What does Computer-Aided Transcription (CAT) mean?

CAT is a process that automatically deciphers a court reporter's notes and converts them into a computer-readable format.

What is E-Discovery?

Electronic discovery, or e-discovery, is a type of cyber forensics (also referred to as *computer* or *digital forensics*) and describes the process by where law enforcement can obtain, secure, search and process any electronic data for use as evidence in a legal proceeding or investigation. Electronic discovery may be limited to a single computer or a network-wide search. *(webopedia.com)*

What is computer forensics?

Computer forensics is the collection, preservation, analysis and presentation of electronic evidence. Computer forensics uses tools and procedures to make sure that data recovered from a computer will comply with the rules of "best evidence", which can be admissible in criminal or civil proceedings. (*TRACEVIDENCE* FAQ sheet, *E-Discovery,* PBI, 2004).

What is the difference between computer forensics and electronic discovery?

Computer forensics is the recovery of computer-based information. It is the science of examining and piecing back together the who, what, when, where, and how of computer-related conduct. Computer forensics is more in-depth than electronic discovery, which involves only active computer-based information. (*TRACEVIDENCE* FAQ sheet, *E-Discovery,* PBI, 2004).

What is Sedona Conference ® Working Group?

The Sedona Conference® Working Group Series is a series of think-tanks consisting of leading jurists, lawyers, experts and consultants brought together by a desire to address various "tipping point" issues in each area under consideration. We have Working Groups up and running in all three areas of our focus (antitrust law, complex litigation and intellectual property rights), and the output of our Working Groups is frequently submitted for peer review at our Regular Season Conferences, other legal education programs and otherwise.

What are the bright lines among the Sedona principles related to E-Discovery?

Principle 5: reasonable and good faith preservation – not every conceivable
Principle 3: early conference on preservation and production
Principle 6: responding parties best situated to select preservation methods
Principle 9: no duty to preserve or produce deleted data
Principle 12: no duty to preserve or produce metadata
Principle 8: primary source active data
Principle 14: no sanctions absent intentional or reckless failure Thomas Y. Allman,
   The New Federal E-Discovery Rules, LegalTech West Coast, 2007)

What are 2006 amendments to Federal Rules of Civil Procedure?

The 2006 Amendments to the Federal Rules of Civil Procedure (the "Amendments") place electronically stored information ("ESI") on the same footing as "documents" for purposes of discovery and make a variety of targeted changes designed to provide uniform national treatment of ESI in discovery. The Amendments, which impact Rules 16, 26, 33, 34, 37, 45 and Form 35, were developed by the Civil Rules Advisory Committee over a six year period before being approved by the Supreme Court on April 12, 2006. They became effective on December 1, 2006. *(Thomas Y. Allman, The New Federal E-Discovery Rules: LegaTech West Coast, 2007)*

What are some new general FRCP rules?

The following provides a rough outline of the keywords associated with the following rules:

Rule 16: Pretrial Conference; Scheduling; Management

Rule 26(b)(2): General Provisions Governing Discovery; Duty of Disclosure; Discovery Scope and Limits; Limits; Inaccessible Data

Rule 26(b)(5)(B): General Provisions Governing Discovery; Duty of Disclosure; Discovery Scope and Limits; Claims of Privilege or Protection of Trial Preparation Materials; Information Produced

Rule 26(f)(3) and (4): General Provisions Governing Discovery; Duty of Disclosure; Conference of Parties; Planning for Discovery

Rule 34(a) and (b): Data Archiving Requirements

Rule 26(f) and 26(b)(2)(B): Data Protection and Production

Rule 37(f): Data Resource Management *(Karen A. Schuler, ONSITE, Best Practices Discovery Checklist, Legal Tech, West Coast, 2007)*

What are some of the implications of new FRCP rules?

- Survey and assess all potential sources early
- Disclose sources claimed to be inaccessible
- Define and explain "burden of costs" of production
- Attempt to secure agreements on sequencing
- Seek cost shifting where appropriate (Tom Allman, Law Tech, West coast, 2007)

What needs to be disclosed?

The new FRCP requires an exhaustive search for all electronically stored information, including email, that is "in the possession, custody, or control of the party." It must be disclosed "without awaiting a discovery request" (Rule 26(a)(1)). The only exception is for privileged information.

The search must be done at the beginning of a legal case and certainly no later than the first pre-trial discovery-related meeting, which is required to be within 99 days (Rule 16(b)).

As a result of the search, a "copy of, or a description by category and location" of all electronically stored information that "the disclosing party may use to support its claims or defenses" must be presented. In the case of email, this disclosure likely includes every relevant piece of email that may be stored, including back-up tapes employee PCs, or Blackberry devices. (Rule 26(a)(1)).

Even if the one party "identifies (information) as not reasonably accessible because of undue burden or cost," its description, category, and location must be disclosed (Rule 26(b)(2)(B)).

What are Zubulake decisions?

Laura Zubulake, an employee of UBS Warburg, LLC, filed a sexual discrimination suit against the company in the United States District Court for the Southern District of New York. The court instructed UBS to provide emails from all optical and servers and from select backup tapes.

The case citations are: 216 F.R.D. 280 (2003); 217 F.R.D. 309 (2003); 220 F.R.D. 212 (2003); 94 Fair Empl. Prac. Case. (BNA) (2004)

In April 2005, a New York jury awarded Zubulake $29 million.

What is the verdict in the Morgan Stanley case?

Morgan Stanley, a Wall Street giant, was slammed with the whopping judgment of $1.45 billion fraud verdict mainly because it repeatedly failed to produce e-documents in a timely fashion, primarily e-mails stored on backup tapes, in response to routine discovery requests.

What is ESI (electronically stored information)?

This is a new term used by FRCP. ESI (electronically stored information) can be in a variety of different forms, including, CDs, DVDs, servers, backup tapes, desktops, laptops, PDAs, portable hard drives, USBs, home computers etc.

What are native files?

When you save a file using a certain program, the file is often saved in a proprietary format only that program can recognize. For example, if you save a Microsoft Word document, it is saved as a Word document (.doc), Excel (.exl) etc. These are native files to the Microsoft Word application and may not be recognized by other programs. In the production phase of the discovery process the native files will be converted into TIFF or PDF etc.

What is a TIFF document?

TIFF is an acronym for *tagged* image file format, one of the most widely supported file formats for storing bit-mapped images on personal computers (both PCs and Macintosh computers). Other popular formats are BMP and *PCX*.

TIFF graphics can be any resolution, and they can be black and white, gray-scaled, or color. Files in TIFF format often end with a *.tif* extension. *(webopedia)*

What is spoliation?

Spoliation is the intentional or negligent loss or destruction of evidence.

All too often, a party's position in litigation is impaired by the destruction, alteration or loss of crucial evidence during -- and sometimes even before -- litigation has begun. This is commonly referred to as "spoliation" of evidence. When the spoliation occurs, sanctions include the striking of pleadings, entering of a default on the issue of liability, imposition of a negative evidentiary presumption and the dismissal of a claim. (Jeffrey Shapiro, *Spoliation of Evidence Can Spoil Litigation*)

What does the chain of custody means?

The purpose of a chain of custody log is to prove that the integrity of the evidence has been maintained from seizure through production in court. Chain of custody logs document how the data was gathered, analyzed, and preserved for production. This information is important, as electronic data can be easily altered if proper precautions are not taken. A chain of custody log for electronic data must demonstrate the following: the data has been properly copied, transported, and stored, the information has not been altered in any way, and all media has been secured throughout the process *(LexisNexis – Applied Discovery fact sheet)*

What is legal hold?

Legal Hold is a process by which an organization must preserve and prepare all forms of electronic communication when litigation is reasonably anticipated. Potential custodians need to be notified that they should not delete any relevant information. (*Exterro*)

What is the good faith safe harbor rule?

FRCP Rule 37(f) precludes federal courts from imposing discovery sanctions against a party for failing to produce electronically stored information that was lost as a result of the routine, good faith operation of an electronic information system.

What is the seven factors test in cost shifting?

Based on the modifications to Rowe Entertainment Inc. v. William Morris Agency, Inc. 205 F.R.D. 421 (2002), the court in Zubulake's case set forth the following seven factors:

1. The extent to which the discovery request is specifically tailored to discovery relevant information;
2. The availability of that information from other sources;
3. The total cost of production compared to the amount in controversy;
4. The total cost of production compared to the party's ability to bear that cost;
5. The relative ability of and incentive to each party to control costs;
6. The importance of the issues at stake; and,
7. The relative benefits to the parties in obtaining the information.

What is LexisNexis FRCP watch?
LexisNexis Applied Discovery has a web site, www.tinyurl.2aha92 that offers updated case law, news and information related to recent changes to the FRCP. It includes case summaries, case analysis and provides links to relevant documents.

What is the checklist for the e-discovery process?
1. Plan for conference early when considering your response to a discovery request.
2. Understand your retention policy and your method for responding to discovery requests.
3. Determine if you are able to locate and access necessary data.
4. Stop document destruction and enforce a litigation hold.
5. Evaluate your document/email review software.
6. Identify a team of experts and advisors.
7. Identify possible issues regarding potential destruction.
8. Assign tasks to key technology professionals.
9. Identify a team of computer forensic experts.
10. Test your plan

   (Karen A. Schuler, *ONSITE, Best Practices Discovery Checklist*, Legal Tech, West Coast, 2007)

Do states have e-discovery rules?
Several states have their own electronic discovery rules and some adopted partially or in full of the new FRCP amendments.

Mirroring the Federal Rules:

Arizona; Indiana; Iowa; Maryland; New Jersey.

Selective adoption:

New Hampshire (adopted meet and confer); New Mexico (all but preservation safe harbor); Washington (all but mandatory meet and confer)

What is electronic records management?

Electronic Records Management, simply put, is the conversion of paper documents and existing electronic records into one system. Data is entered into the system by scanning or other various import tools and is then indexed and organized to mimic your current paper-based products. (mccinnovations.com)

What is metadata?

Metadata, often described as "data about data," is electronically stored information that generally is not visible from the face of a document that has been printed out, or as first seen on a computer screen. Embedded in the software, metadata gives information about the creation or modification of the document--- information which often is mundane but at other times, can be quite significant and perhaps even privileged. (Marcia Coyle, v30, no. 23 NLJ 1)

What is document imaging?

This is a litigation support system in which documents are scanned into a computer and the document's actual images (similar to photographs) are retained in the computer.

What are the names of some litigation support software programs?

Several programs are available to assist law firms in litigation support including Lexis-Nexis and Westlaw. The following are a few of the many popular software programs. To find additional programs, use journals such as *Legal Management* or *Legal Technology News* to find the litigation support software programs.

CaseMap (www.casemap.com)
Summation (www.summation.com)
PerfectLaw (www.perfectlaw.com)
Omega (www.omegalegal.com)
Compulaw (www.compulaw.com)
RealLegal (www.reallegal.com)

What is branding?

A brand is a combination of name, words, designs and symbols that identifies a service and its provider and, through persistent use, differentiates the entity from its competitors. Law firms are seeking to build brands with everything from image and graphic identity programs (including logos, firm :colors" and so forth) to tag lines, positioning statements and points of differentiation. (Sally J. Schmidt, Marketing, 60 *Law Practice*, March 2008.)

What is CRM (client relationship management)?

CRM systems are software applications that manage information on the firm's clients, prospects and other contacts. The sophisticated programs integrate with the firm's time and billing system. In addition, these multi-user programs allow firms to track contacts made, produce reports and, of course, create customized lists. The most popular products in the legal world are InterAction, ContactEase and the emerging CRM4Legal. (Sally J. Schmidt, Marketing, 60 *Law Practice*, March 2008.)

What is CI (competitive intelligence)?

The following are some of the definitions offered by Ben Gilad.

A systematic and ethical program for gathering and analyzing information about your competitors' activities and general business trends to further your own company's goals.

The purposeful and coordinated monitoring of your competitors within a specific marketplace.

A collection of information pieces that have been filtered, distilled and analyzed and turned into something that can be acted upon. (Ann Lee Gibson, How to Create and Use Competitive Intelligence, 60 *Law Practice* March 2008.)

What are some of the CI gathering tools?

Zoominfo.com, Linkein.com (people's backgrounds, their networks and their interests), LexisNexis's Atvantage, Strategic Profiles, Google Alerts, West Monitor Suite, CourtLink are some of the useful tools for law firms.

CHAPTER 17

PUTTING IT ALL TOGETHER

How do I know that I have collected all necessary information?
Primary materials first and then use secondary sources.

When do I stop researching?
When one keeps on finding the same materials after reviewing both primary and secondary sources.

What if I did not find anything for my topic?
It is possible to have difficulty in finding an answer to a question. It may be necessary for you to expand your research to other jurisdictions and additional secondary sources.

When should I go to the law library?
Depending on the topic to be researched, it may be necessary to go to the library to obtain primary and secondary sources that may or may not be available free online or in a fee-based services. If someone cannot afford to purchase fee-based systems, the researcher probably will have to go to a physical law library to research digests to obtain case law. Trial court cases may not be available online in any fee-based system. Annotated statutory codes are also available in law libraries for constitutions, statutes, and rules. In addition, there are many secondary sources like treatises, encyclopedias, periodicals, newspapers, etc. that may or may not be available online but only accessible in a law library.

If the law library is not available where should I go?
It is possible that university/college libraries and public libraries may have legal collections. Throughout the country, there are federal depository libraries in academic and public libraries that possess the basic law collections such as *United States Reports, United States Code,* and *Code of Federal Regulations/Federal Register*. Some libraries are also state depository libraries containing both primary and

secondary sources. Many of the same depository libraries may also be a depository for United Nations materials.

Is information available on the Internet reliable?

Legal information from official web sites such as government agencies or courts may be considered authentic; links available by academic institutions on their web sites may also be considered reliable.

Shall I pay what the online services are asking?

There are a number of fee-based services offering access to primary sources at different rates. Before subscribing to any one service, shop around to determine who may have the coverage of what you need and can supply it to you at a reasonable cost. For example, subscribe to LawNet or Loislaw instead of LexisNexis/ Westlaw.

When do I stop collecting research information?

When you have pursued all primary and secondary sources, updated your research, and continue to find duplicated materials, then it is time to stop your research.

Do the fee-based programs have any cost-saving programs?

Both LexisNexis and Westlaw provide flat-fee charges by jurisdiction or topic for research purposes. While performing research, one can use functions such as book browse or next section to move between documents, use alerts to be kept current on new information.

How do I start my research?

Identify the key words, facts and issues found in the research issue. Key words can include general words, alternative words, synonyms, and antonyms that may be needed to search a digest. So for death penalty, the indexes may use capital punishment or vice versa.

Shall I start my research first with the secondary materials?

If you do not know much about the topic, secondary sources are a good place to start. They may provide overview of a topic (encyclopedia), summary of cases upon a specific subject (A.L.R. annotations), or a periodical article on a topic that provides both summary and analysis of a subject.

Shall I start my research first with primary authority?

It may depend on your expertise in using legal resources. If you do not know much about your topic, you may wish to start with secondary sources. However, familiarity may lead you to the primary sources like a case or statute as a starting point.

What is the best way to use the Internet for my research?
One should start their research with the relevant blawgs, Wikis, RSS feeds, and web sites on your topic.

How do I update my research?
For book research, one should always check pocket parts, pamphlets, and advance sheets as well as citators (Shepards Citations).

For online research, it will depend on the topic whether one can use free web sites or a fee-based service like LexisNexis or Westlaw. Free web sites may offer RSS feeds to deliver updates to the researcher. LexisNexis and Westlaw offer an Alert service to provide update information. Both Shepard's Citations and Westlaw's KeyCite provide updating services as well.

What is meant by research plan?
A research plan provides the steps involved in preparing and performing the research needed to complete the assignment. It is necessary to frame the research questions that you need to address to complete an assignment. Once the questions are framed, it is necessary to determine whether it is useful to examine either primary or secondary sources first to understand what you are looking for. Case law research may require going to digests, statutory research may require going to an annotated code, etc.

Are there any software packages or system that provide citing sources to

In addition, there are several programs like CiteIt.com as well as brief checking citators (LexisNexis' Briefcheck and Westlaw's Westcheck) to update briefs and table of authorities that can be created and updated right before submitting briefs to court.

APPENDIXES

A. 50 Legal Research Internet Sites
B. 50 Law Firm Technology Sites
C. 50 Legal Blawgs
D. Library of Congress Classification System KF
E. Guide to Popular Subjects of Law
F. Guide to Popular Titles
G. Legal Words
H. Bibliography

APPENDIX A

50 LEGAL RESEARCH INTERNET SITES

The following list contains popular web sites for legal research. The list is in no order of preference. Most of the sites are comprehensive in scope, but some are topic specific, e.g., Thomas.loc.gov for Congressional materials only. There are numerous other sites also available for legal research. This list is intended to guide users to sites that the authors found most useful to those in the legal profession for a variety of reasons.

1. FindLaw
   www.findlaw.com
2. HierosGamos
   www.hg.org
3. Legal Information Institute
   www.law.cornell.edu
4. Thomas
   http://Thomas.loc.gov
5. Government Printing Office (Access)
   www.gpoaccess.gov
6. WashLaw
   www.washlaw.edu
7. FirstGov
   www.firstgov.gov
8. MegaLaw
   www.megalaw.com
9. AllLaw
   www.alllaw.com
10. American Law Source
    www.lawsource.com
11. Virtual Chase
    www.virtualchase.com
12. LexisOne
    www.lexisone.com
13. GalleryWatch
    www.gallerywatch.com
14. Court TV
    www.courttv.com
15. Westlaw
    www.westlaw.com
16. LexisNexis
    www.lexisnexis.com
17. Loislaw
    www.loislaw.com
18. VersusLaw
    www.versuslaw.com
19. Justia
    www.justia.com
20. Internet Legal Resource Guide
    www.ilrg.com
21. Lectric Law Library
    www.lectlaw.com
22. American Lawyer Media
    www.law.com

23. American Bar Association
www.abanet.org
24. United Nations
www.un.org
25. US Legal Forms
www.uslegalforms.com
26. Federal Government Statistics
www.fedstats.gov
27. Law Guru
www.lawguru.com
28. Australasian Legal Information Institute
www.austlii.org
29. United States Courts
www.uscourts.gov
30. CourtLink
www.courtlink.com
31. State and Local Government
www.statelocalgov.net
32. HeinOnline
www.heinonline.org
33. IndexMaster
www.indexmaster.com
34. U.S. Department of Justice
www.usdoj.gov
35. Martindale-Hubbell
www.martindale.com
36. Association of Trial Lawyers of America
www.atla.org
37. Legal Abbreviations
www.legalabbrevs.cardiff.ac.uk
38. Law Library of Congress
www.loc.gov/law
39. United States Supreme Court
www.supremecourtus.gov/
40. WhiteHouse
www.whitehouse.gov
41. Uniform Law Commissioners
www.nccusl.org
42. Citeit!
www.sidebarsoft.com
43. National Association of Legal Assistants
www.nala.org
44. *i*Courthouse
www.icourthouse.com
45. Brief Serve
www.briefserve.com
46. Expert Pages
www.expertpages.com
47. VoirDireBase
www.voirdirebase.com
48. Law Library Resource Exchange (LLRX)
www.llrx.com
49. Jurist
www.jurist.law.pitt.edu
50. Law Technology News
www.lawtechnews.com

APPENDIX B

50 LAW FIRM TECHNOLOGY SITES

The following list contains popular web sites for law firm technology. The selected list is based on the web sites' own information about the services and legal topics they provide and cover. The list is in no order of preference. There are hundreds of vendors providing services to law firms today in areas of law firm management, such as case management and electronic discovery. The technology is changing rapidly

1. AbacusLaw
   www.abacuslaw.com
2. Legal Files
   www.legalfiles.com
3. CompuLaw
   www.compulaw.com
4. Orion Law
   http:orionlaw.com
5. PCLaw
   www.pclaw.com
6. RealLegal
   www.reallegal.com
7. Client Profiles
   www.clientprofiles.com
8. Blumberg Law Products
   www.blumberg.com
9. Summation
   www.summation.com
10. Discovery Resources
    www.discoveryresources.com
11. LiveNote
    www.livenote.com
12. Sanction
    www.sanction.com
13. Case Central
    www.casecentral.com
14. DecisionQuest
    www.decisionquest.com
15. ESILaw
    www.esilaw.com
16. DepoNet
    www.deponet.com
17. Robert Half Legal
    www.roberthalflegal.com
18. Transcription Gear
    www.transcriptiongear.com
19. Lighthouse Document Technologies
    www.lighthousedt.com
20. PerfectLaw
    www.perfectlaw.com
21. Tabs3
    www.tabs3.com

22. Verdatum
www.verdatumsys.com
23. TrialSmith
www.trialsmith.com
24. Amicus Attorney
www.amicusattorney.com
25. Interwoven
www.imanage.com
26. IPRO Tech
www.ipro.com
27. On Site E-Discovery
www.onss.com
28. SER Solutions
www.ser.com/search
29. Image Capture Engineering
www.imagecap.com
30. Paychex
www.paychex.com
31. Visual World System
www.visualworldsytem.com
32. Vestige Ltd.
www.vestigeltd.com
33. CaseData
www.casedata.com
34. Omega Legal
www.omegalegal.com
35. Lex Solutio
www.lexsolutio.com
36. Spherion Deposition
Services www.spheriondeposi-
tionservices.stormer.com

37. RainMaker
www.rainmakerlegal.com
38. GlowPoint
www.glowpoint.com
39. nQueue
www.nqueue.com
40. Xact
www.xactids.com
41. Spi Litigation Direct
www.spilitigationdirect.com
42. CaseSoft
www.casemap.com
43. Fios
www.fiosinc.com
44. CyberMatrix Timesheets
www.cyber-matrix.com
45. Lexicon
www.lexicon-projects.com
46. BlackBerry
www.blackberry.com
47. Hudson Legal Resources
www.hudson.com/us
48. LexisNexis Time Matters
www.timematters.com
49. West km
www.westthomspn.com/westkm
50. Aderant
www.aderant.com

APPENDIX C

50 BLAWGS

"Blawgs" are the legal profession's equivalent of "blogs"; the word combines the words "blogs" and "law." New blawgs are launched each day —some with mixed results and others that are destined to become mainstays in the legal profession. The selected list is in no order of preference.

1. Blawg Review
   www.blueblanket.net/blawgreview
2. Blawg
   www.blawg.org
3. Debt and Credit Law
   www.creditwrench.com
4. Bag and Baggage
   http://bgbg.blogspot.com
5. Legal References
   http://legalreferences.blogspot.com
6. Terra Nova
   http://terranova.blogs.com
7. Law Professors
   www.lawprofblogs.com
8. My Shingle
   www.myshingle.com
9. Overlawyered
   www.overlawyered.com
10. Tech Law Advisor
    http://techlawadvisor.com
11. Out of the Box Lawyering
    www.outoftheboxlawyering.com
12. Workplace Fairness
    www.workplacefairness.org.pblog.php

13. Tax Prof Blog
    http://taxprof.typepad.com/taxprof_blog
14. Patently-O: Patent Law Blog
    www.esilaw.com
15. SCOTUSblog
    www.scoutsblog.com/movabletype
16. Benefits Blog
    www.benefitscounsel.com/benefitsblog
17. Statutory Construction Zone
    www.statconblog.blogspot.com
18. Workers Comp Insider
    www.workerscompinsider.com
19. Discourse.Net
    www.discourse.com
20. Legal Theory Blog
    http://lsolum.blogspot.com
21. Leiter Reports
    http://leiterreports.typepad.com/blog
22. Bespacific
    www.bespacific.com
23. Esqlawtech Weekly
    www.lawyerlounge.com
24. 10B-5 Daily
    www.the10b-5daily.com/
25. Louisiana Supreme Court Report
    www.la-legal.com/supreme
26. Government Podcasts
    http://freegovinfo.info
27. Rory Perry's Weblog
    http://radio.weblogs.com/0103705/
28. Grep Law
    http://grep.law.Harvard.edu
29. Blawg Republic
    www.blawgrepublic.com
30. Electronic Discovery of Evidence
    http://arkfeld.blogs.com/ede/
31. Law Practice Today
    www.abanet.org/lpm/home.shtml
32. LawMeme
    http://research.yale.edu/lawmeme/

33. Ernie the Attorney
www.ernietheattorney.net
34. Evan Schaeffer's Legal Underground
www.legalunderground.com
35. Dennis Kennedy
www.denniskennedy.com
36. Daily Rotation
www.dailyrotation.com
37. May It Please the Court
www.mayitpleasethecourt.com/journal.asp?
38. Inter Alia
www.inter-alia.net
39. Net Law Blog
www.netlaw.com
40. Chess Law
www.chesslaw.com
41. Law Pundit
www.lawpundit.com
42. Sports Law Blog
www.sportslaw.blogspot.com
43. How Appealing
http://legalaffairs.org/howappealing
44. Law Geek
http://lawgeek.typepad.com/lawgeek/
45. Point of Law
www.pointoflaw.com
46. The Legal Reader
www.legalreader.com
47. You and Yours Blawg
http://youandyoursblawg.blogspot.com
48. jd2b
http://jd2b.com
49. CrimLaw
http://crimlaw.blogspot.com
50. Healthcare Law Blog
http://healthcarebloglaw.
blogspot.com

APPENDIX D

LIBRARY OF CONGRESS
SUBJECT CLASSIFICATION SYSTEM

KF SCHEDULE

American law books are classified according to the Library of Congress Subject Classification system under the KF Schedule followed by a number arrangement from 1 to 9999. Some law-related books may be found under H (Social Science), J (Political Science), and K (International Law).

The following is the table of American law under **KF** call number.

1-8	Bibliography
16-49	Legislative Documents
50-51	Session Laws
53-68	Monographic compilations
70	Administrative regulations
101	U. S. Supreme Court Reports
110-117	U. S. Circuit Courts Reports
120-122	U. S. District Court Reports
125	Other Courts
127-128	Digests
135-146	Regional Reporters
154	Encyclopedias
190	Legal Directories
240-247	Legal Research books
297-334	Legal Profession (includes ethics and law office management)
353-379	Biography & History
380	Treatises
398-400	Equity
410-418	Conflicts of Law

501-553	Family Law
556-698	Real Property
726-745	Trusts & Trustees
746-750	Estate planning
753-780	Succession Upon Death--Probate and Wills
801-951	Contracts
956-1062	Banking law
1066-1084	Marketing of securities
1146-1238	Insurance law
1244	Restitution, quasi contracts, unjust enrichment
1246-1329	Tort law
1341-1348	Agency
1355-1480	Corporation law
1501-1548	Bankruptcy
1600-2940	Regulation of industry trade and commerce (includes retail, services, utilities, professions)
2971-3198	Intellectual and Industrial Property.
3300-3559	Labor law
3566-3589	Occupational safety & health
3600-3771	Social Security, Unemployment Insurance, Public assistance
3775-3816	Public Health--Sanitation
3821-3845	Medical legislation
4101-4257	Education law
4270-4330	Science and the arts
4501-4869	Constitutional law
4880-5399	Organs of the Government
5401-5425	Administrative law
5500-5677	Public property
5691-5710	Zoning law
5900-6075	Government measures in time of war, emergency
6200-6265	Public Finance
6271-6795	Taxation
7201-7755	Military law
8201-8228	Indian law
8700-8807	Courts including organization and officers
8810-9075	Civil procedure
9084-9085	Negotiation settlement; arbitration and award
9201-9479	Criminal law
9601-9720	Criminal procedure
9730-9763	Imprisonment & prison administration
9771-9827	Juvenile criminal law and procedure

APPENDIX E

GUIDE TO POPULAR SUBJECTS OF LAW

Accounting Law	KF 1357	Estate Planning	KF 750
Administrative Law	KF 5401	European Community	KJE
Admiralty	KF 1104	Evidence	KF 8931
Agency	KF 1341	Family Law	KF 510
Antitrust	KF 1631	Federal Practice	KF 8884
Arbitration	KF 3416	Immigration Law	KF 4819
Banking Law	KF 974	Insurance Law	KF 1164
Bankruptcy Law	KF 1501	Intellectual Property	KF 2979
Business Law	KF 1355	International Law	JX, KZ
Canon Law	KBG	Jury Instructions	KF 8964
Civil Procedure	KF 8840	Labor Law	KF 3319
Civil Rights	KF 4750	Medical Jurisprudence	KF 2910
Commercial Law	KF 871	Municipal Law	KF 5304
Computer Law	KF 390.5	Patents	KF 3114
Conflicts of Law	KF 410	Personal Property	KF 705
Constitutional Law	KF 4501	Philosophy of Law	KF 379
Contracts	KF 801	Products Liability	KF 1296
Corporations	KF 1384	Real Property	KF 566
Criminal Law	KF 9319	Secured Transactions	KF 1050
Criminal Procedure	KF 9619	Tax Law	KF 6271
Damages	KF 445	Torts	KF 1250
Drunk Driving	KF 2231	Trusts and Trustees	KF 730
Educational Law	KF 4119	Uniform Commercial Code	KF 871
Environmental Law	KF 3775	Workers' Compensation	KF 3632
Equity	KF 398	Zoning	KF 5697

APPENDIX F

GUIDE TO POPULAR TITLES

ALR (American Law Reports) Annotations	KF 105, KF 132
Am. Jur.2d (American Jurisprudence, Second)	KF 154
Am. Jur. Proof of Facts	KF 8933
Am. Jur. Trials	KF 8917
Causes of Action	KF 1250
C.F.R. (Code of Federal Regulations)	KF 70
Congressional Record	KF 35
C.J.S. (Corpus Juris Secundum)	KF 154
Decennial Digest	KF 141
English Reports	KD 200
Federal Appendix	KF 105
Federal Practice and Procedure	KF 8840
Federal Register	KF 70
Federal Reporter	KF 105
Federal Rules Decisions	KF 8830
Federal Rules of Court	KF 8816
Federal Supplement	KF 120
Martindale-Hubbell Law Directory	KF 190
Moore's Federal Practice	KF 8820
Nimmer on Copyright	KF 2991.5
Pacific Reporter	KF 135
Restatement of the Law	KF 395
Statutes at Large	KF 50
Supreme Court Reporter	KF 101
Tax Management Portfolios	KF 6289
U.S. Attorney General Opinions	KF 5406
U.S.C. (United States Code)	KF 62
U.S. Law Week	KF 175
U.S. Reports (United States Reports for Supreme Ct.)	KF 101

U.S.C.A. (United States Code Annotated)	KF 62
U.S.C.C.A.N. (United States Code, & Congressional Administrative News)	KF 48
U.S.C.S. (United States Code Service)	KF 62
United States Supreme Court Reports	KF 101
West's Federal Forms	KF 8836
West's Federal Practice Digest	KF 127
West's General Digest	KF 141
Words and Phrases	KF 156

APPENDIX G

LEGAL WORDS (Latin and French)

Following is the selected list of the frequently used Latin/French words in the legal documents and legal literature. Consult any legal dictionary for full explanation of the words with examples.

animus furandi	intent to steal
actus reus	a criminal act
amicus curiae	friend of the court
certiorari	to be informed of
corpus deliciti	the body on which a crime has been committed
corpus juris	body of law
corpus delicti	body of the crime
crimen falsi	a crime of deceit
de facto	actually
de jure	legitimate
ejusdem generic	of the same class
en banc	by the full court
et seq	and the following
ex gratia	out of grace
ex officio	by virtue of his office
ex parte	by or for one party
ex post facto	after the fact
forum non conveniens	an inconvenient court
habeas corpus	you have the body
ibid	in the same place or manner
in forma pauperis	in the form of a pauper
in limine	in the beginning
in re	in the matter of
ipse dixit	he himself said it
ipso facto	by the fact itself

locus sigilli (L.S.)	the place of the seal
mala in se	wrongs in themselves
mala prohibita	prohibited wrongs
mandamus	we command
mens rea	criminal intent
modus operandi	the manner of operation
non assumpsit	he did not promise
non sequitur	it does not follow
nudum pactum	a barren promise with no consideration
per curiam	by the court
per diem	by the day
per se	by means of itself
pro forma	as a matter of form
pro rata	in proportion
pro se	for himself
quasi	almost
quid pro quo	something for something
ratio legis	legal reasoning
remittitur	reduction
res ipsa loquitur	the things speaks for itself
res judicata	a thing decided
sin qua non	without which not
stare decisis	to stand by that which was decided
stare decisis et non	to adhere to precedent and not to unsettle things which are
quieta movere	settled
status quo	the position or condition that exist
subpoena	under penalty
supra	above
voir dire	to speak the truth

Source: *Barron's Dictionary of Legal Terms*, 4th ed., 2008.

APPENDIX H

BIBLIOGRAPHY OF SOURCES

The following bibliography is a selective bibliography of legal research titles, newspapers, and journals published since the late 1980s, that we consulted to compile this book. We remind the reader that there are several other good legal research books available.

Armstrong, J. D. S. and Christopher Knott. *Armstrong and Knott's Where the Law Is: An Introduction to Advanced Legal Research*. 2d ed. Eagan, Minn: Thomson/West, 2006.

Bae, Frank S., Edward J. Bander, Francis R. Doyle, Joel Fishman, and Paul Richert. *Searching the Law*. 3rd ed. Ardsley, N.Y.: Transnational Publications, 2005.

Bast, Carol and Margie Hawkins. *Foundations of Legal Research and Writing*. 3rd ed. Thomson/Delmar Learning, 2006.

Biehl, Kathy and Calishain Tara. *The Lawyer's Guide to Internet Research*. Lanham, Maryland: The Scarecrow Press, Inc. 2000

Blackman, Josh. *How to Use the Internet for Legal Research*. New York, New York: Find/ SVP, 1996.

Bouchoux, Deborah E. *Legal Research and Writing for Paralegals*. 4th ed. N. Y.: Aspen, 2006.

Chip special (computing in focus). A magazine from India.

Cohen, Morris L. *Legal Research in a Nutshell*. 8th ed. Eagan, Minn: Thomson/West 2005.

Cohen, Morris L., Robert C. Berring and Kent Olson. *How to Find the Law*. 9th ed. St. Paul, Minn.: West, 1989.

Dernbach, John C. et al. *A Practical Guide to Legal Writing & Legal Method*. New York, N.Y.: 3d ed. Aspen, 2007.

E-Content. Medford, N.J.: Information Today Inc.

Elias, Stephen, Susan Levinkind. *Legal Research: How to Find and Understand the Law*. 13th ed. Berkeley, CA: Nolo Press, 2005.

Emmett Fitzpatrick, III. *Internet Essentials for the Pennsylvania Attorney and Other Legal Professionals*, Philadelphia: George T. Bisel Co. Inc. 2000.

Feinberg, Lawrence. Consolidation and the Consolidation Counsel: A Report to the Board of Governors and House of Delegates of the Pennsylvania Bar Association. *Legislative Process, Statutory Drafting, Regulatory Process and Update*. Mechanicsburg: PBI, 2008. pp. 317-52.

Harvey, Greg. *Adobe Acrobat 6 PDF for Dummies*. New York: wiley Publishing Inc., 2003.

Hazelton, Penny, ed. *Specialized Legal Research*. N.Y. Aspen Publishers, 2005.

Hock, Randolph. The *Extreme Searcher's Guide to Web Search Engines*. Medford, NJ: Cyberage Books, 2000.

Howstuffworks, www.howstuffworks.com

Information Today. www.infotoday.com

Johnson, Nancy P. Robert C. Berring, and Thomas A. Woxland. *Winning Research Skills*. Minneapolis : West Pub. Co., 1996.

Jones, Vivian Catherine. *Legal Research for Non-lawyers : A Self-study Manual*. Washington, DC : Special Libraries Association, 1994.

Kelso, J. Clark. *Studying Law : An Introduction to Legal Research*. New York, NY: M. Bender, 1990.

Klein, Deborah J. *Legal Research Materials*. Dubuque, Iowa : Kendall/Hunt Pub. Co., 1989.

Kozlowski, Ken. *The Internet Guide for the Legal Researcher*, 3d ed. Teaneck, N.J.: Infosources Publishing, 2001.

Kunz, Christina L. et al. *The Process of Legal Research*. 6th ed. New York, N.Y. Aspen, 2004.

Larsen, Sonja and John Bourdeau. *Legal Research for Beginners*. Hauppauge, NY : Barron's Educational Series, 1997.

Levitt, Carol A. and Mark E. Rosch. *The Cybersleuth's Guide to the Internet: Conducting Effective Investigative and Legal Research on the Web*. 8th ed. Culver City, CA: Internet for Lawyers, 2006.

Law Technology News, www.lawtechnologynews.com

Lawyers Weekly USA, www.lawyersweeklyusa.com

Legal Management (Magazine) www.alanet.org/digimag

Legal Times, Washington D.C.

Levitt, Carol A. and Mark E. Rosch. *The Lawyer's Guide to Fact Finding on the Internet*. 3rd ed. Chicago: ABA, Law Practice Management Section, 2006.

Lewis, Alfred J. *Using American Law Books : Including Online and CD-Rom Services*. Dubuque, Iowa : Kendall/Hunt Pub. Co., 1995.

LLRX, www.llrx.com

Logan, R. G. *United States Legal Research*. West Yorkshire, Eng. : Legal Information Resources, 1990.

Long, Judy A. *Legal Research Using the Internet*. St. Paul, Minn: West Legal Studies, Thomson Learning, 2000.

Low, Kathleen. *Legislative Reference Services and Sources* . Binghamton, N.Y. : Haworth Press, 1995.

Mandall, Steven L. *Busy Lawyer's Guide: Online Services*, St. Paul, Minn: West Publishing Co., 1990.

Marke, Julius J. and Richard Sloane. *Legal Research and Law Library Management*. N.Y. Law Journal Seminars-Press, 1990-.

Masters David L. *The Lawyers Guide to Adobe Acrobat*. Chicago: American Bar Association, 2004.

Masters, David L. *Adobe Acrobat 8 for Legal Professionals*. (White Paper, Adobe Acrobat, 2007).

McCully, Brian J. and Grace I. Robinson. *The Legal Research Workbook*. Cincinnati, Ohio : Anderson Pub. Co., 1996.

McKinney, Ruth Ann. *Legal Research : A Practical Guide and Self-instructional Workbook*. St. Paul, Minn. : West Pub. Co., 2003.

Mersky, Roy M. and Donald Dunn. *Fundamentals of Legal Research*. 8th ed. New York, N.Y.: Foundation Press, 2002.

Morris, Roberta A., Bruce D. Sales and Daniel W. Shuman. *Doing Legal Research : A Guide for Social Scientists and Mental Health Professionals*. Thousand Oaks, Calif. : Sage Publications, 1997.

Morville, Peter, Rosenfeld Louis, and Janes Joseph, Second Edition revised by Decandido Grace Anne A. *The Internet Searcher's Handbook: Locating Information people and Software*. New York, New York: Neal-Schuman Netguide Series, 1999.

Murray, Michael D. and Christy Hallam De Sanctis. *Legal Research Methods*. New York, N.Y.: Foundation Press, 2006.

Murray, Michael D. And Christy Hallam De Sanctis. *Legal Research, Writing and Analysis*. New York, N.Y. : Foundation Press, 2006.

National Law Journal, www.nlj.com

Neacsu, Dana. *Introduction to U.S. Law and Legal Research*. Ardsley, N.Y. : Transnational Publishers, 2005.Nedzel, Nadia E. *Legal Reasoning, Research, and Writing for International Graduate Students*. New York, NY : Aspen Publishers, 2004.

Nemeth, Charles P. and Hope I. Haywood. *Learning Legal Research : A How-to Manual*. Upper Saddle River, N.J. : Pearson Prentice Hall, 2005.

Oates, Laurel Currie and Anne Enquist. The Legal Writing Handbook: Analysis, Research and Writing. 4ᵗʰ ed. Aspen, 2006.

Online. Medford, N.J.: Information Today Inc.

Pagel, Scott B., ed. *The Legal Bibliography : Tradition, Transitions, and Trends*. New York : Haworth Press, 1989.

Park, Roger C., Douglas D. McFarland. *Computer-Aided Exercises on Civil Procedure*, Saint Paul, Minn: Thomson West, 2004.

Pittsburgh Tribune Review, Pittsburgh, P.A.

Putnam, William. *Legal Research*. Clifton Park, N.Y.: Thomson/Delmar Learning, 2006.

Rao, Dittakavi N. and Ryan L. Dansak. *Internet Resources for Legal Professionals: 50 Legal Research Sites, 50 Law Firm Technology Sites*. McDonald, Pa.: D. Rao, 2007.

Rao, Dittakavi. *Internet Legal Research: Q & A*. McDonald, Pa.: D. Rao, 2007.

Roper, Brent. *Using Computers in the Law Office*, 4ᵗʰ ed. Eagan, Minn.: Thomson, 2004.

Scaros, Constantinos E. Learning About the Law. New York: Aspen Law & Business, 1997.

Search Engine Watch. www.searchenginewatch.com

Searcher. E-Content, Online (magazines). Medford, N.J.: Information Today Inc.

Sherman Chris and Price Gary. *The Invisible Web*. Medford, New Jersey: CyberAge Books, 2001.

Sloan, Amy and Steven D. Schwinn Sloan. *Basic Legal Research Workbook*. N. Y.: Aspen Publishers, 2005.

Sloan, Amy. *Basic Legal Research: Tools and Strategies*. 3ʳᵈ ed. N. Y.: Aspen Pubishers, 2006.

SmartComputing in Plain English. www.smartcomputing.com

Tech Briefs from *The Philadelphia Lawyer*.

The Internet Connection, www.glasserlegalwks.com

The Internet Law Researcher, www.glasserlegalwks.com

The Internet Lawyer. www.Internetlawyer.com

The Pennsylvania Lawyer (Legal Tech column)

Using the Internet for Legal Research. [Harrisburg]: Pennsylvania Bar Institute, 2006.

Wikipedia, www.wikipedia.org

Zich, Joanne and Gary McCann, eds.; Susan Ryan and William Ryan, Internet eds., *A Lawyer's Research Companion: A Concise Guide to Sources*. Buffalo, N.Y. : W.S. Hein & Co. 1998.

Index

CPSIA information can be obtained at www.ICGtesting.com
Printed in the USA
LVOW120835131111

254742LV00005B/53/P